PRAISE FOR MYSTERY BABYLON

"Once again, Joel Richardson has shaken the foundations of the prophecy world and just about everything we thought we knew about Mystery Babylon. This highly original and thought-provoking book just may provide the solution to this age-old mystery that we've been searching out for millennia."

—TOM HORN, BESTSELLING AUTHOR AND CEO SKYWATCH TV

"Richardson's new volume is brilliantly researched, Scripturally solid, and fluently written. It is quite evident that 'MYSTERY, BABYLON THE GREAT, THE MOTHER OF HARLOTS' may no longer be a mystery. This book is must-reading for everyone with a passion for prophetic truth and an interest in the last days."

—MARVIN J. ROSENTHAL, EXECUTIVE DIRECTOR, ZION'S HOPE

"Once again, bestselling author Joel Richardson connects the geo-political and prophetic dots and presents a compelling, straightfor-ward, and redemptive case for one of the Bible's most enigmatic prophecies. If you want to understand the times like the sons of Issachar, I heartily recommend Joel's latest excellent work."

—CHRIS MITCHELL, MIDDLE EAST BUREAU CHIEF, CHRISTIAN BROADCASTING NETWORK

"Joel Richardson has provided us with an important and very systematic work, laying out the possibilities of who or what is the identity of Mystery Babylon. This book will definitely make you rethink your previously held positions."

—PASTOR MARK BILTZ

MYSTERY BABYLON

MYSTERY BABYLON

UNLOCKING THE BIBLE'S GREATEST PROPHETIC MYSTERY

JOEL RICHARDSON

MYSTERY BABYLON

Copyright © 2017 by Joel Richardson

Published by WND Books, Washington, D.C. WND Books is a registered trademark of WorldNetDaily.com, Inc. ("WND")

Book designed by Mark Karis

WND Books are available at special discounts for bulk purchases. WND Books also publishes books in electronic formats. For more information call (541) 474-1776, e-mail orders@wndbooks.com, or visit www.wndbooks.com.

Hardcover ISBN: 978-1-944229-31-3
eBook ISBN: 978-1-944229-32-0

LCCN 2016027972 (print) | LCCN 2016047316 (ebook)
LC record available at https://lccn.loc.gov/2016027972

Printed in the United States of America
17 18 19 20 21 LBM 9 8 7 6 5 4 3 2

To the uncountable numbers of Christians globally who have lost everything because of the name of Jesus. Be patient just a little longer. Justice is coming.

CONTENTS

ACKNOWLEDGMENTS

TO JESUS, the yearning of my heart, thank You for pouring yourself out to the fullest.

To my beautiful wife and kids, you are my polestar ever calling me home. I am so grateful to and for you all.

My deepest thanks to those supporters who have blessed me these past few years. Once again, you have made this book possible.

Thanks also to Samuel Whitefield, D. Williamson, Stephen Holmes, Jeremy Johnson, Greg Maxwell, Donnie Williams, Julie Jenkins, Ralph Woodrow, David Lindhjem, and Dax Cabrera for reading the early manuscript and giving me feedback.

Finally, I want to express my deep gratefulness to Joseph and Elizabeth Farah for your support. Thanks also to the whole WND team. Thanks to editorial director Geoffrey Stone for all of your hard work, as well as your input and advice on the manuscript. Thanks to Renee Chavez, my editor. Thanks to Mark Karis for creating another scary good cover design. Thanks also to marketing coordinator Michael Thompson. What a great team to work with. Thanks again and many blessings to you all.

INTRODUCTION

FEW PASSAGES OF THE BIBLE have been more mysterious, more perplexing, than Revelation 17–18. Together these two chapters comprise
the single longest prophecy in the New Testament. Its subject is "the
great city" (Rev. 17:18), described metaphorically, using the imagery
of an absolutely grotesque woman. She is at once a queen, a prostitute,
and a cold-blooded killer. High in the air, she proudly waves a gold cup.
Though it gleams on the outside, it is filled with a horrific mixture of the
shed blood of God's holy martyrs and the sickening, "impurities of her
prostitution" (17:4 HCSB). Not only has she drunk from this cup, but she
has also enticed "the kings of the earth" and even entire nations to drink
from it (17: 2). The woman is full of arrogance, rebellion, and raw self-
glorification. Like the proverbial ring of gold in a swine's snout, though
masquerading as a queen, she is in fact a vile and classless prostitute. She
is decked out in royal "purple and scarlet, and adorned with gold and
precious stones and pearls" (v. 4). Not only does she lavish herself with
extravagant material excess, but she has seduced the kings of the earth
to live "luxuriously with her" (18:9 HCSB).

Adding to all of this abhorrent and perplexing imagery, this woman is riding atop a most bizarre and horrific red beast—a monster, really—with seven heads and ten horns. The woman and this "beast," rider and steed, both scarlet, are truly a match made in hell.

God's judgment, about to be poured out, looms over this woman, as an angelic voice from heaven trumpets a thunderous warning to the inhabitants of the earth, "Come out of her, my people, so that you will not participate in her sins and receive of her plagues; for her sins have piled up as high as heaven, and God has remembered her iniquities" (Rev. 18:4).

Anyone who has sought to understand this passage can surely identify with the apostle John, who declared, "when I saw her, I wondered greatly" (17:6). Then, in a sudden and shocking turn of events, the monster the harlot sits upon turns on her, devouring her body and burning what remains. Across the heavens, angels rejoice aloud, declaring the news of her death as a momentous victory for God and His people: "Fallen, Babylon the Great has fallen!" (18:2 HCSB). Earthly bystanders look on in shock and horror as the ascending smoke of her destruction is seen from a distance. Throughout the world, wealthy businesspeople, merchants, seafarers, and the rulers of the earth all join in mourning her loss—and the loss in revenue that her death means to them.

The title this woman is given by God Himself, has also mystified many interpreters: "Mystery, BABYLON THE GREAT, THE MOTHER OF ALL HARLOTS AND OF THE ABOMINA-TIONS OF THE EARTH" (17:5). Alternately, she is called "the great harlot" (17:1) or, in other translations, "the great whore" (KJV) or "the great prostitute" (NIV).

So who or what does this woman represent? Is she active today in our world? She is described repeatedly as a city, but what city does she represent? Can she be identified? Does properly understanding this passage have any actual real-world implications or application for us today? Could there be any relationship between this woman and the global rise of radical Islam? Does this passage have anything to say about the future of the United States? Bible students and teachers alike have wrestled with many of these questions, literally for millennia.

It is unfortunate that many pastors and teachers today view the answers to these questions—attempting to actually identify Babylon the Great—as the purview of fringe armchair theologians and end-time fanatics. No doubt, for some, this is the case, but these answers are much more than strange prophetic trivia. We cannot expect, after all, to rightly understand the very culmination of God's grand plan of redemption while outright ignoring two of the final chapters of the Bible. When responsible and careful interpreters of the Bible avoid a particular topic, they only surrender it to those who are less than responsible and careful in their interpretations. Certainly, many fringe Bible teachers have planted their stakes and laid claim to this segment of the Bible, but this is no excuse to avoid it. Quite the contrary. This is not a portion of the Scriptures that we can afford to abandon. As we will see, properly interpreting and wrestling through this prophecy and answering the many questions the text brings up indeed have some very real-world implications and pastoral application today. We will discuss many of these implications as we move forward.

I've arranged this book into three parts. The first part is more expositional, but not necessarily verse by verse. Rather, I work through Revelation 17–18 systematically and thematically, drawing out all the various descriptions of the great harlot so you will know what to look for as I weigh the different positions that various interpreters have offered. In the second part of the book, I examine each of the more common positions, weighing their strengths and weaknesses. Finally, in part 3, I work extensively through the view that I am suggesting as the solution to this great mystery. If you are not so much interested in what I *don't* think the harlot Babylon is, then you can simply skip the second part of the book altogether and jump right into part 3.

It is my most sincere hope that this book, which takes a very serious look at a position that has not been given much serious consideration, will become a valuable contribution to the discussion.

I have striven as much as possible to make this study simple and straightforward. I truly hope I've succeeded. I pray this work will help shed greater light on a prophecy that is only going to become more and more relevant, particularly as we draw closer to that final day and the return of the glorious King—Jesus the Messiah.

PART ONE

THE BIBLE'S GREATEST
PROPHETIC MYSTERY

1

THE HISTORY OF THE MYSTERY

FROM THE EARLY DAYS OF CHRISTIANITY, believers have struggled to understand the mystery of the great harlot. Scholars and students alike have arrived at many different conclusions. The purpose of this chapter is to survey the primary interpretations of this passage and their development and evolution throughout church history.

ROME

Roughly two hundred years after the book of Revelation was written, Lactantius, an early Christian writer from North Africa, believed the harlot was the city of Rome, which was still dominated by paganism at the time.[1] Tertullian, Irenæus, and Jerome all used the term "Babylon" to refer to the Roman Empire.[2] But with the steady decline of pagan Rome, this view begin to lose favor among Christians. By the sixth century, Andrew of Caesarea openly expressed his doubt concerning Lactantius's view, stating, "For old Rome lost its power of dominion a long time ago, and we do not suppose that ancient status will return to it." Rather than pointing to any particular city of his day, Andrew contended that Mystery Babylon represents a city that will arise in the last days and hold sway over much of the earth.[3]

ISLAM

A thousand years later, after Islam had arisen and swept much of the world under its control, many Christians began to wonder if it was the solution to the mystery of the great harlot. We find this view expressed in the writings Nicholas of Lyra, a French Franciscan monk often referred to as the greatest exegete of the fourteenth century. As was common for European Christian writers from the later medieval era, Nicholas often referred to Muslims either as "the saracens," a generic term used for Muslims during this era, or simply as "the Turks," who ruled much of the Muslim world at the time. Nicholas referred to Islam as "Great Babylon, that is the Saracen sect, which is called Babylon."[4] He said that John the apostle used the term "Mystery Babylon" to "show that he is not speaking of the city Babylon, but more concerning the Saracen sect in relation to the Turks, [who have] drawn the eastern peoples into the error of their sect."[5] Although Lyra's views were highly influential during the later medieval period, they soon fell out of favor during the Reformation, when Protestants shifted much of their focus back to Rome.

THE ROMAN CATHOLIC CHURCH

As the great division between Roman Catholics and Protestants swept across Europe, the Reformers dusted off the earlier, Rome-as-Babylon view, modified it, and began pointing to the Roman

Catholic Church. In 1522, Martin Luther's good friend Lucas Cranach created the now-famous woodcut images that Luther would use so effectively in his propaganda war against the Vatican. Lucas's woodcuts portrayed the pope as the great harlot riding the seven-headed beast. This new view—namely, that Roman Catholicism is the great harlot—quickly became almost universally accepted among Protestants. William Tyndale, the famous Reformation scholar and translator, would declare that Catholics had "set up that great idol, the Whore of Babylon, antichrist of Rome, whom they call the pope."[6] For the next five hundred years, such views defined how Protestants would relate to the Catholic Church. Since that time, numerous men have breathed fresh life into this perspective.

Foremost among these champions was a Scottish minister named Alexander Hislop, author of a nineteenth-century book titled *The Two Babylons: The Papal Worship Proved to Be the Worship of Nimrod and His Wife*. It is difficult to overstate the impact that Hislop's work has had on popular Protestant thinking concerning the Roman Catholic Church. Hislop argued that the ancient Babylonian religion of Tammuz worship eventually crept into and permeated virtually every aspect of the Roman Catholic liturgy. According to Hislop, if an ancient Babylonian priest, or even Belshazzar himself, were to "enter St. Peter's [Basilica] at Rome and see the Pope in his pontificals, in all his pomp and glory . . . surely he would conclude that he had only entered one of his own well-known temples, and that all things continued as they were at Babylon."[7] Later we'll take a whole chapter to discuss Hislop's work (as well as its countless problems).

Another champion of the view that Roman Catholicism is the harlot (along with every other Protestant group that worships on Sunday) was Ellen G. White, founder of the Seventh-day Adventist movement. To this day, based on White's prophecies, many traditionalist Adventists are convinced the day is coming when the pope will suddenly enforce global "Sunday laws," and behead everyone who does not conform to his authority.

The Scofield Reference Bible, published in 1917 but still very popular today, has also contributed greatly toward preserving the popularity of the view that the Roman Catholic Church is the last-days Babylon.[8] Other books, such as the late prophecy teacher Dave Hunt's 1991 work, *A Woman Rides the Beast: The Roman Catholic Church and the Last Days*, continue to have a great impact among many Protestant students of prophecy.

Although the belief that the Roman Catholic Church is the great harlot has lost some ground among many Protestants today, the shockwaves of this interpretation continue to affect the popular Protestant consciousness in many profound ways. Just skim through the comment section that follows nearly any Internet article or any social media post that refers to the pope or Roman Catholicism, and the legacy of this view will be quite apparent.

Already, we can see why having a proper understanding of this passage is so critical for Christians. No doubt, Protestants and Catholics continue to have many significant differences. These disagreements, however, are matters that can generally be discussed between two reasonable adults. It is one thing, though, to say, "Let us discuss our disagreements, that perhaps we might understand each other better," and another thing entirely to say, "You are the great whore!" When one party views the other as a willful participant in a religious organization that is the actual embodiment of Satan on the earth, then even simple dialogue becomes impossible. This dynamic has often plagued the relationship of Roman Catholics and Protestants for the past five hundred years. This is just one reason, albeit a rather important one, why gaining a proper understanding of this passage is a deeply relevant matter for Christians.

NEW YORK CITY / UNITED STATES

In more modern times, another position that has gained tremendous popularity is the view that the United States of America, or New York City, specifically, is harlot Babylon. In their book *The Final Babylon: America and the Coming of Antichrist*, coauthors Kreiger,

McGriff, and Woodward claim that identifying Mystery Babylon "requires only a minute amount of analytical skills. Indeed it is only the United States of America that can muster the money and the might to be THE FINAL BABYLON of Revelation 18."[9] In recent years there has actually been an explosion of popular prophecy books that champion this view. The titles are almost impossible to distinguish one from another: *The End of America; The Fall of America Babylon the Great; The Judgment of Babylon: The Fall of America; and America Will Burn*, for example. All of these titles tell a very similar story. As a result of many embracing this new interpretation, there has actually developed a growing movement of Christians who are fleeing—or seeking to flee—the United States for safety from the coming judgment and destruction that await her. A few of the aforementioned titles even offer detailed escape plans for those seeking to get out. As I travel and speak to congregations all over North America, concerns and questions about this matter are brought up quite frequently. I recently spoke with a Canadian pastor who has received several inquiries from Americans considering moving to Canada in the hope of escaping the coming destruction of the United States. Needless to say, if America is indeed the last-days Babylon, the very real-world implications are profound. Once more we see why a proper interpretation of these two chapters in the book of Revelation is so important.

MODERN APOSTATE JERUSALEM

Another, less popular interpretation holds that this passage refers to Jerusalem. Most who espouse this view are preterists, meaning they believe this prophecy is already long past, having been fulfilled when Jerusalem was destroyed by the Romans in AD 70.[10] The most influential voice who supports this view today is New Testament scholar N. T. Wright. Wright explains his interpretation of Revelation 17–18 thus:

It is from Jerusalem that the true Israel must now flee, lest they partake in her destruction. It is Jerusalem whose destruction will be the sign that the God whom Jesus has proclaimed is now indeed manifestly the king of the whole earth . . . Jerusalem and its hierarchy have taken on the role of Babylon, Edom and Antiochus Epiphanes. They are the city whose fall spells the vindication of the true people of Israel's God. The prophecies of rescue from the tyrant have come true in and for Jesus and in his people. When this city falls they must leave quickly; this is their moment of salvation and vindication.[11]

Though rare, there are also some who believe the harlot represents a future last-days judgment on apostate Israel. One book promoting this perspective declares, "The Bible tells us exactly which city will be the capital city of the Antichrist in the last days, it tells us the city that will promote the Antichrists [sic] worship to the rest of the world and the city in which the Antichrist will institute the greatest persecution of all time. That city is Jerusalem."[12] We will discuss some of the problems with this view as we move forward.

LITERAL BABYLON

Another interpretation is that the literal city of Babylon (the remnants of which are located fifty-three miles south of Baghdad, Iraq, in a town called Hillah) will be rebuilt in the last days. Although the ruins of this once magnificent city are little more than a tourist attraction today, those who hold this view believe that, in the days to come, a reconstructed Babylon will far surpass the ancient city's former glory. They argue that this is the most straightforward and literal of all the various options. This view has been espoused by a handful of notables throughout the past two hundred years. Among them were classic commentators E. W. Bullinger, B.W. Newton, and Joseph Augustus Seiss in the early nineteenth century. In the twentieth century, such well-respected commentators as G. H. Lang, Arnold Fruchtenbaum, Robert Thomas, Pastor Mark Hitchcock, and Joel C. Rosenberg have promoted this view. We will discuss the viability of this interpretation in part 2 of this book.

APOSTATE CHRISTENDOM OR INTERFAITH ECUMENISM

Another perspective holds that all segments of apostate Christianity will someday join together in the last days to form some kind of organized ecumenical body. The World Council of Churches, at least since its founding in 1975, has been the most common candidate— or culprit—that is expected to bring all of these apostate bodies together. John Walvoord, former president of Dallas Theological Seminary, specifically believed that the harlot "system" would indeed be an apostate form of ecumenism. Walvoord declared of the harlot:

> The woman symbolizing the apostate religious system, was drunk
> with the blood of the saints. This makes it clear that the apostate
> religious system of the first half of the last seven years leading up
> to Christ's second coming will be completely devoid of any true
> Christians. As a matter of fact the apostate church will attempt
> to kill all those who follow the true faith.[13]

Others are awaiting an even more broadly defined ecumenism, one that will combine all religions and beliefs together under a yet larger umbrella. In this imagined scenario, it is the United Nations that is often looked to as the perfect vehicle for the Antichrist to assume control of the whole world.

THE ILLUMINATI

For some, no umbrella is big enough unless it recognizes a full-blown, pan-historical, transnational conspiracy of exceedingly secretive, occult globalists, power brokers, and bankers whose wicked tentacles extend into every nook and cranny of the entire planet. This is a conspiracy so all-encompassing that it is somehow able to bring together such diverse bodies as the Roman Catholic Church, the World Council of Churches, the United Nations, a global body of Jewish Zionists, the Illuminati, and just about every other group we might imagine. For those who hold this position, it is not merely an interpretation of these two chapters in Revelation; rather, it is a complete worldview, complete with a way of understanding nearly every event that occurs in the news. It is a conspiracy so far-reaching, in fact, that even I am apparently deeply involved. "Joel Richardson is also an Illuminati agent, who works for the Zionist agenda,"[14] one Internet writer warned. Ironically, my involvement in a secret satanic conspiracy is proven by the fact that I've appeared on many Christian television programs, which, as everyone apparently should know, "is the mind-control central for the Illuminati. . . . And these facts are undeniable evidence of him being one of them, NO DOUBT."[15] Appearing in any form of visible media seems to be a common concern among these conspiracists, as another writer has similarly warned:

> Richardson projects a convincing Christian jargon and appears to be well-schooled in the Bible. But the first alert my spirit had re: Joel, was his overwhelming acceptance by powerful people and the media. That was a red flag right there. I often wonder if he is part of what I call "white propaganda."[16]

Yet another conspiracy theorist mirrored similar sentiments, this time casting the blame primarily on a Jewish-Zionist conspiracy: "It doesn't take a conspiracy theorist to see that Jewry has long been running serious psyops."[17] In the early 1990s I spent several months backpacking around the Middle East, getting to know the people and the region, and praying about moving there as a missionary. But according to this particular individual, my time there was actually "really intense training at the Mossad Institute." The proof is clear. "I mean, look at the guy—he looks seriously Jewy."[18] But beyond my physical features, the crowning proof of my involvement in the global Babylonian system is that, according to the first conspiracist just cited, "I have seen him shapeshift."[19]

MECCA / SAUDI ARABIA

In more recent years, with many Christians increasingly embracing the idea of an Islamic Antichrist leading a Middle Eastern empire, some are now looking at the city of Mecca and the Kingdom of Saudi Arabia as the last-days Babylon. Although this view is gaining considerable traction within the world of popular Bible prophecy, to date, it has not been explored in a thorough or complete manner. Part 3 of this book is devoted exclusively to discussing this interpretation.

CONCLUSION

Some of these positions obviously have far more merit than others. A few are, at least in my opinion, rather unsupportable. Some are fairly wacky. I will nevertheless examine each of the views and consider all the possibilities. In this sense, this book is unique. Although I will argue for one particular position over the others, I will seek to honestly weigh the strengths and weaknesses of all the options. As we all seek to properly understand what the Lord is conveying to His people through this prophecy, it is imperative that we do so responsibly, carefully considering all of the various criteria the Lord has given us, and not just a few select clues, as is too often the case.

If you have opened this book with your mind somewhat made up as to the meaning of this prophecy, I only ask that you also keep both your Bible and your mind open. I am confident that if we will give ourselves to understanding this text in a careful, prayerful, and humble manner, the Lord will bring much-needed clarity and clear away much of the accumulated confusion that has attached itself to this truly critical portion of Scripture. Thus, as I always like to do, I would invite you to consider reading this book not simply with an intellectual curiosity, but with much prayer and a truly contrite and trusting heart, believing indeed that the Lord will open up His secrets to all "those who fear Him" (Ps. 25:14).

2

THE GREAT CITY

AS WE SEEK TO UNRAVEL THE MYSTERY of the great harlot, the first thing that needs to be made clear is that she is a literal city. Although the harlot indeed represents an ungodly religious and financial system—she is in fact the heart of the system—she is not merely a system or concept, but is a very real, identifiable geographic hub. The Bible not only clearly states that the harlot is a city; it also gives us some very specific and important details concerning the nature and geography of this city. Let's jump right in and consider these descriptions.

A REAL CITY

While our introduction to the great harlot begins with symbolic terms—as a vile, murderous prostitute—the literal interpretation and explanation of what she represents immediately follows. Eight times in Revelation 17–18, she is referred to as a "city." Many commentators, I believe, have overcomplicated the mystery by claiming that not only are the lurid descriptions of the woman symbolic, but so is the repeated use of the term "city." This is not, however, a double metaphor. The woman riding the beast, drunk on the blood of the saints—that is the portion of this prophecy that all commentators agree is metaphorical.[1] But first, in Revelation 17:18, and then several more times, we are given the interpretation of the metaphorical woman: "The woman whom you saw is the great city, which reigns over the kings of the earth." The grotesque, murderous prostitute described throughout the first half of the prophecy is a literal city on the earth. The city is not, as some commentators have claimed, merely a metaphor for conceptual or vague ideas, such as a "seductive world system," or "apostate Christianity." We are most certainly dealing here with a tangible, definable, and specific city.

As we apply ourselves to understanding the mystery of the harlot, we must have confidence that the Lord is not sitting in heaven trying to confuse us with overly difficult apocalyptic symbolism and metaphors within metaphors. Throughout the apocalyptic portions of Scripture, the pattern is fairly consistent. First there is a revelation, dream, or vision using symbolic imagery. Then that symbolism is explained in fairly straightforward and literal terms. Quite often, a messenger angel is sent to explain the meaning of the symbolism. This is exactly the case here in Revelation, where the interpreter angel assures John, (and us too, if we will listen), "I will tell you the mystery of the woman" (17:7). Then the angel states plainly that the harlot is a city—an actual, physical city.[2]

A CONSUMER CITY

Beyond being directly referred to as a city eight times, the great
harlot is also described in ways that can only apply to a literal city.
After she is destroyed, we are told "the merchants of the earth weep
and mourn over her, because no one buys their cargoes any more."
What kinds of cargoes?

> Cargoes of gold and silver and precious stones and pearls and
> fine linen and purple and silk and scarlet, and every kind of
> citron wood and every article of ivory and every article made
> from very costly wood and bronze and iron and marble, and
> cinnamon and spice and incense and perfume and frankincense
> and wine and olive oil and fine flour and wheat and cattle and
> sheep, and cargoes of horses and chariots and slaves and human
> lives. (Rev. 18:11–13)

While certainly not exhaustive, the list includes some of the
city's primary imports. If the harlot were not a literal city, then
it would be very strange to include such a list of goods in the
prophecy. Why would the Scriptures take the time to give us what
is essentially a grocery list of a symbolic city? That wouldn't make
any sense. Obviously, this portion of the prophecy is not symbolic.
There are some things within Scripture (just as in everyday life) that
were never intended to be taken symbolically. This list is a perfect
example. Our job here is not to decode the deeper spiritual meaning
of cinnamon, flour, or cattle. If you were to write out a grocery list
today, only a delusional individual would pick up that list and try
to explain the deeper spiritual meaning of each item through some
alleged symbolic lens. Efforts to read deeper spiritual meaning into
the harlot Babylon's list of imports would be equally irrational. It
is nothing more than a listing of merchandise shipped to this city.

We can learn much about Babylon by the items she imports.
That she imports them implies that she cannot, or simply does
not, produce them herself. The specific products on this list can be

divided into three categories. Let's look at each category:

Luxury Items: This category includes expensive building materials, clothing, perfumes, and precious metals, gems, and pearls. From this we see that Babylon is likely not a nation that mines, quarries, or even harvests many of the fine materials that she cherishes. We also see the mention of "carriages" (18:13 HCSB). While I am usually hesitant to read modern equivalencies in ancient descriptions, I think it is quite fair here to equate "carriages" with automobiles. Babylon will not be a major auto manufacturer. Instead, whatever forms of transportation that she uses will be largely imported.

Food Items: This category includes both livestock and produce. Babylon must import even the basics. Babylon as a city will not be a "breadbasket," as is often said of America. It is not a nation rich in pastureland or farming.

Humans: Babylon imports people for various reasons. While most would like to imagine that slavery is a thing of the past, the truth is that today, slavery is indeed thriving in various forms in many places throughout the world. For whatever reason, Babylon will be a city that will import all sorts of people, no doubt to maintain and bolster its excessively luxurious lifestyle.

SHE SITS IN A DESERT

As chapter 17 begins, an angel approaches the apostle John and says, "Come here, I will show you the judgment of the great harlot who sits on many waters. . . . And he carried me away in the Spirit into a wilderness; and I saw a woman sitting on a scarlet beast" (vv. 1, 3). Of all the clues we are given concerning the harlot, one profound detail that is often missed is the description of her location: most Bible translations call it "a wilderness."[3] The word wilderness can be misleading. For many, this word conjures up images of a vast forest. The Greek word used, however, is *erēmos*. It connotes a lonely, deserted, solitary place[4]—in other words, a desert. When the Israelites wandered in the "wilderness" for forty years, they wandered through the Sinai, the Negev, and the Jordanian deserts. I've traveled throughout these regions, and I assure you, they are quite the opposite of a forest. Likewise, when Jesus went out into the "wilderness" to fast and pray for forty days (see Matt. 4:1–11), he did not go out into the woods. Jesus went into the barren Judean desert. I've been there also. It's rocky, dry, and desolate. If the prophecy intended to point to a forest, the writer would have used the Greek word *hule*, meaning a wooded forest, used elsewhere in the Bible to refer to such.

Many miss the importance of the woman sitting in a desert because they interpret desert only in a spiritual sense. While the word may also carry some deeper spiritual meaning, I do not believe it should be understood as purely metaphorical. In Revelation 17:15, the interpreting angel explains to John that "the waters" upon which the harlot sits represent "peoples, multitudes, nations and languages" (HCSB). We understand this to mean that she exerts a strong measure of influence over a great number of peoples and nations. However, the angel never explains some deeper spiritual or metaphorical meaning to the desert. We have no basis to assume, then, that this is anything other than a very real description of her location in a desert.

We also know the intention is to reveal the city itself as being in an actual desert because this imagery is drawn directly from Isaiah 21, a prophecy that begins by specifically describing Babylon as "the Desert by the Sea" (v. 1 HCSB).

We should also note that in Revelation 21, John has an identical experience, but this time, rather than being carried away into a desert, he was carried away to "a great and high mountain," where he was shown "the holy city, Jerusalem, coming down out of heaven from God" (v. 10). The mountain was not merely a movie theater of sorts, irrelevant to and disconnected from the vision. No, it was a reference to Mount Zion, the actual and literal location where New Jerusalem will come to rest.[5] So also should we understand the desert where the woman sits as an actual physical description of the topography where the harlot city is located. The desert where John was taken—where he saw the harlot—cannot be separated from the content of the vision. When interpreters just brush aside details such as this, they miss critical clues in the text. In this case, the desert is an important indicator helping us identify the city in question. Whatever our interpretation regarding the great harlot, it must be a city geographically located in a desert region.

A PORT CITY

Beyond being a desert city or nation, the last-days Babylon will also be a port city, or at least close to the shore. After Babylon is judged and destroyed by God, a great lament arises specifically from three groups of people: kings, merchants, and seafarers. They mourn because of their loss in revenue, specifically, that no one buys their "cargoes" any longer. The word for cargoes is *gomos* and refers specifically to freight carried by ship or boat. The text tells us that "every shipmaster and every passenger and sailor, and as many as make their living by the sea, stood at a distance, and were crying out as they saw the smoke of her burning . . . All who had ships at sea became rich by her" (Rev. 18:17, 19). The fact that all these seafarers can see the smoke of her destruction seems to indicate that she is located either directly on or in close proximity to the seashore. So once more, we are given an important clue, a unique geographical feature of this city, that will help us zero in on her identity.

THE MEGACITY

While acknowledging that the last-days Babylon is a very real city, we should not rigidly limit our interpretation to a city. The term city is used, not to restrict the harlot's identification, but rather to distinguish her as something very real, an actual geographically identifiable location. The harlot Babylon is repeatedly described with the Greek words *polis hē megalē*. She is a megacity, as it were, a megalopolis, or as most Bible translations simply translate it, "the great city." Her greatness could rest in her size, though the text would seem to emphasize her far-reaching and vast influence. As commentator G. K. Beale has stated, "The whore is contrasted with the city of God and represents the ungodly metropolis, whose hub radiates economic and religious institutions."[6] So, she is not merely a city. Any great city of renown during the biblical period was not only a city, but the heart of the various city-states that reigned over large segments of the world. As the prototype for the last-days Babylon, the ancient city of Babylon was a great city-state. The city of Rome also was a great empire. When referring to nations, kingdoms, or even empires, it is quite common to simply name its capital city. Thus, to refer to the ancient empire of Babylon, one might simply mention the city of Babylon, the capital and the very heart of that empire. The same is true of Rome. Today it is no different. When we refer to the capital city of any nation, it is a way of referring to the whole nation. Instead of saying that the United States and Russia are at odds, one might simply say that Washington is in conflict with Moscow. This figure of speech is called synecdoche, and it is used abundantly throughout the Bible.[7] The great cities of Babylon and Rome were not merely the capitals, but the epicenters, the very hearts of massive spheres of economic and religious influence and authority. This is precisely why the angel in Revelation 17:15 states that "the waters" on which the great harlot sits represent "peoples, multitudes, nations, and languages" (HCSB). Like the great city-states of ancient times, the last-days Babylon will also wield great influence over a large portion of the peoples of the earth. She is the heart of a much larger religious and economic sphere.

CONCLUSION

In conclusion, already we have been given some very specific and fairly unique criteria to help us identify the harlot Babylon. She is a literal city or a nation that sits in a literal desert, yet seems to be located on or very close to the coast. Right from the start, then, such specific descriptions will help us greatly as we seek to understand this great prophetic mystery.

3

BABEL OR BABYLON?

TO UNDERSTAND THIS GREAT MYSTERY, we must begin with the things within the prophecy that are the most obvious. In this case, we begin simply with the name that the Scriptures assign to the great harlot. Before we attempt to decipher all of the strange symbolism and metaphor attached to her, we must remember that the woman is repeatedly called "Babylon." From a simple biblical perspective, what does this mean?

There are actually two "Babylons" in Scripture. On one hand, both are the same city, with the same name, built on the same spot. On the other hand, these two Babylons are separated by roughly seventeen hundred years, and each carries its own very distinct story within the biblical narrative. This would be similar to, for example, the city of Rome. There is ancient pagan Rome, ruled by the various Caesars, so famous in ancient history, and there is the modern city of Rome, home to the Vatican, the very heart of the Roman Catholic Church. Though they are the same city, with the same name, built on the same location, they are separated by two millennia and are quite distinct cities, representing two very different realities. So it is with Babylon. First, there was the most ancient city of Babel, seemingly founded by Nimrod—literally the first city to be built after the great flood. Then there is what we normally call Babylon, the city made great by Nebuchadnezzar, built upon the remains of the original Babel. In the Hebrew Bible, both Nimrod's city and Nebuchadnezzar's city are called "Babel." But because the Greek name for the city is *Babylōn*, English translations of the Bible generally translate Nimrod's city as "Babel," and the later revival of that city as "Babylon."

As we attempt to discern what God is trying to show us by calling this last-days city Babylon, we need to ask which of the two cities He is primarily pointing to as a prophetic foreshadower of the last-days Babylon. Is it Nimrod's city or Nebuchadnezzar's? Or is it both? Exploring this question is important, because the biblical stories involving each city, the sins associated with each city, and how those sins affected God's people are quite different. Let's consider what each city represents within the biblical accounts.

NIMROD'S BABEL

According to the book of Genesis, after the great flood, Babel was the first city built by humankind. It was planted in Mesopotamia, in the plains of Shinar, on the Euphrates River. This is roughly sixty miles south of modern-day Baghdad, Iraq. In Genesis 10, we're told that Nimrod, son of Cush, grandson of Ham, and great-grandson of Noah, not only became "a mighty hunter" (v. 9) but also built a kingdom for himself. "The beginning of his kingdom," the Bible says, "was

Babel . . . in the land of Shinar" (v. 10). Following is the account of this massive building project (and the Lord's disruption of that plan):

> Now the whole earth used the same language and the same words. It came about as they journeyed east, that they found a plain in the land of Shinar and settled there. They said to one another, "Come, let us make bricks and burn them thoroughly." And they used brick for stone, and they used tar for mortar. They said, "Come, let us build for ourselves a city, and a tower whose top will reach into heaven, and let us make for ourselves a name, otherwise we will be scattered abroad over the face of the whole earth." The Lord came down to see the city and the tower which the sons of men had built. The Lord said, "Behold, they are one people, and they all have the same language. And this is what they began to do, and now nothing which they purpose to do will be impossible for them. Come, let Us go down and there confuse their language, so that they will not understand one another's speech." So the Lord scattered them abroad from there over the face of the whole earth; and they stopped building the city. Therefore its name was called Babel, because there the Lord confused the language of the whole earth; and from there the Lord scattered them abroad over the face of the whole earth (Gen. 11:1–9).

This great effort to build Babel, along with its legendary tower, seems to have stood in conflict with God's command to humankind to "be fruitful and multiply, and fill the earth" (Gen. 9:1). Instead of spreading out, the people congregated together in this city, ultimately to make "a name" for themselves.

THE GATE OF GOD

Interestingly, there is a play on words within the name Babel. In the ancient Akkadian language, *bav-ili* meant "Gate of God." This was most likely a reference to the Tower of Babel, the goal for which was to enable man to reach "into heaven." In Hebrew, however, *bav-il* means, "confusion," referring to that which gripped the people after the Lord confused their languages.

As we assess the Babel story to determine its relation to the last-days Babylon, we actually do not have much information to work with. The sin of ancient Babel might be summarized as a massive and unified rebellion against God. It is quite likely, then, that this same dynamic will be found in the last-days Babylon. Beyond this, however, we can only speculate. Somewhat awkwardly, the biblical story concerning Babel is lacking in detail. Unfortunately, this has led many throughout history to look to extrabiblical sources and to engage in much speculation. Somewhat shockingly, when we examine any number of Christian books about the last-days Babylon, we find all kinds of information about Nimrod, his wife, their religion, and the Tower of Babel. Entire books have been written about these things. We will discuss the Nimrod traditions in much detail in the next chapter. For now, however, we will simply say that these extrabiblical traditions about Nimrod are just that: traditions, many of which are demonstrably not true. For the purpose of our study, we will remain focused solely on what the Scriptures say.

NEBUCHADNEZZAR'S BABYLON

Fourteen hundred years after the ancient builders of Babel were scattered, in the sixth century BC, the city of Babylon would reach the height of its ancient glory. King Nebuchadnezzar, standing on the roof of the royal palace, declared, "Is this not Babylon the great, which I myself have built as a royal residence by the might of my power and for the glory of my majesty?" (4:30). It is this specific phrase uttered by Nebuchadnezzar, "Babylon the Great," that the Lord used in Revelation to describe the great last-days city (14:8; 16:19; 17:5; 18:2). This is the proud city known for its stunning architectural features, such as the towering Ishtar Gate (an impressive reconstruction of which can now be seen in Berlin's Pergamon Museum) and the legendary Hanging Gardens, one of the seven wonders of the ancient world. It was under Nebuchadnezzar's reign that Babylon expanded its regional power to become a mighty empire of ancient history. When we consider Nebuchadnezzar's Babylon, and specifically how it affected Jerusalem and the Jewish people, it is very easy to see multiple ways in which it was a powerful foreshadower of the last-days Babylon.

THE ROD OF THE LORD'S CHASTISEMENT

Upon becoming king, Nebuchadnezzar began conquering many of the smaller kingdoms around Judah. It had already been more than a hundred years since the Assyrians had defeated the northern kingdom of Israel and carried away most of its citizens into captivity. In 598 BC, Nebuchadnezzar and his forces besieged Jerusalem. King Jehoiachin and his family surrendered and were taken as prisoners. Worse yet, Nebuchadnezzar "led away into exile all Jerusalem and all the captains and all the mighty men of valor, ten thousand captives, and all the craftsmen and the smiths. None remained except the poorest people of the land" (2 Kings 24:14). Yet as devastating as this was, this was only the first wave. After taking the first round of prisoners, Nebuchadnezzar installed Zedekiah, the uncle of Jehoiachin. Rather than submitting to Nebuchadnezzar, however, he forged a series of alliances with the surrounding kingdoms, the foremost of which was Egypt. These alliances failed miserably, and the end result was the utter devastation of the kingdom of Judah and its capital city of Jerusalem.

On the ninth of Av, 586 BC, Nebuchadnezzar and his armies invaded Jerusalem and brought the city and the temple to ruin. The writer of 2 Chronicles recorded the catastrophic events leading to the downfall of Judah and its last king:

> Zedekiah was twenty-one years old when he became king, and he reigned eleven years in Jerusalem. He did evil in the sight of the Lord his God; he did not humble himself before Jeremiah the prophet who spoke for the Lord. He also rebelled against King

Nebuchadnezzar who had made him swear allegiance by God. But he stiffened his neck and hardened his heart against turning to the Lord God of Israel. Furthermore, all the officials of the priests and the people were very unfaithful following all the abominations of the nations; and they defiled the house of the Lord which He had sanctified in Jerusalem. The Lord, the God of their fathers, sent word to them again and again by His messengers, because He had compassion on His people and on His dwelling place; but they continually mocked the messengers of God, despised His words and scoffed at His prophets, until the wrath of the Lord arose against His people, until there was no remedy. Therefore He brought up against them the king of the Chaldeans [Babylon] who slew their young men with the sword in the house of their sanctuary, and had no compassion on young man or virgin, old man or infirm; He gave them all into his hand. All the articles of the house of God, great and small, and the treasures of the house of the Lord, and the treasures of the king and of his officers, he brought them all to Babylon. Then they burned the house of God and broke down the wall of Jerusalem, and burned all its fortified buildings with fire and destroyed all its valuable articles. Those who had escaped from the sword he carried away to Babylon; and they were servants to him and to his sons until the rule of the kingdom of Persia, to fulfill the word of the Lord by the mouth of Jeremiah, until the land had enjoyed its sabbaths. (2 Chron. 36:11–21)

Far more disturbing than the historical ruin of the city and the temple is the fact that this catastrophic period of Judah's history is actually a foreshadowing of what will occur yet again in the last days during the reign of the Antichrist. In describing this three-and-a-half-year period, the angel Gabriel said it would not be completed until the Antichrist and his armies "finish shattering the power of the holy people" (Dan. 12:7). Elsewhere in the prophecies of Daniel, we're told that the leaders of Israel will be given over to the Antichrist, who "will fling truth to the ground and perform

[his] will and prosper" (8:12). Such warnings are repeated multiple times. The Antichrist "will destroy to an extraordinary degree and prosper and perform his will; he will destroy mighty men and the holy people" (8:24, cf. 11:36).

Among the worst horrors the Antichrist will succeed in accomplishing is taking many of the present-day citizens of Jerusalem and Israel as captives. References to this unimaginably painful future reality are found throughout the Scriptures. The prophet Zechariah, for example, wrote that half of the citizens of Jerusalem will be taken as prisoners of war:

> For I will gather all the nations to battle against Jerusalem; the city shall be taken, the houses rifled, and the women ravished. *Half of the city shall go into captivity*, but the remnant of the people shall not be cut off from the city. (Zech. 14:2 NKJV, emphasis added)

Jesus also, in his Olivet Discourse, warned of the future day when many of the inhabitants of Judah would be taken as prisoners of war into the surrounding nations:

> But when you see Jerusalem surrounded by armies, then recognize that her desolation is near. Then those who are in Judea must flee to the mountains, and those who are in the midst of the city must leave, and those who are in the country must not enter the city; because these are days of vengeance, so that all things which are written will be fulfilled. Woe to those who are pregnant and to those who are nursing babies in those days; for there will be great distress upon the land and wrath to this people; and they will fall by the edge of the sword, *and will be led captive into all the nations*; and Jerusalem will be trampled under foot by the Gentiles until the times of the Gentiles are fulfilled. (Luke 21:20–24, emphasis added)

Offering hope in the midst of this trouble, multiple passages speak of these Jewish captives being delivered when Jesus the Messiah returns:

"Therefore thus says the Lord God: 'Now I will bring back the captives of Jacob, and have mercy on the whole house of Israel.'" (Ezek. 39:25 NKJV)

For in Mount Zion and in Jerusalem there shall be deliverance, as the Lord has said, among the remnant whom the LORD calls. "For behold, in those days and at that time, when I bring back the captives of Judah and Jerusalem" . . . (Joel 2:32–3:1 NKJV)

The Spirit of the Lord God is upon me . . . He has sent me to bind up the brokenhearted, to proclaim liberty to the captives, and the opening of the prison to those who are bound; to proclaim the year of the Lord's favor, and the day of vengeance of our God; to comfort all who mourn; to grant to those who mourn in Zion . . . (Isa. 61:1–3 ESV)

You will arise and have pity on Zion; it is the time to favor her; the appointed time has come . . . From heaven the LORD looked at the earth, to hear the groans of the prisoners, to set free those who were doomed to die. (Ps. 102:13, 19, 20 esv)

As the king who led many of the Jews into captivity, Nebuchadnezzar is a clear prefigurement of the coming Antichrist, the last-days "king" of Babylon. It is in this way that the ancient empire of Babylon, under Nebuchadnezzar's rule, is a picture of the last-days Babylon, which represents the Lord's final chastisement of His own people, before He draws them to Him and makes them His forever.

THE GOLDEN IDOL

When we consider the harlot Babylon's description as a great persecuting entity, "drunk with the blood of the saints, and with the blood of the witnesses of Jesus" (Rev. 17:6), it brings to mind an episode recorded in the book of Daniel that surely conveys the spirit of Babylon that will rise again in the last days. It is the story of the three Hebrews Hananiah, Mishael, and Azariah, most often known by their given Babylonian names, Shadrach, Meshach, and Abednego. According to Daniel, King Nebuchadnezzar had set up an "image of gold" in the plain of Dura (Dan. 3:1). This massive idol was 90 feet tall. Compare this to the colossal Christ the Redeemer statue overlooking Rio de Janeiro, which, not counting its large base, is 98 feet tall. The Statue of Liberty, from the base to the tip of the torch, is 151 feet. This was a mammoth, imposing statue.

After completing the construction of this great idol, Nebuchadnezzar commanded all the people in Babylon to bow down and worship before it. If they refused, they were to be burned alive in a raging fire. The decree read:

> To you the command is given, O peoples, nations and men of every language, that at the moment you hear the sound of the horn, flute, lyre, trigon, psaltery, bagpipe and all kinds of music, you are to fall down and worship the golden image that Nebuchadnezzar the king has set up. But whoever does not fall down and worship shall immediately be cast into the midst of a furnace of blazing fire. (Dan. 3:4–6)

Some of the Chaldeans, devotees of the Babylonian religion, were furious that Hananiah, Mishael, and Azariah refused to bow down and worship before the idol. Indignant, a group came forward and denounced them before the king.

> O king, live forever! You, O king, have made a decree that every man who hears the sound of the horn, flute, lyre, trigon, psaltery, and bagpipe and all kinds of music, is to fall down and worship the golden image. But whoever does not fall down and worship shall be cast into the midst of a furnace of blazing fire. There are certain Jews whom you have appointed over the administration of the province of Babylon, namely Shadrach, Meshach and Abednego. These men, O king, have disregarded you; they do not serve your gods or worship the golden image which you have set up. (Dan. 3:9–12)

And so these faithful Hebrews were called before Nebuchadne-zzar. I've always loved the humility with which they defied him, even at the threat of death. It is an example for all servants of the Lord:

> O Nebuchadnezzar, we do not need to give you an answer con-cerning this matter. If it be so, our God whom we serve is able to deliver us from the furnace of blazing fire; and He will deliver us out of your hand, O king. But even if He does not, let it be known to you, O king, that we are not going to serve your gods or worship the golden image that you have set up. (Dan. 3:16–18)

A typical dictator, Nebuchadnezzar burst into a rage. The fire was stoked seven times hotter than usual and the men were bound and tossed into the flames. Of course, the story doesn't end there. After being astounded to see the men walking around alive in the midst of the inferno (along with a fourth and divine being), Nebu-chadnezzar set the Hebrews free and allowed them to live. The result was a profound acknowledgment of the power of the God of the Jews. This was a powerful divine deliverance. The point to be emphasized, however, for our purposes here, is the enforced worship at the threat of death. No doubt, this is a preview, a prophetic type of the last-days Babylon. This city will be integrally connected to the religious-economic system of the Antichrist. Whoever refuses to accept the "mark of the beast" and bow down and worship the god of the Antichrist will do so at the expense of his own life (see Rev. 13). This is precisely why the woman Babylon is portrayed as being drunk on "the blood of the saints, the blood of the martyrs of Jesus" (17:6 ESV). Like Shadrach, Meshach, and Abednego, faithful believers in the last days will also be called to stand firm, even unto death. This will become one of the defining dynamics governing the relationship of the last-days Babylon and the people of God on the earth during that time.

CONCLUSION

As we assess the biblical narratives concerning Nimrod's Babel and Nebuchadnezzar's Babylon, we find that although Nimrod's Babel provides very little insight into the nature of the last-days Babylon, Nebuchadnezzar's Babylon offers an abundance of information. Even as Nebuchadnezzar's Babylon was used as a rod of chastisement against the Lord's people in history, so also will the last-days Babylon be the source of great chastisement to Israel, the Jewish people, and Christians all over the world. Many Jews were taken into captivity by the Babylon of old; similar events will be repeated in the last days. Ancient Babel represented a united rebellion against the Lord; the last-days Babylon will represent a satanically empowered global rebellion against the one true God of the Bible. It will also represent a profoundly adversarial and persecuting religion that demands that all peoples bow before its god. Though Nebuchadnezzar's Babylon shed an abundance of Jewish blood, the last-days Babylon, in partnership with the devil, will shed more Jewish—and Christian—blood than any previous persecution. As we are told in Revelation 12: "So the dragon was enraged with the woman, and went off to make war with the rest of her children, who keep the commandments of God and hold to the testimony of Jesus" (v. 17). But just as ancient Babylon provided the Lord's faithful an opportunity to stand firm in the face of tremendous pressure, so also will the last-days Babylon provide God's people with the opportunity to stand firm, even unto death.

4

THE NIMROD MYTH

IN THE LAST CHAPTER, we discussed the difference between the ancient city of Babel and the slightly less ancient Babylon of Nebuchadnezzar. As we noted, although there is abundant information in the Bible about Nebuchadnezzar's Babylon, the Scriptures give us only nine verses regarding ancient Babel. Unfortunately, this has led many Christian authors down through history to turn to and rely on a series of legends outside of the Bible that I refer to collectively as "the Nimrod myth." For faithful students of God's Word, this is simply not an option. Our understanding of Revelation 17–18 must be rooted in the revealed Word of God, not extrabiblical myths that, as we will see, probably have no basis in truth whatsoever.

Some years ago, when I began studying numerous Christian treatments of the harlot Babylon, I was repeatedly confronted with a veritable tower of information about Nimrod and Babel. All of this literature seemed to relay very well-developed stories about Nimrod, his wife, their religion, and how that religion eventually came to infiltrate every other religion throughout world history. It was these stories about Nimrod that actually formed the very foundation for many theologians' understanding of Mystery Babylon. Basically, what many of these books taught is that through the ancient Babylonian religion, every religion in the world would be brought under one umbrella, controlled by the Antichrist, a sort of last-days Nimrod. This picture created the perfect grand narrative that pulled many seemingly conflicting religions and ideologies all into one unified tent. While this did provide a very neat and convenient explanation for how the Antichrist could unite the whole world under one banner, the entire narrative rested on these stories about Nimrod. As I came to realize just how foundational these stories were to this picture that was so often painted, seeking to be a faithful Berean I knew it was critical to investigate their origins. Since virtually none of these Nimrod stories are found in the Bible, I needed to understand where they came from. When and where did they originate? As I began to dig into these matters, I uncovered a wide variety of Jewish, Christian, and even Islamic traditions. Though some of these traditions arose sometime around the first century, they continued to develop into a larger and much more detailed narrative, expanding right up to our present day. As fascinating as I found these tales, the problem was that none of them could be verified as true. In fact, many of them were actually in conflict with the biblical record or with other known facts of history. If we desire to be responsible in our interpretation of Revelation 17 and 18, then we must address this issue. The last thing we want to do is validate, rely on, and even perpetuate traditions that "nullify the word of God" (see Mark 7:13 NIV). In this chapter, then, we will briefly examine where these various Nimrod stories came from, when they developed, and why we should not look to them to help us understand the mystery of the last-days harlot Babylon.

PHILO OF ALEXANDRIA

The first reference to Nimrod outside of the Bible is found in the writings of Philo Judaeus (20 BC–AD 50). Philo was a first-century Jewish philosopher from Alexandria who sought to combine Greek philosophy with biblical theology.

Philo's approach to biblical interpretation was very strange. For him, a person's character was determined by the deeper allegorical or spiritual meaning of his or her name. According to Philo, Ham, Nimrod's grandfather, "is the name of wickedness in a state of inactivity"[1] Cush, Nimrod's father, represented "the sparse nature of earth," and "the name Nimrod, being interpreted, means, 'desertion.'"[2] Thus, Philo argued, Nimrod was "the first to set the example of this desertion [of God and His ways]."[3] Because Nimrod was a "mighty (Hebrew: *gibbor*) hunter," to Philo he was also "a giant born of the earth, [who] prefers earthly to heavenly things . . . for in truth he who is an emulator of earthly and corruptible things is always engaged in a conflict with heavenly and admirable natures."[4] Elsewhere, Philo stated that Nimrod should be translated as "Ethiopian" or the black one, because in Nimrod there is no spiritual light.[5]

Philo also claimed that Nimrod built the Tower of Babel, not to reach out to the gods, as many claim, but rather, "as a bulwark against heaven,"[6] a fortress to protect him from God. Concluding his denunciation of Nimrod, Philo stated:

> There is much propriety in the expression, "he was a giant against God," which thus declares the opposition of such beings to the deity; for a wicked man is nothing else than an enemy, contending against God: on which account it has become a proverb that every one who sins greatly ought to be referred to him as the original and chief of sinners, being spoken of as "a second Nimrod."[7]

There is little doubt that Philo's completely negative portrayal of Nimrod set the tone for many others who would follow.

FLAVIUS JOSEPHUS

Writing roughly forty years later, Flavius Josephus, the Jewish historian, presented a different, yet more developed Nimrod tradition. According to Josephus, for a few generations after the Great Flood, humankind was terrified that the Lord would send another flood. Being obedient to the Lord's commands to spread out over the earth, Noah's sons, Shem, Ham, and Japheth, were the first to come down out of the mountains to inhabit the plains. The remainder of humanity, however, not trusting the Lord, "were greatly afraid of the lower grounds on account of the floods and so were very loth to come down from the higher place, to venture to follow their examples."[8] In time however, due to the persuasions of Noah's sons, people began to repopulate the plains. Those who did, multiplied rapidly and experienced great blessings. According to Josephus, it was here that Nimrod emerged, agitating the people into a "contempt of God":

> He persuaded them not to ascribe [their blessings] to God as if it was through his means they were happy, but to believe that it was their own courage which procured that happiness. He also gradually changed the government into tyranny,—seeing no other way of turning men from the fear of God, but to bring them into a constant dependence upon his power. He also said he would be revenged on God, if he should have a mind to drown the world again; for that he would build a tower too high for the waters to be able to reach! and that he would avenge himself on God for destroying their forefathers![9]

According to Josephus, the purpose of the Tower of Babel was to provide a safe haven for those who lived in the plains. Should the Lord decide to send another great flood, the tower was to be their refuge.[10]

THE SIBYLLINE ORACLES

The Sibylline Oracles are a collection of controversial prophecies delivered sometime during the first century by a woman called Sibyl. Although some ancient writers refer to several or as many as ten Sibyls, both Philo and Josephus refer singularly to "the Sibyl." The Sibylline Oracles are cited frequently, and sometimes favorably, within Jewish and early Christian writings. One of the Sibylline Oracles refers to the Tower of Babel:

> When all men were of one language, some of them built a high tower, as if they would thereby ascend up to heaven; but the gods sent storms of wind and overthrew the tower, and gave everyone his peculiar language; and for this reason it was that the city was called Babylon.[11]

Already we can see a diversity of views concerning the purpose for building the tower. Whereas Philo saw it as a "bulwark against heaven," Josephus saw it as a means to survive a flood, and the Sibyl cast it as a means to reach into heaven. Three completely different and contradictory stories.

PSEUDO-PHILO

We know almost nothing about Pseudo-Philo, other than he was the author of another expanded history of the Bible, referred to as *The Biblical Antiquities of Philo*. This work was probably written during the second half of the first century. Although this author wrote under the name Philo, in actuality he was simply a Philo pretender. Adopting the name of other famous writers to give weight to one's own works was a fairly common practice in ancient times. Pseudo-Philo has provided us with a very well-developed Nimrod story. In commenting on Genesis 10:9, he wrote that Nimrod[12] "began to be proud before the Lord."[13] Later, after Nimrod is chosen as the leader of the sons of Ham, we read an intriguing story about a direct spiritual confrontation between Nimrod and Abraham. All the people said, "Let us take bricks, and let us, each one, write our names upon the bricks and burn them with fire: and that which is thoroughly burned shall be for mortar and brick."[14] Each man then took a brick and wrote his name on it—all except twelve men, including Abraham. The people of the land, filled with rage,

> laid hands on them and brought them before their princes and said: These are the men that have transgressed our counsels and will not walk in our ways. And the princes said unto them: Wherefore would ye not set every man your bricks with the people of the land? And they answered and said: We will not set bricks with you, neither will we bejoined with your desire. One Lord know we, and him do we worship. And if ye should cast us into the fire with your bricks, we will not consent to you.[15]

Furious at their rebellion, Nimrod had Abraham thrown alive into the furnace used to fire the bricks. The story is nearly identical to the story of Shadrach, Meshach, and Abednego and the fiery furnace recorded in Daniel 3. When an earthquake caused the furnace to spew forth fire, 83,500 men died, but Abraham escaped completely unscathed.[16] This story, or some version of it, is repeated in numerous other, later Nimrod traditions where Abraham and Nimrod have a series of conflicts.

THE TALMUD

The next significant family of Nimrod stories, perhaps the most influential of all, is found in the Talmud. In his classic work, *The Legends of the Jews*, renowned nineteenth-century rabbi Louis Ginzberg summarized many of these traditions. In perhaps the most unique story, Ginzberg detailed the events that led to Nimrod becoming a great king of the ancient world:

> The first among the leaders of the corrupt men was Nimrod. . . . [His father, Cush,] gave him the clothes made of skins with which God had furnished Adam and Eve at the time of their leaving

Paradise. Cush himself had gained possession of them through Ham. From Adam and Eve they had descended to Enoch, and from him to Methuselah, and to Noah, and the last had taken them with him into the ark. When the inmates of the ark were about to leave their refuge, Ham stole the garments and kept them concealed, finally passing them on to his first-born son Cush. Cush in turn hid them for many years. When his son Nimrod reached his twentieth year, he gave them to him. These garments had a wonderful property. He who wore them was both invincible and irresistible. The beasts and birds of the woods fell down before Nimrod as soon as they caught sight of him arrayed in them, and he was equally victorious in his combats with men. The source of his unconquerable strength was not known to them. They attributed it to his personal prowess, and therefore they appointed him king over themselves.[17]

Ginzberg recounted another unique story that features Nimrod building a massive throne for himself, upon which he sought to be worshipped as a god:

The great success that attended all of Nimrod's undertakings produced a sinister effect. Men no longer trusted in God, but rather in their own prowess and ability, an attitude to which Nimrod tried to convert the whole world. Therefore people said, "Since the creation of the world there has been none like Nimrod, a mighty hunter of men and beasts, and a sinner before God." And not all this sufficed unto Nimrod's evil desire. Not enough that he turned men away from God, he did all he could to make them pay Divine honors unto himself. He set himself up as a god, and made a seat for himself in imitation of the seat of God. It was a tower built out of a round rock, and on it he placed a throne of cedar wood, upon which arose, one above the other, four thrones, of iron, copper, silver, and gold. Crowning all, upon the golden throne, lay a precious stone, round in shape and gigantic in size.

This served him as a seat, and as he sat upon it, all nations came and paid him Divine homage.[18]

Both of these stories are certainly interesting, even if some elements, such as Nimrod's cloak of invincibility, make them rather impossible to believe.[19]

Within rabbinic Judaism, many of these stories are viewed as part of the "Oral Torah," sacred tales not found in the written Torah, or Bible but, nevertheless, true stories passed down through the millennia. There are, however, some huge flaws with such claims. First, we do not find a single example of any of these traditions even written down until the first and second centuries AD. Yet Nimrod lived approximately two thousand years before these traditions. Second, in the fifth century BC, after the Jewish exiles had returned from Babylon, when a copy of the written law was found in the temple and was read aloud before the people, they had all but forgotten it. How could they have remembered the so-called Oral Torah if they had all but forgotten the written Torah? Instead of being some long-preserved tradition, all evidence points to the fact that these Nimrod traditions likely were created sometime around the first century.

AUGUSTINE

We cannot fail to mention Nimrod's treatment by Augustine, arguably the most influential post-apostolic theologian in Christian history. Writing in the early fifth century, Augustine, like so many before him, cast Nimrod in a purely negative light:

> And so this giant is to be recognized as a "hunter against the Lord." And what is meant by the term "hunter" but deceiver, oppressor, and destroyer of the animals of the earth? He and his people therefore, erected this tower against the Lord, and so gave expression to their impious pride; and justly was their wicked intention punished by God, even though it was unsuccessful.[20]

THE APOCALYPSE OF PSEUDO-METHODIUS

The Apocalypse of Pseudo-Methodius, a spurious, seventh-century Christian work, perpetuated the idea that Nimrod was one of the giants of the ancient world. It is there that we also find the first reference to Nimrod being taught astronomy, through which he gained the power to rule humankind:

> Jonitus, the son of Noah, entered into the East as far as the sea, which is called "Hiliu Chora," that is "the Country of the Sun," in which the rising of the sun takes place, and he lived there. This Jonitus received from God the gift of wisdom; not only this alone, but he also became the inventor of every division of astronomy. Nimrod, who was a giant, came down to him and learned from him and received from him the counsel by which he might begin to rule. This Nimrod was descended from the sons of heroes; he was a son of Shem and he was the first to rule as a king over the earth. In the 790th year of the third millennium, which is the passing of three thousand years, Babylon the Great was built and Nimrod ruled in it.[21]

THE BOOK OF ROLLS

An early ninth-century Arabic Christian work known as the *Kitab al-Magall*, or the *Book of Rolls*,[22] part of what is called the Clementine Homilies, features more familiar elements, such as Nimrod being a giant. It does add, however, some previously unknown traditions. Here's one example:

> Nimrod the giant reigned over the whole earth. The beginning of his kingdom was from Babel. It was he who saw in the sky a piece of black cloth and a crown; he called Sasan the weaver to his presence, and commanded him to make him a crown like it; and he set jewels in it and wore it. He was the first king who wore a crown. For this reason people who knew nothing about it, said that a crown came down to him from heaven. The length of his reign was sixty-nine years.

Later, the book describes how Nimrod established the practice of fire worship and idolatry, and received instruction in divination from someone named Bouniter, the fourth son of Noah.[23]

THE BOOK OF JASHER

The Book of Jasher, which has experienced a tremendous resurgence of popularity in recent times, should not be confused with the book of Jashar mentioned in the Bible (see Josh.10:13; 2 Sam. 1:18). *The Book of Jasher*, also known as *Sefer haYashar*, is actually a Jewish midrashic work from the sixteenth century. Jasher features an extensive section on Nimrod that includes many of the elements of previous traditions. One unique aspect of Jasher's account features the builders of the Tower of Babel and their intentions to dethrone God:

> And all these people and all the families divided themselves in three parts; the first said We will ascend into heaven and fight against him; the second said, We will ascend to heaven and place our own gods there and serve them; and the third part said, We will ascend to heaven and smite him with bows and spears.[24]

Later, we are told of three distinct judgments leveled against each of these groups. The first group was killed, the second group were turned into apes and elephants, and the third group the Lord dispersed throughout the earth. Jasher also recounts what became of the tower after the Lord dispersed the people:

> And as to the tower which the sons of men built, the earth opened its mouth and swallowed up one third part thereof, and a fire also descended from heaven and burned another third, and the other third is left to this day, and it is of that part which was aloft, and its circumference is three days' walk.[25]

Finally, Jasher recounts a story concerning how Abraham's grandson Esau, also a hunter, stalked, ambushed, and beheaded Nimrod, then stole the animal skin clothes that had been given to him by his father. Similar accounts are found in earlier Talmudic traditions.[26]

NIMROD AS A HISTORICAL FIGURE

Beyond these traditional expansions of the biblical narrative, several scholars have sought to equate Nimrod with various mythological or historical figures, such as (1) Ninurta, the Assyrian god of hunting; (2) Gilgamesh, the Babylonian epic hero, who was also described as a hunter; (3) Marduk, a Babylonian god; (4) Amenhotep III (1408–1369 BC) of Egypt's Eighteenth Dynasty; (5) Tukulti-Ninurta, Assyrian monarch and another reputed hunter who conquered Babylon; and (6) Sargon of Akkad Naram-Sin, grandson of Sargon of Akkad. As *The Lexham Bible Dictionary* concludes, "This list shows the stark disagreement among biblical scholars over the identification of Nimrod."[27] While some scholars equate Nimrod to a sort of god or demigod, others link him to human kings. None of these suggestions are convincing.

NIMROD THE RIGHTEOUS?

In the margin notes of the most widely used Bible of seventeenth-century Protestantism—the 1599 Geneva Bible—Nimrod is referred to as "a cruel oppressor and tyrant . . . [whose] tyranny came into a proverb as hated both by God and man: for he did not cease to commit cruelty even in God's presence."[28] Despite the fact that the Bible nowhere overtly supports the idea that Nimrod was actually an evil tyrant of the ancient world, the acceptance of this idea and its impact on Christianity down through the centuries have been widespread.

Amazingly, many alternate traditions actually cast Nimrod as righteous. To the surprise of some, at least one early Jewish tradition actually equates Nimrod with Noah, claiming they are actually the same person.[29] Both Targum Yerushalmi and Targum Pseudo-Jonathan state that Nimrod specifically emigrated to Assyria because he refused to participate in the building of the Tower of Babel. According to these Talmudic traditions, because of this righteous act, the Lord rewarded Nimrod with four cities.[30] Later, toward the close of the fourth century, John Chrysostom argued on Nimrod's behalf as a man blessed by God with bravery and strength:

"Now, Cush became the father of Nebrod [Nimrod], who began to be a giant on earth. He was a giant hunter before the Lord." While some people say the phrase "before the Lord" means being in opposition to God, I on the contrary do not think sacred Scripture is implying this. Rather, it implies that [Nimrod] was strong and brave. But the phrase "before the Lord" means created by him, receiving from him God's blessing.[31]

Ephrem the Syrian, another renowned fourth-century Christian theologian, also spoke of Nimrod in glowing terms, casting him not as one who built the Tower of Babel, but as a hero before the Lord who actually chased the builders of the tower away:

Concerning Nimrod, Moses said, "He was a mighty hunter before the Lord," because, according to the will of the Lord, it was he who fought with each of these nations and chased them out from there, so that they would go out and settle in the regions that had been set apart for them by God. "Therefore it is said, like Nimrod a mighty hunter before the Lord." One used to bless a chief or a ruler by saying, "May you be like Nimrod, a mighty hunter who was victorious in the battles of the Lord."[32]

Obviously Nimrod cannot have been both the very embodiment of wickedness and a man of legendary righteousness. Yet we have absolutely no way of knowing which stories are true—if any!

CONCLUSION

As we've seen, the various Nimrod traditions are filled with contradictions. Some accounts say Nimrod's rise to power was due to the animal skins he acquired from Adam and Eve. Another tradition says it was because he learned astronomy. Yet another tradition says he rose to power because he was both a giant and a mighty hunter. Philo described the Tower of Babel as Nimrod's defensive bulwark against God, while Josephus portrayed it as a tower of refuge in case God sent another flood. Sibyl cast it as the means whereby man could "ascend up to heaven." Finally, Jasher portrayed it as a means to actually attack the inhabitants of heaven. Yet for all their diversity, none of these accounts aligns with the biblical account. The Bible simply says the builders were seeking to make a name for themselves and to avoid being scattered throughout the earth. It says nothing about avoiding being drowned in a flood or reaching into heaven. What's more, the Bible doesn't even say that Nimrod actually built the Tower of Babel. The only thing it says relating Nimrod to Babel is, "The beginning of his kingdom was Babel" (Gen. 10:10). That's it. Anything beyond this is simply conjecture.

While the Nimrod traditions began as rather simple expansions of the biblical story, the more we move forward in history, the more they've expanded and grown more complex. Each new tradition seems to inflate larger than those traditions that came before it. Clearly, in these stories, we do not have the preservation of ancient truths; rather, we have a snowballing myth. For roughly two thousand years, this myth has continued to evolve. Nowhere, however, has the expansion of this myth found a greater champion than in the imaginative mind of a Scottish minister named Alexander Hislop. It is to this man, and his voluminous work, that we will dedicate the next chapter.

5

ALEXANDER HISLOP'S TWO BABYLONS

IN 1853, THE REVEREND ALEXANDER HISLOP published a pamphlet titled *The Two Babylons*. Five years later, the pamphlet was revised, dramatically expanded, and rereleased as a book by the same title. *The Two Babylons* has come to be one of the most deeply influential Christian works of the nineteenth century, having profound reverberations even today throughout various segments of Protestantism.

HISLOP'S NARRATIVE

The basic premise of Hislop's work is that modern Roman Catholicism is entirely pagan, having received its practices, symbols, and structure, not from any Christian tradition, but directly from Nimrod and Semiramis, the founders of ancient Babylonian paganism.

From the very outset, Hislop's narrative begins with a strong note of patently offensive racism. "Nimrod," we are told, "was a Negro . . . the real original of the black Adversary of mankind . . . the recognised representative of the Devil."[1] According to Hislop, because Nimrod was a son of Cush, who is most often associated with the African lands south of Egypt, he must have been black,[2] and because he was black, he must have therefore been the original representative of the devil. Sadly, this is the quality of logic that underpins so much of Hislop's work.

Next, because Nimrod was called "a mighty hunter before the Lord" (Gen. 10:9), Hislop reasoned that he must have been a giant, a descendant of the Nephilim (Gen. 6:4). The problem, of course, is that a more careful reading of the text shows that Nimrod "became a mighty one" (10:8). "Mighty" in this context simply means that Nimrod was an exceedingly excellent hunter. Thus, Hislop cast Nimrod as an evil giant black man. On the other hand, Nimrod's wife, Semiramis, is portrayed as an exceedingly beautiful blonde, blue-eyed woman. As we will see later, however, Nimrod and Semiramis couldn't have actually been married, as the two lived well over a thousand years apart!

As Hislop told it, shortly after marrying Nimrod and becoming pregnant with his child, Semiramis killed him. When the child was born, she claimed that her baby was a reincarnation of Nimrod. The child was named Tammuz. According to Hislop, the Babylonian religion of Ishtar, created by Nimrod and Semiramis, came to worship both Semiramis and Tammuz, this mother-and-child pair. Later, as this religion spread out across the globe, the names of Semiramis and Tammuz were changed from one nation to another. In Egypt, Semiramis was called Isis; in Greece and Rome she was called Venus, Diana, Athena, Fortuna, and a host of other names. In this way, wrote Hislop, the original satanic Babylonian religion has spread into every corner of the earth, forming the basis for every false religion. And because the last-days Babylon is referred to as "the Mother of Harlots" (Rev. 17:5), that ancient Babylonian religion is obviously the "mother," quite literally, of every false religion that exists—including Christianity!

BABYLON INFECTS CHRISTIANITY

Hislop claimed that in the early fourth century, Emperor Constantine very purposefully deceived the whole world by claiming to convert to Christianity, when in fact he remained entirely pagan. According to Hislop, Constantine renamed the Babylonian gods and goddesses he worshipped with Christian names in order to secretly mix the two religions. The end result of this great satanic conspiracy is that modern Roman Catholicism, and by extension, Eastern Orthodoxy and Anglicanism, are not simply tainted by paganism, but are actually a modern manifestation of ancient Babylonian satanism. Hislop believed that the Roman Catholic Church's "doctrine and discipline, in all essential respects, have been derived from Babylon."[3] None of the practices, symbols, or liturgical structures of the traditional branches of Christianity, then, come from any apostolic or even postapostolic tradition whatsoever, but instead they all come directly from ancient Babylon. Unfortunately, some Christian groups have even used Nimrod's general premise to cast every other Protestant denomination (apart from their own) as the pagan "daughters" of Babylon.

Unfortunately, it is not only fringe groups that have come to embrace Hislop's theories. As we will see, numerous Christian teachers, some of them very well respected and mainstream, have perpetuated various elements of Hislop's narrative. It would be difficult to understate the profound impact that Hislop's work has had on modern Christianity.

GLOBAL BABYLON

For those seeking some all-encompassing satanic religious conspiracy

through which every false religious system in the world is intercon-
nected, Hislop has provided the perfect story. He is viewed as the
great historical detective who first exposed Satan's grand plan, having
demonstrated a direct historical connection from the very beginning of humankind's rebellion at the Tower of Babel to this very day.
For this reason, Hislop's work has become the primary basis for the
interpretation of those who see "Mystery Babylon" as relating to the
"New World Order" or Illuminati and so forth. The problem is that
the overwhelming majority of Hislop's claims are simply bogus. His
larger narrative is thoroughly detached from both reality and history.

REVEREND RALPH WOODROW: DEBUNKING HISLOP

Originally influenced by Hislop's work, the Reverend Ralph
Woodrow, an American evangelist and minister, wrote his own
updated version of Hislop's work, titled *Babylon Mystery Religion*.
For years, Woodrow was a modern Hislop, traveling and lecturing
on the Babylonian connections to Catholicism and every world religion. Quite amazingly, however, after being challenged to reexamine
the historical accuracy of Hislop's work (and thus his own book),
Woodrow became convinced that it was indeed all a massive fraud.
As a result, he did what very few authors have the courage to do;
not only did he withdraw his own book (an action that has caused
him much financial loss), but he also took the time to write another
book, actually renouncing Hislop's work and correcting that which
he himself had previously written. This book is called *The Babylon
Connection?* With Mr. Woodrow's permission, I have printed the
following portion from the introduction to his book:

> In my earlier Christian experience, certain literature fell into my
> hands which claimed paganism had been mixed into Christianity.
> While the Roman Catholic Church was usually the target, it
> seemed other churches had also been contaminated by customs
> and beliefs for which pagan parallels could be found.
> *The Two Babylons* by Alexander Hislop (1807–1862), with its
> alarming subtitle, the papal worship proved to be the worship of

nimrod and his wife, was the textbook on which much of this teaching was based. Over the years, this book has impacted the thinking of many people—ranging all the way from those in radical cults to very dedicated Christians who hunger for a move of God and are concerned about anything that might hinder that flow. Its basic premise is that the pagan religion of ancient Babylon has continued to our day, in disguise, as the Roman Catholic Church and is described in the book of Revelation as "Mystery Babylon the Great" thus, the idea of two Babylons, one ancient, and one modern. Because this book is very detailed, having a multitude of notes and references, I assumed, as did many others, it was factual. We quoted "Hislop" as an authority on paganism, just like "Webster" might be quoted on word definitions.

As a young evangelist I began to share a sermon on the mixture of paganism into Christianity, and eventually wrote a book based on Hislop—*Babylon Mystery Religion*. In time, my book became quite popular, went through many printings, and was translated into Korean, German, Spanish, Portuguese, and several other languages. I came to be regarded by some as an authority on the subject of pagan mixture. Even a noted Roman Catholic writer, Karl Keating, said: "Its best-known proponent is Ralph Woodrow, author of *Babylon Mystery Religion*."

Many preferred my book over *The Two Babylons* because it was easier to read and follow. Sometimes the two books were confused with each other, and I even had the experience, on one occasion, of being greeted as "Rev. Hislop"! Letters in a steady flow were received praising my book. Only occasionally would there be a dissenting voice. One who disagreed was Scott Klemm, a high school history teacher in southern California. Being a Christian, and appreciating other things I had written, he began to show me evidence that Hislop was not a reliable historian. As a result, I realized that I needed to go back through Hislop's work, my basic source, and prayerfully check it out!

As I did this, it became clear—Hislop's "history" was often only mythology. Even though myths may sometimes reflect events that actually happened, an arbitrary piecing together of ancient myths can not provide a sound basis for history. Take enough tribes, enough tales, enough time, jump from one time to another, from one country to another, pick and choose similarities—why anything could be "proved"![4]

Not only are Woodrow's honesty, courage, and humility to be commended, but his analysis of Hislop's work is piercing, yet done with a great sense of wit and humor. Because Woodrow has done such a thorough job refuting Hislop, I highly recommend that everyone who reads this book also take the time to read Woodrow's book as well.[5]

ALEXANDER HISLOP'S BEAUTIFUL MIND

In the 2001 film *A Beautiful Mind,* actor Russell Crowe portrays John Nash, a brilliant mathematician who suffered from paranoid schizophrenia. Nash is recruited by the Pentagon to decrypt Russian communications. To the shock of his recruiters, Nash is able to decipher encryptions mentally without any external assistance. Sliding into a delusion that he has been given a secret government assignment, Nash begins obsessively scanning magazines and newspaper headlines to uncover secret codes and Soviet propaganda. One of the most memorable features in the film is a large wall where Nash pins hundreds of pages from magazines and newspapers. Crisscrossing the wall with dozens of strings and pins, Nash seeks to make various "connections" between random words and images. It is all very classic schizophrenic behavior. It also is terribly reminiscent of Alexander Hislop's *Two Babylons.* In fact, I would even be willing to say that if Hislop did not suffer from some degree of mental illness, then he was a deliberate fraud. Personally, I suspect he actually believed the things he taught. Although Hislop was a tireless researcher with regard to his actual historical methodology, his work is often frightfully illogical. Let's consider just a few examples of his claims and his methodology to see what I mean.

CONNECTIONS, CONNECTIONS, CONNECTIONS

Perhaps the most common argument that Hislop repeatedly fell back on is known as the logical fallacy of false equivalence. Whenever Hislop found two things that shared any similarity whatsoever, for him this was absolute, irrefutable proof that they were the same thing. Using this kind of faulty logic could prove that I, Joel Richardson, am in fact Joel C. Rosenberg. After all, we both are called Joel, both of our last names begin with R, we are both authors, we live during the same period of history, and we both write and teach frequently about very similar issues. We must be the same person. Case closed. Or so Hislop would reason. It is no exaggeration to say that it is this very kind of thought that dominates Hislop's work. Each time he discovered another similarity between two things, he stretched another string across his wall, building a veritable spider's web of connections. Let's look at just a few examples.

NIMROD AS OSIRIS

Because Hislop wished to prove that Nimrod was the original source of literally every false god that has ever existed, he sought points of similarity between his description of Nimrod and other false gods of history. Scouring other works, Hislop discovered an image of the Egyptian god Osiris from Sir J. Gardner Wilkinson's 1841 work, *The Manners and Customs of the Ancient Egyptians*. In observing Wilkinson's image of Osiris, Hislop claimed to have found "unequivocal evidence" that Osiris is actually Nimrod. Hislop said that Osiris "was also represented as a veritable Negro. In Wilkinson may be found a representation of him with the unmistakable features of the genuine Cushite or Negro."[6] Please follow Hislop's logic here. Because Nimrod was black (according to Hislop), and based on the drawing in Wilkinson's book, Osiris was also black, Nimrod and Osiris must be one and the same.

But wait; the "evidence" mounts. In further observing Wilkinson's image of Osiris, Hislop also noticed another incontrovertible proof. Osiris is seen to have a spotted garment. What could

Fig. 18.

this mean? After going into great detail (three whole pages' worth) concerning the use of leopards in ancient hunting rituals, Hislop concluded that because Nimrod was himself a hunter, he definitely would have been associated with leopards. And so, "that dress directly connects him with Nimrod. This Negro-featured Osiris is clothed from head to foot in a spotted dress."[7] How does this prove that Osiris is Nimrod? Well, obviously, leopards have spots, and thus, "we may be sure," that the spotted dress was intended to identify Osiris with Nimrod.[8] That's right; the proof is in the polka dots. This is simply downright bizarre.

DIONYSUS AS NIMROD

Moving forward to prove that the worship of Nimrod infected not only Egypt, but also Greece and pagan Rome, Hislop set out to connect yet another thread in his web, this time to Dionysus the Greek god of wine and harvest. Later, the Romans would change Dionysus's name to Bacchus. Sharing another image of an ancient Assyrian divinity, this time holding a spotted fawn,

Fig. 21.

Hislop wondered how anyone could miss the obvious symbolism. Leopards have spots and fawns have spots. Obviously, then, Dionysus is just another name for Nimrod. The "connections" are undeniable.

IS THE POPE A PRIEST OF DAGON?

Because Hislop wanted to show that every aspect of Roman Catholicism is thoroughly pagan, he cast nearly every aspect of the historical Christian faith as being rooted in Babylonian paganism. According to him, the practice of confessing to a priest found its origins in pagan Babylon. The doctrine of baptismal regeneration, he argued, also comes from Babylon. The use of any form of pillar in architecture is Babylonian too. Of course, Hislop failed to consider the fact that the Lord Himself ordained the use of pillars within the holy tabernacle (see for example Exod.24:4; 26:32,37; 27:11, 17; 1 Kings 7). According to Hislop, however, because a steeple is basically a pillar, any church with a steeple is simply a modern Babylonian temple. Seeking to cast the Roman Catholic communion wafer as pagan, he even claimed that the very circle is pagan, representing the Babylonian worship of the sun. Hislop's greatest efforts, however, were directed toward the pope. According to Hislop, the pope's hat, known as the "papal mitre" is actually a symbol of Dagon, the Babylonian fish god; therefore, the pope is a priest of Dagon. How did Hislop come to this conclusion? He found a picture in Sir Austen Henry Laylard's 1853 work, *Discoveries Among the Ruins of Nineveh and Babylon*, and noted someone wearing an outfit designed to resemble a fish. The head and mouth of the fish bear a resemblance to the mitre worn by the pope. So far, his observations are partially accurate. The problem, however, is that there is no historical connection between the hat worn by the pope today and the costume observed in Laylard's work. The papal mitre has undergone a series of gradual changes over the centuries. Initially, in the eleventh century, the pope's hat was short, round, and only slightly pointed, looking nothing like any fish head whatsoever. Over the years, the hat gradually evolved to become what it is today. Simply stated, there is absolutely no way the pope's tall mitre of modern times can be tied back to the ancient Dagon cult. Hislop simply saw an image that sort of resembled the pope's hat and did what he did hundreds of other times throughout his book; he simply assumed a connection where no such connection actually exists.

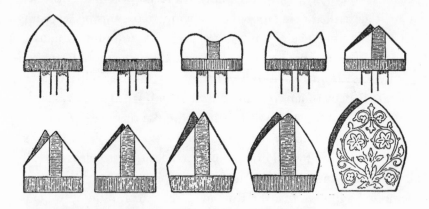

Development of the mitre from the eleventh century until modern times. Source: Braun, J. (1911). Mitre. In *The Catholic Encyclopedia*. New York: Robert Appleton Company. Retrieved July 15, 2008 from New Advent: Published in the public domain Catholic Encyclopedia.

Laylard's *Discoveries Among the Ruins of Nineveh and Babylon*. Note the second person on the left wearing a fish costume.

IS THE CROSS A SATANIC SYMBOL?

In his overly zealous efforts to tie anything associated with Roman Catholicism to Babylon, Hislop even went so far as to claim the very symbol of the cross is a satanic idol. He wrote:

> There is yet one more symbol of the Romish worship to be noticed, and that is the sign of the cross. In the Papal system as is well known, the sign of the cross and the image of the cross are all in all. No prayer can be said, no worship engaged in, no step almost can be taken, without the frequent use of the sign of the cross. The cross is looked upon as the grand charm, as the great refuge in every season of danger, in every hour of temptation as the infallible preservative from all the powers of darkness. The cross is adored with all the homage due only to the Most High.[9]

To establish his point, Hislop shared a picture of Bacchus (from *Smith's Classical Dictionary*), portrayed wearing a headband adorned with the ancient Greek *tau*, and stated, "The cross thus widely worshipped, or regarded as a sacred emblem, was the unequivocal symbol of Bacchus, the Babylonian Messiah, for he was represented with a head-band covered with crosses."[10]

According to Hislop, the "pagan symbol" of the cross was never used in the early church; it infected the church much later:

> Now, this Pagan symbol seems first to have crept into the Christian Church in Egypt, and generally into Africa. A statement of Tertullian, about the middle of the third century, shows how much, by that time

the Church of Carthage was infected with the old leaven. Egypt especially, which was never thoroughly evangelised, appears to have taken the lead in bringing in this Pagan symbol. The first form of that which is called the Christian Cross, found on Christian monuments there, is the unequivocal Pagan Tau, or Egyptian "Sign of life."[11]

So is it true that ancient pagans used symbols that resembled the cross? In some cases, it is. Does this mean the church was "infected with the old leaven" of paganism, as Hislop claimed? Of course not! Again, simply because two things are similar, in no way does it follow logically that the two things are the same. I am reminded of a picture I once saw of George W. Bush flashing a hand sign that supposedly proved that he is a Satan worshipper. Of course, the satanists' hand gesture and the gesture used by the Texas Longhorns college football team are basically the same. Can we conclude that every Texas Longhorn fan is actually a secret worshipper of Satan? Of course not. Even if the tau, or something else resembling a cross, was used long ago as a pagan symbol, it doesn't follow that the cross of Christ is thus a symbol of Satan worship. Yet this is exactly what Hislop claimed: "At first it was the emblem of Tammuz, at last it became the emblem of Teitan, or Satan himself."[12] This is absolute lunacy.

Reason with me here for a moment. Long before the temple in Jerusalem was established with its system of priests and sacrifices, various ancient pagans also had temples with holy of holies, priesthoods, and animal sacrifices. Shall we conclude then that the very temple which the Lord Himself ordained is actually pagan and satanic? Who would suggest something so absurd? Pagan precedence does not necessarily mean that any symbol or practice is forever the property of paganism. Something is not pagan based on its possible origins, but on how it is perceived today by those who use or observe it.

What do the Scriptures say? Is the cross really a symbol of paganism that infected the church? Was Jesus really crucified on a stake, as the Jehovah's Witnesses (and Hislop) claim?[13] When the apostle Thomas made his famous statement of doubt regarding the resurrection, what did he say? "Unless I see in His hands the imprint of the nails, and put my finger into the place of the nails, and put my hand into His side, I will not believe" (John 20:25). If Jesus had been crucified on a simple upright stake, with his hands above his head, only one nail would have been used. That His hands were spread out on a crossbeam shows why there would have been the need for nails—plural—and why Thomas spoke of nails. Also, the sign was hung not above Jesus' hands, but "above His head" (Matt. 27:37). All evidence points to Jesus having been hung on a cross.

Elsewhere in the Scriptures, we find an amazing clue concerning the sign of the cross in the prophecy of Ezekiel. In chapter 9, the Lord commands six angels to walk through Jerusalem and kill those who are unrighteous. To one angel, specifically "a man in linen" the Lord said, "Go through the midst of the city, even through the midst of Jerusalem, and put a mark on the foreheads of the men who sigh and groan over all the abominations which are being committed in its midst" (v. 4). What was the sign that the angel was to mark the righteous with? It was the paleo-Hebrew *tav*, which, like the Greek *tau*, is simply a cross. As Woodrow correctly reminds us,

> It was the Lord who ordered the + to be placed on the foreheads of the righteous. If this was a recognized evil, Babylonian symbol of Tammuz, why would the Lord designate this as the mark? Why would it be placed on the righteous? This was not a case of some wicked person placing a mark on the foreheads of wicked people. This was the mark of God! If pagans worshipped the cross as the symbol of Tammuz, as Hislop speculates, placing this mark on the righteous would be especially inconsistent when considered in context, for it is only eight verses before that Tammuz worship is condemned! (Ezek. 8:14).[14]

SEMIRAMIS

The most important and foundational component of Hislop's thesis, however, is his claim that Nimrod married a woman named Semiramis. As we have discussed, according to Hislop, together Nimrod and Semiramis built Babel, along with its legendary tower, and created the ancient Babylonian religion. This is the very basis for his entire work. It is from this ancient Babylonian religion, created by Nimrod and Semiramis, that every false religion in the earth today has its origin. The problem is that none of this ever happened. There is literally no historical or biblical evidence to support Hislop's most basic claims. Let's begin with Semiramis; who was she, and is there any actual historical connection between her and Nimrod?

Hislop's Semiramis, most historians agree, is merely a mythological figure initially created by the classical Greek historians. Although numerous legends of Semiramis can be found throughout the Middle East, historians are unable to pinpoint an actual historical Semiramis from Nimrod's period. Some scholars believe the mythological Semiramis stories to be rooted in the life of a real, ninth-century Assyrian queen named Sammuramat. Sammuramat was the wife of the Assyrian king Shamshi-Adad and the mother of Adad-Nirari. When her husband died, she ruled for several years as a temporary regent-queen until her son reached the age when he would take his father's throne. She seems to have been quite active, both expanding the Assyrian Empire through war and making improvements to the city of Babylon. This all took place between 823 and 806 BC.[15] Hislop also drew heavily from the life of Sammuramat to paint his picture of Semiramis. What he ignored, however, is that Nimrod lived sometime around 2600–2100 BC; Sammuramat lived at least twelve hundred years later. Needless to say, this completely rules out the notion that the two were ever married or formed a religion together. They did not even live in the same millennium! The most basic foundation of Hislop's claims are not only fundamentally wrong but easy to debunk. Hislop's method, however, was not to study history to discover truth. Instead he began with his preconceived storyline, then sought any proof he could scare up, whether historically or logically valid or not. When the facts did not line up, he simply ignored them. Throughout Hislop's book, the notion that Nimrod married Semiramis, and together they formed a religion, is treated as an unassailable fact. The fact, however, is that this story has absolutely no basis in historical reality. In the words of Joshua J. Mark, contributor to the *Ancient History Encyclopedia*, "The historical inaccuracies in [Hislop's] work are too numerous to mention."[16]

As we have seen, Alexander Hislop lacked a basic understanding of the historical method and even simple logic. Like John Nash in *A Beautiful Mind*, he was a diligent, if not obsessive, researcher, scouring every source he could find for "connections" that were little more than weak similarities. Worse, when he failed to find such similarities, he manufactured them wholesale, along with new "facts" based on an often mind-numbing series of assumptions. That Hislop's delusions affected him is unfortunate by itself, but when we consider how widespread his impact on twentieth-century Protestant Christianity has been, it is truly a great embarrassment.

THE IMPACT OF HISLOP ON CHRISTIAN INTERPRETATION
Even before Alexander Hislop, the Nimrod traditions were little more than unverifiable myths, completely detached from history. None of these traditions can be substantiated by the Bible. Even before Hislop, Christian interpreters, and commentators' reliance on the Nimrod myth was deeply problematic. Their embrace of Hislop's monumentally disastrous work, however, is outright scandalous. Whereas Hislop's work should have been immediately exposed and rejected, it has instead been widely embraced within large segments of mainstream Protestantism.

In his classic commentary series, famed American Baptist pastor and commentator Warren Wiersbe accepted and promoted the same narrative that Hislop did:

The "Babylonian system" of false religion has been a part of history since Nimrod founded his empire. Scholars have discovered it is amazingly like the true Christian faith! Alas, it is Satan's counterfeit of God's truth. Babylonians practiced the worship of mother and child, and even believed in the death and resurrection of the son.[17]

So also did John Walvoord, one of the most well-respected and widely cited Bible prophecy teachers in modern times, mirror Hislop's perspective. For example, in his massive work *Every Prophecy of the Bible*, Walvoord wrote:

> The wife of Nimrod, who was the founder of Babylon, headed up the mystery religion which characterized Babylon. She was given the name Semiramis, and according to the adherents' belief, she had a son conceived miraculously whose name was Tammuz. He was portrayed as a savior who fulfills the promise of deliverance given to Eve. This was, of course, a satanic description which permeates pagan religions.[18]

Today, countless Christian interpreters continue to draw from Hislop's polluted well to build their case for their view of Mystery Babylon. A very recent work that champions this perspective states:

> To solve the Bible's greatest riddle, we need to go far back into the distant past to a time not long after Noah's flood in ancient Babylon. Here, in the cradle of civilization along the Euphrates River, are the clues we need to piece together a cosmic jigsaw puzzle that predicts what is happening in our world today.[19]

Having established the hermeneutic that the only way we can truly understand Mystery Babylon is by understanding Nimrod's Babylon, these authors then begin to unpack exactly what kind of essential information we gain when we refer to the most ancient Babylon: "Since ancient Babylon, members of secret societies have acted as a kind of invisible elite wielding an inordinate degree of

control over the affairs of mankind and the direction of civilization."[20] According to these authors, Babylon is "the birthplace of the
moneychangers, mystery religions, and pagan worship of the Virgin
and Child."[21] Semiramis, we are told, is the "Queen of Heaven"
who "called for blood sacrifices, man sacrifices. She instituted the
shrine prostitutes that we read about in the Bible."[22] Again, as we
have already seen, none of this is true. Yet despite having no basis
in reality, this storyline of Nimrod and Semiramis as the leaders of
an ancient secret religion has become a foundational belief of many
Christians who hold that the system of the Antichrist will be some
form of occult New World Order, headed by a Roman Catholic
pope. To be very clear, my point here is not to personally criticize
Weirsbe or Walvoord or anyone else. I am simply demonstrating
just how widespread the impact of Hislop and his fanciful pseudo-
scholarship really is. Neither Weirsbe nor Walvoord is a fringe personality. The impact of Hislop's fraud is far more widespread than
many wish to admit.

CONCLUSION
Though the extrabiblical Nimrod myth began sometime around the
first century, it was not until the middle of the nineteenth century,
through the writings of Alexander Hislop, a man with a penchant
for horrific scholarship, that the Nimrod myth reached the bound-
aries of the truly bizarre. Tragically, however, even to this day, many
interpreters continue to rely on this muddled invention as the very
foundation for their interpretation of Revelation 17–18. I hope that
after reading these last two chapters, you agree that this is simply
no longer an option for any honest interpreter.

If the true key to understanding the identity of harlot Babylon
were to be found in this vast collection of traditions and even myths
about Nimrod and Semiramis, then the Lord would have included
this information in the Bible. As fascinating as these stories may be,
they must remain in the category of fiction, on par with *Harry Potter*

or *Star Wars*, but having no place within the house of responsible biblical interpretation. Nowhere in the Bible does it say or even hint that Nimrod claimed to be a god, that he started a religion, or that his wife initiated human blood sacrifices and cult prostitution. Dr. Walvoord himself noted that, because none of this information about Nimrod's religion is found in the Bible, the only way one can actually understand the truth concerning Mystery Babylon is if God Himself reveals it directly: "Because the religion of Babylon was in the form of secret religious rite . . . , it requires divine revelation to understand completely what they held."[23] This is a stunning admission. It requires divine revelation to understand even the most essential information needed to properly interpret Revelation 17–18. Divine revelation, though, for all its potential benefits, is subjective. It is most certainly not the foundation for responsible biblical interpretation. Relying on subjective, personal revelation as the basis for understanding the Bible is literally the hermeneutic of cults. For this reason we must agree with Martin Luther, who, long before Hislop, scoffed at the degree of speculation often associated with Genesis 10–11:

> Opinions vary both about the structure or tower itself and about the sin of its builders. The more daring a man is in answering each of these two questions, the more outspokenly he expresses himself. And the common people too did not refrain from inventing stories. Thus they say that the height of the tower was nine miles, but that when the languages were confused, a third of it was destroyed by the force of wind and weather, and the rest sank into the earth so that now only one third of it is still in existence. Moreover, they claim that it was so high that from it one could hear the voices of the angels singing in heaven. *But we disregard these Foolish tales.*[24] (emphasis mine)

As we seek to understand the last-days harlot Babylon, those of us who desire to be careful and responsible interpreters of the Bible must flee from reliance on such spurious and extrabiblical sources. As we seek to understand the admittedly challenging prophecy of Revelation 17 and 18, our understanding must come from the Word of God—a solid foundation that we all agree is unchanging, ever-reliable, and most of all, *true*.

THE MOTHER OF ALL HARLOTS

WE MUST NOW TURN TO ANOTHER of the most critical clues concerning the identity of the harlot Babylon. Despite the importance of this clue, most interpretations of the harlot seem to completely miss it.

Whenever I come to this passage, I am always reminded of a terribly unedifying event from my high school years, before my salvation. I apologize beforehand for sharing it, but it is simply too illustrative to skip over. One late afternoon after school, several of my neighborhood friends and I had been drinking pretty heavily. One of my friends (we'll just call him "Zeke") had drunk way too much and passed out cold on another friend's couch. As punishment, those of us still awake painted his face with clownishly heavy makeup. Next, with a black marker, in big letters across his fore-head, we wrote the word DRUNK. Then came the fun part. All in a feigned fluster, we woke him up and told him that his father had called and wanted him home immediately. Barely aware of where he was, he jumped up and practically ran out the door, rushing home. Needless to say, when he arrived, it wasn't difficult for his parents to figure out what their son had been up to that day. As clear as day, in big, solid-black letters, it was spelled out across his forehead: Zeke was drunk.

With regard to the harlot Babylon, the Lord has given us pre-cisely the same kind of brazenly obvious clue. Yet for some reason, virtually every commentary I've read has missed it. In Revelation 17:5, the apostle John tells us that across the forehead of the harlot, in big, bold letters, "a name was written, a mystery, 'BABYLON THE GREAT, THE MOTHER OF HARLOTS AND OF THE ABOMINATIONS OF THE EARTH.'" It doesn't get any more direct than this. If there had been neon lights in the first century, perhaps the Lord would have hung a blinking neon sign around her neck. Do you understand this? The Lord obviously wants us to get this clue. As biblical scholar and commentator G. K. Beale stated, "The nature of the woman is revealed in greater detail by the name written on her forehead. In the Apocalypse names written on foreheads reveal the true character of people and their ultimate relationship, whether to God (7:3; 14:1; 22:4) or to Satan (13:16; 14:9; 20:4)."[1] What then does this phrase mean as it relates to her true character and relationship to God? Let's break it down.

The mysterious phrase written on the woman's forehead is actu-ally two titles. The first is "Babylon the Great," and the second is "the mother of all harlots and of the abominations of the earth." These two titles are appositional, which means they're simply reiterating the same point. Of the two, the second is the title that most seem to misunderstand. Most often, it is interpreted to mean that she is a mother prostitute who has given birth to many other, daughter pros-titutes. Accordingly, classic commentator Matthew Henry wrote:

She is named from her infamous way and practice; not only a harlot, but a mother of harlots, breeding up harlots, and nursing and training them up to idolatry, and all sorts of lewdness and wickedness—the parent and nurse of all false religion and filthy conversation.[2]

The title "the mother of all harlots," however, has nothing to do with actual or metaphorical motherhood. It is not, as Henry said, about "breeding" or "nursing." No, the phrase "the mother of" is figure of speech that means "major" or "best."[3] For instance, Saddam Hussein famously declared that if the United States invaded Iraq, the result would be "the mother of all battles," meaning the biggest ever. The largest storm of the century might be referred to as "the mother of all storms." Again, this simply means it is the biggest or most extreme storm, not that it will give birth to every other storm in history. Similarly, one who discovered a large vein of gold during the nineteenth-century California gold rush might be said to have struck "the mother lode," or the largest one yet. That this is the meaning of the phrase here in Revelation becomes even more clear when the two appositional phrases are considered side by side. Both "Babylon the great," and "the mother all harlots and of the abominations of the earth," mean that the last-days Babylon will be the biggest, greatest, most significant "harlot" humankind has ever witnessed. Or as commentator R. C. H. Lenski says, "This is, indeed, the supreme whore."[4] She quite literally represents the greatest abomination that has ever existed.

PROSTITUTION

Although a side note, I think it is important to make a qualifier here before moving forward. To communicate the nature of the last-days Babylon, the Lord chose to use the metaphor of prostitution. In modern times, with the explosion of human trafficking across the earth, in what too frequently amounts to forced prostitution and outright slavery, it is worth stating that not every form of prostitution is necessarily equal. We must consider the reality that today many prostitutes, millions in fact, are young women who are prisoners, captives, slaves. They are exploited, most against their own will, for the supremely selfish gain of those who traffic and exploit them. Consider the torment that many of these woman experience. Many have literally been kidnapped, captured, repeatedly beaten, drugged, threatened, blackmailed, raped, and scarred beyond comprehension. They are terrified, disoriented, hopeless, abused. These modern slaves, though we call them prostitutes, are of a very different kind from what John saw and described in his vision. What the Lord is conveying concerning the harlot of the book of Revelation is a very deliberate form of prostitution. This woman is brazen and proud of her lifestyle; she seeks to lure as many as she can into joining her. For this reason the woman is rightly referred to as "the great whore" (Rev. 17:1 KJV).

SPIRITUAL HARLOTRY

The sin of the last-days Babylon, of course, is not literal prostitution, but spiritual. What does spiritual harlotry refer to? Throughout the Scriptures, harlotry refers to idolatry, the worship of any god other than Yahweh, the one true God of the Bible.[5] It is a term applied to both the Israelites, when they began to worship other gods, and to Gentiles, who worshipped their own pagan gods. In Exodus, for example, when the Gentiles worship their gods, the Lord refers to it as playing the harlot:

> You shall not worship any other god, for the Lord, whose name is Jealous, is a jealous God—otherwise you might make a covenant with the inhabitants of the land and they would play the harlot with their gods and sacrifice to their gods, and someone might invite you to eat of his sacrifice, and you might take some of his daughters for your sons, and his daughters might play the harlot with their gods and cause your sons also to play the harlot with their gods. You shall make for yourself no molten gods. (Ex. 34:14–17)

In Leviticus, consulting spiritists or mediums is also referred to as harlotry: "As for the person who turns to mediums and to spiritists, to play the harlot after them, I will also set My face against that person and will cut him off from among his people" (20:6). The Lord forewarned Moses concerning the idolatry the Israelites would fall into after they entered the promised land:

> "Behold, you are about to lie down with your fathers; and this people will arise and play the harlot with the strange gods of the land, into the midst of which they are going, and will forsake Me and break My covenant which I have made with them." (Deut. 31:16)

Later, during the time of the judges, Israel engaged in harlotry with its veneration of Gideon's ephod as a holy relic: "Gideon made it into an ephod, and placed it in his city, Ophrah, and all Israel played the harlot with it there, so that it became a snare to Gideon and his household" (Judg. 8:27). Later yet, the Lord rebuked Israel for being like the Gentile nations, stating, "You have played the harlot, forsaking your God" (Hos. 9:1).

It is clear, then, that harlotry is a symbol for idolatry or any form of worship or devotion apart from worship and devotion to Yahweh, the only true God. It is consistently used this way throughout the Bible. The last-days Babylon therefore represents not simply false religion, but the greatest of all false religions. You might say harlot Babylon is "the big mamma" of all false and idolatrous religious systems.

THE HARLOT'S RELIGION

The woman represents not only the greatest false religion humankind has ever known, but also a profoundly tyrannical faith system, one that persecutes and even seeks to exterminate all who worship Christ. Revelation 17:6 tells us she is drunk on "the blood of the saints, and with the blood of the witnesses of Jesus," God's faithful martyrs. This would strongly suggest that she is in cahoots with the Antichrist, who is described earlier as being given power "to make war with the saints and to overcome them" (Rev. 13:7).

The woman is also seen to be riding the beast. We will discuss the beast in much greater detail as we move forward. For now, however, we must understand that the ten-horned beast represents the kingdom of the Antichrist. At least at the outset of the vision, the harlot and the beast are portrayed as a team. They are rider and steed, sharing a very close, even symbiotic relationship. This is a demonic parody (albeit nineteen hundred years early) of the Lone Ranger and Silver, his trusted steed. Even more, as the beast is "scarlet" (17:3), so also is the harlot "clothed in purple and scarlet" (17:4). Like high school sweethearts, they are wearing the same colors, cheering for the same team. That's why it is such a deeply ironic and shocking turn of events when the beast turns on the harlot and devours her. But in the beginning, a close partnership exists between the woman and the beast.

By seducing "the kings of the earth," and "those who dwell on the earth" into becoming "drunk with the wine of her immorality" (17:2), the harlot is actually a great evangelist of sorts for the religion of the Antichrist. As Beale has written, "That the woman here is 'mother' of idolaters connotes her authoritative influence over and inspiration of the system of idolatry."[6] The kings who are drunk on her false religion are specifically the same kings who come to form the primary leadership for the kingdom of the Antichrist. More than simply being in partnership with the Antichrist and his alliance, the false religion the harlot represents is one and the same with the religion of the Antichrist. As Lenski stated, "The woman, the whole antichristian seduction, is thus connected with the whole antichristian power. The connection, too, seems significant: she sits upon this beast; by her seduction to whoring she exercises the power of the beast."[7]

That the harlot's false religion is the same as the Antichrist's is further validated in Revelation 14. There we find three angels loudly proclaiming a message to the inhabitants of the earth. Although each angel has a separate message, all of their comments flow together into one very cohesive statement. The first angel calls upon all people to reject idolatry and worship God alone: "And he said with a loud voice, 'Fear God, and give Him glory, because the hour of His judgment has come; worship Him who made the heaven and the earth and sea and springs of waters'" (v. 7). The second angel declares the good news that the last-days Babylon (which represents the greatest system of idolatry to ever exist) has finally met its judgment and destruction: "Fallen, fallen is Babylon the great, she who has made all the nations drink of the wine of the passion of her immorality" (v. 8). The third angel then states that "if anyone worships the beast and his image, and receives a mark on his forehead or on his hand, he also will drink of the wine of the wrath of God, which is mixed in full strength in the cup of His anger; and he will be tormented with fire and brimstone in the presence of the holy angels and in the presence of the Lamb. And the smoke of their torment goes up forever and ever; they have no rest day and night, those who worship the beast and his image, and whoever receives the mark of his name" (vv. 9–11). When the full message is considered together, it is a call to the inhabitants of the earth to worship God alone, lest they, like Babylon, be judged by the Lord and destroyed eternally.

I AM, AND THERE IS NO OTHER

The final indicator that the woman represents a great anti-Yahweh religion is seen in a peculiar statement the woman makes of herself. In Revelation 18:7, she says in her heart, "I sit as queen and I am not a widow, and will never see mourning." This verse is taken directly from Isaiah 47:8, where the "daughter of Babylon,"[8] says, "I am, and there is no one besides me. I will not sit as widow." This proclamation of "I am" is a direct challenge to Yahweh, the God of the Bible, whose very name is "I AM" (see Ex. 3:14). This allusion to Isaiah 47:8 creates a possible context for the great harlot of Revelation to represent a direct challenge to the one true God.

CONCLUSION

In conclusion, "Babylon the great, the mother of all harlots, and of the abominations of the earth" represents the greatest and largest false religion that humankind will ever know. It is portrayed as a violent and murderous religion, guilty for the shed blood of God's holy martyrs. The harlot Babylon is also a source of great religious seduction, luring many of the earth's inhabitants to join this false system of worship and opposition to the Lord. Of all of the various hints we are given, this one is absolutely critical. In the next chapter, we will further develop this theme.

7

THE WOMAN AND THE BEAST

UPON SEEING THE HARLOT IN ALL OF HER UGLINESS, the apostle John was appalled. As John's angelic guide addressed his shock, he gave us one of the most critical clues concerning the harlot's identity.

Strangely, though the angel told John that he was about to unravel "the mystery of the woman *and* of the beast that she rides upon" (17:7, emphasis added), he instead launched into a very detailed explanation of the beast alone. For the remainder of the chapter, the angel focused almost entirely on describing the beast. The woman is not even mentioned. This is no accident. Simply put, understanding the meaning of the woman requires that we first understand what the beast represents. Once we establish this and understand the woman's relationship to the beast, then we will have a much better idea of what the woman represents within this prophecy. For this reason, we will devote the remainder of this chapter to understanding this mysterious portion of the vision.

First, what does the beast represent? What does it mean that the beast has seven heads? And what of the mysterious eighth kingdom that is mentioned? What is that about? Answering these questions is absolutely critical if we are to rightly understand the mystery of the last-days Babylon.

SEVEN SATANIC EMPIRES

If trying to understand the meaning of a seven-headed monster with ten crowns seems impossible, don't worry. Once we recognize that the symbolism in this vision has already been explained in other parts of the Bible, then understanding this mysterious prophecy becomes much simpler. To begin with, the concept of "the beast" is first found in Daniel 7, where four beasts are used as symbols of various pagan empires. Unlike the beasts of Daniel 7, however, the beast described in Revelation 17 does not represent just a single empire, but a conglomerate of seven historical pagan empires. Each head, as we will see, represents a different empire.[1]

This seven-headed beast, which represents seven historical satanic empires, is actually first introduced back in Revelation 12–13. There this beast is revealed to, in essence, be the very embodiment of Satan on the earth. In Revelation 12, Satan himself is first described as a "great red dragon having seven heads" (v. 3). Then, in chapter 13, as the great dragon stands on the seashore, from out of the sea before him, this second beast arises. The first thing we notice is that the beast is nearly identical to the satanic dragon. Both are red monsters with seven heads.

Why is the beast revealed to be a near mirror image of Satan? There is a very important point being made here. No doubt, Satan and the other rebellious angelic beings wage war against humankind under cover of darkness: subtly, secretly, covertly. In fact, most people would say that Satan works by luring, tempting, and laying traps for the unwitting—but always remaining out of sight, in the shadows. Of course, Satan does work this way. The Scriptures warn that "the devil prowls" (1 Peter 5:8). What we learn from this particular picture in Revelation, however, is that Satan's primary way of carrying out his activity on earth is actually overt. It has been that way down through history: Satan effects his plans and purposes—in plain sight, for all to see—through pagan empires and their armies. This is why the beast, which represents seven historical pagan empires, is essentially a mirror image of Satan himself. These historical pagan empires have essentially been the devil's puppets to carry out his work of resisting the Lord's unfolding plan of redemption. This is exactly why it is said that Satan will bestow upon the beast "his power and his throne and great authority" (Rev. 13:2). Even as Satan has worked through these historical beast kingdoms, his greatest work will be carried out through the final kingdom of the beast.

Though there have been many satanically empowered empires and nations throughout history, the seven heads of the beast represent seven very specific empires through which Satan has sought to wage war against God's purposes. These are the primary empires that have at one time or other ruled over the promised land and most often have sought to destroy God's people. While Daniel 7 gives us a partial picture, revealing only four pagan kingdoms (Babylon, Medo-Persia, Greece, and the empire of the Antichrist), Revelation 13 and 17 convey a much fuller picture, spanning all of biblical history. So, which empires do the seven heads represent?

IDENTIFYING THE FIRST SIX EMPIRES

The first head of the beast represents the ancient pagan empire of Egypt. This is the Egypt of Pharaoh, which enslaved the Hebrews and chased them into the desert for extermination. This Egypt represented the first great satanic attack on God's chosen people,

THE WOMAN AND THE BEAST | 73

the Hebrews. The second pagan empire to assault God's people was Assyria, which, under Sennacherib, attacked and carried into exile the ten northern tribes of Israel. After this, it was Babylon, under Nebuchadnezzar, who attacked the southern kingdom of Judah, destroying Jerusalem and carrying the nation away into exile. The fourth great pagan empire was Medo-Persia, from which came Haman and his devilish plot to exterminate the Jewish people, as recorded in the book of Esther. Then came the Greeks, led by Alexander the Great, who conquered the whole of the Middle East. After Alexander's death, it was through the Greek king Antiochus IV Epiphanes that Satan once more waged a horrific assault against the people of God. The next satanically empowered kingdom, of course, was Rome, which oppressed and occupied the promised land during Jesus' day. It was under the Roman empire that Jesus Himself was crucified. Forty years later, under Emperor Titus, Jerusalem and the temple would be destroyed and many of the citizens of the land killed or exiled. So far, then, these are the first six empires:

1. Egyptian Empire

2. Assyrian Empire

3. Babylonian Empire

4. Medo-Persian Empire

5. Grecian Empire

6. Roman Empire

Most futurist commentators would agree with the names on this list.[2] From the late-nineteenth-century commentator Joseph Augustus Seiss to the late-twentieth-century commentators George Eldon Ladd and John Walvoord, scholars generally identify the beast's first six heads with these empires. Not surprisingly, though, there is some controversy surrounding the identity of the beast's seventh head. Many interpreters suggest it represents a revived Roman empire, one that will be led by the Antichrist. There is a glaring problem with this view, however. Beyond the seventh head or kingdom, the angel went on to describe another, mysterious, eighth kingdom. What are we to make of this? Surely the eighth kingdom cannot be a double-revived Roman Empire. Rome cannot be the sixth, the seventh, and the eighth, can it? This wouldn't seem to make any sense. Consistency requires that we see each head as a distinct empire. The eighth is the only exception, as it is mysteriously linked to the one before it. The key, then, is to identify the seventh head first. The eighth is the revival of the seventh head. So what empire might this be? Which empire came after Rome?

THE SEVENTH HEAD: THE ISLAMIC EMPIRE

I would suggest that the only real candidate, the only empire in history that follows in the footsteps of and completes the clearly established pattern set by the previous six empires, is what we could refer to as the historical Islamic empire. Most refer to this historical empire as the "Caliphate," from the Arabic word *Khalifa*, which simply refers to the Islamic government that succeeded Muhammad, the founder of Islam. After Muhammad died, his successors conquered the Middle East with lightning speed. The Islamic empire quickly came to engulf much of the ancient world, reaching from India to Spain, and most important, over the promised land. It was far larger than even the Roman Empire at the time of its greatest extent. In its day, the historical Islamic empire, like the previous empires, was the primary satanic steward of the anti-Semitic, Jew-hating spirit. Like the other great empires before it, the Islamic empire has long been possessed with the same lust to conquer and possess the promised land of Israel. If the identity of the seventh head after Rome is the Islamic Caliphate, then this would mean that a revived caliphate, the final yet short-lived empire of the Antichrist, is the eighth kingdom. The following list would then complete the vision:

1. Egyptian Empire

2. Assyrian Empire

3. Babylonian Empire

4. Medo-Persian Empire

5. Grecian Empire

6. Roman Empire

7. Islamic Empire

8. Revived Islamic Empire of the Antichrist

We must note that this interpretation would seem to be the only way we might understand this passage without violating the pattern previously established in Daniel 2 and 7. In both of those chapters, the final empire is portrayed as a single empire with two distinct phases. In Daniel 2, we are shown a statue comprised of five distinct segments, each representing various historical empires. The final two sections of the statue, the legs of iron and the feet of mixed iron and clay, represent two distinct phases of the same kingdom. Likewise, in Daniel 7, which describes a vision of four beasts, each representing different historical empires, the fourth beast, and then the ten horns that arise "out of this kingdom" (v. 24), represent two distinct phases of the same kingdom.[3] This would mean that the legs of iron in Daniel 2 and the fourth beast of Daniel 7 represent the historical Islamic empire, while the feet of iron and clay in Daniel 2 and the ten horns of the beast in Daniel 7 represent the revival of this empire, which the Antichrist will lead. *Again, we must note that the final kingdom is composed of two phases, not three.* When we get to Revelation 17, this same pattern continues. The legs of iron and the fourth beast correlate to the seventh head. Those who hold the final empire to be Roman are forced to see a three-phased empire in Revelation 17. This interpretation clashes with both Daniel 2 and 7.

But when we understand the seventh and eighth kingdoms to refer to the historical Islamic empire and its revival, then Revelation flows perfectly with Daniel 2 and 7. See the table:

DANIEL 2	DANIEL 7	REVELATION 13
		EGYPT
		ASSYRIA
HEAD OF GOLD	LION	BABYLON
CHEST AND ARMS OF SILVER	BEAR	MEDO-PERSIA
BELLY AND THIGHS OF BRONZE	LEOPARD	GREECE
		ROME
LEGS OF IRON	FOURTH BEAST	ISLAM
FEET OF IRON AND CLAY	TEN HORNS	ANTICHRIST

Some will ask why the Roman Empire is not included in Daniel 2 or 7. The answer is simple. The context of Daniel 2 is a dream that was given to Nebuchadnezzar, the king of Babylon. The vision is about the three specific kingdoms that would succeed his kingdom. The Roman Empire, in all of its long history, reached Babylon for only a few months. In AD 116, under Emperor Trajan, Rome indeed took the ruins of Babylon. After only a very short time there, however, Trajan had a stroke, withdrew, and died shortly thereafter. Both Daniel 2 and 7 speak of Babylon, Medo-Persia, and Greece, and then they move directly to the next major empire that would truly gain control over Babylon (Dan. 2:40). History informs us that this was accomplished by the Islamic Caliphate. Quite simply, no other candidates exist that fulfill the requirements of the text.[4] We will discuss this in some more detail as we move forward.

LEOPARD, BEAR, AND LION

Further substantiating this interpretation, namely, the Middle Eastern or Islamic nature of the seventh and eighth heads of the beast, is the beast's composite description:

And the beast which I saw was like a leopard, and his feet were like those of a bear, and his mouth like the mouth of a lion. And the dragon gave him his power and his throne and great authority. (Rev. 13:2)

This imagery comes directly from Daniel 7. There, the leopard represents the Grecian Empire, the bear represents the Medo-Persian Empire, and the lion represents the Babylonian Empire. The seventh and eighth empires, then, are a composite of these three empires, partially leopard, partially lion, and partially bear. In modern terms, Babylon loosely correlates to Iraq, Medo-Persia to Iran, and the Greek Empire to the Balkans, Turkey, and Syria. These nations, of course, correlate almost perfectly with the historical Islamic empire—but not the Roman Empire. This is critical.

THE EIGHTH KINGDOM: THE REVIVED ISLAMIC EMPIRE

As we ponder the nature of the eighth and final kingdom of Revelation 17, we must note how the angel described it:

The beast that you saw was, and is not, and is about to come up out of the abyss and go to destruction. And those who dwell on the earth, whose name has not been written in the book of life from the foundation of the world, will wonder when they see the beast, that he was and is not and will come. (Rev. 17:8)

The final manifestation of satanic empire is portrayed as an empire that, after a period of existence, descends into the darkness of "the abyss." It dies. Then, at a later time, it arises back from the abyss. Because of the cryptic nature of this portion of the prophecy, many have misunderstood its meaning. First, it is essential to properly understand the end-time context and thus the proper perspective of the angel's words. Admittedly, this is a bit tricky. Think about this. The angel is explaining to John, who lived in the first century, that the beast that he is seeing will, in the last days, have been an empire that formerly existed. The angel is not saying that, from John's perspective in the first century, the beast was already alive and about to come back. No, this riddle makes sense only from the perspective of one living in the actual last days, to which John was temporarily, as it were, transported in the vision. Those in the last days will look at an empire that formerly existed, died, and then comes back. The next verse makes it clear that the angel is indeed speaking of the eighth and final head of the beast: "The beast which was and is not, is himself also an eighth and is one of the seven, and he goes to destruction" (Rev. 17:11). Remember: the eighth kingdom of the beast correlates to the feet of iron and clay in Daniel 2 as well as the ten horns that arise from the fourth beast: "out of this kingdom ten kings will arise" (Dan. 7:24). The ten horns in Daniel 7 are the same ten horns described here in Revelation as being one and the same as the eighth kingdom:

> The ten horns which you saw are ten kings who have not yet received a kingdom, but they receive authority as kings with the beast for one hour. (Rev. 17:12)

The ten kings are the primary leaders of the coming coalition of the Antichrist. This is the final "empire" of the Antichrist, Satan's final, last-ditch effort to resist the completion of the Lord's grand plan of redemption.

A REVIVED EMPIRE, OR A REVIVED MAN?

I should comment briefly here on this revived empire. Many commentators see in this passage a reference to the Antichrist, who will suffer a fatal head wound and then come back to life (see Rev 13:3). For clarity, I do believe the Antichrist will fulfill this prophecy. However, it is also clear that the seventh empire will also experience a death and revival. As we have already discussed, both Daniel 2 and 7 make it clear that the final empire has two very distinct phases.

A WOMAN AND THE BEAST: A PARTNERSHIP MADE IN HELL

Having identified the seventh head of the beast as the historical
Islamic Caliphate, and the eighth kingdom as a revived Islamic alliance, what does this teach us about the identity of harlot Babylon?
First, we must note the relationship between the great harlot and the
beast. The first point that stands out concerning their relationship
is the fact that the harlot is riding this beast. This speaks of a very
close relationship between the two. The woman and the beast share,
as it were, an alliance, a symbiotic partnership. This demonic duo
is a satanic variation of the classic motif of the hero on his trusted
and faithful steed. Beyond this, the two are also wearing the same
team colors. As commentator R. C. H. Lenski reminds us,

> The fact that the beast is now described simply as "scarlet" har-
> monizes with the vision of the woman who is also clothed in
> purple and "scarlet." We regard "scarlet" as the color of sin, the
> opposite of white (see "scarlet" Isa. 1:18) . . . The point to be noted
> here is the whore's connection with the beast, her relation to him.[5]

Outwardly, the two match. They are clearly portrayed as
belonging together; truly, they are a match made in hell. They also
share the same mission. Even as the beast is empowered "to make
war with the saints and to overcome them" (Rev. 13:7), the woman
is "drunk with the blood of the saints, and with the blood of the
witnesses of Jesus"—Christians (Rev. 17:6). Everything about these
two speaks of a partnership.

That is why it comes as such a surprise when later, the beast
suddenly turns on the woman, devours her flesh, and burns her
with fire. Imagine watching Silver turn on the Lone Ranger, as if
out of the blue, and devour him. It is specifically because of their
deep bond, common goals, and close partnership that this sudden
turn of events is so surprising. Yet, this alarming development, as
we will see, is yet another essential key that will help us unlock the
identity of the mysterious harlot.

CONCLUSION

Despite all of the mysterious symbolism and apocalyptic imagery in Revelation, the point is actually somewhat simple. Understanding the woman's identity is largely contingent upon identifying the beast. Although the beast broadly represents seven satanically inspired empires, its ultimate manifestation is the eighth kingdom. This is the kingdom that will thrive during the days of the great harlot. Together, the harlot and the eighth kingdom will function as the great last-days dynamic duo, working together to fulfill the will of their master, the devil. By identifying the eighth kingdom as a revived Islamic empire, we have dramatically narrowed down the options concerning this great end-time city. Mystery Babylon will be the capital, the very heart of the coming revived Islamic empire.

8

THE ISLAMIC EMPIRE

BECAUSE IDENTIFYING THE SEVENTH AND EIGHTH HEADS of the beast of Revelation 17 as Islamic is so critical in identifying the great harlot, it is important that we build a scriptural case for it.[1] If the seventh and eighth kingdoms represent the historical Islamic empire and a revival of that empire, then the identity of the harlot city is dramatically narrowed down. As a city, the harlot Babylon is the religious and financial capital of the final satanic empire. It will be the last great stronghold of Satan in the earth before Jesus returns. We should therefore look to the city that is the primary spiritual and economic heart of the Islamic world.

To make this case, however, it must be shown that the Islamic empire is indeed that which the prophets foresaw and spoke of. Having carefully weighed this matter for well over a decade now, I can say with confidence that the case for an Islamic Antichrist and Islamic empire is one that every serious student of the Scriptures should carefully consider. The remainder of this chapter will summarize the primary biblical arguments for a final Islamic beast empire.

IT'S ALL ABOUT ISRAEL

Anyone who wishes to properly identify the beast—or simply understand the story of the Bible—must grasp a very basic, but profoundly important point. Simply stated, geographically speaking, the story of the Bible is thoroughly centered around Israel and especially Jerusalem. The culmination of the story in particular revolves around this very specific piece of land and this very specific city. Jerusalem, after all, is where Jesus will return and reestablish the throne of David. It is from Mount Zion that Jesus will rule the nations. As difficult as it might be for some Americans to grasp, the United States is not the center of God's unfolding story. Throughout the Scriptures, the world outside of the Middle East and North Africa is most often referred to in such vague terms such as "the coastlands," "far off," or even "the ends of the earth." Now, this isn't to say that those who live outside of the biblical world are less important in God's eyes. Of course not. But in terms of the prophetic story that is unfolding, it revolves around Israel. Any effort to understand the story of the end times must begin by grasping this simple reality. This is the context of the Bible.

THE SURROUNDING NATIONS

Which nations does the Bible say will attack and attempt to take control of Jerusalem? Repeatedly, throughout the Scriptures, it is "the surrounding" nations or peoples. Let's consider just a few examples.

Speaking of the armies of the Antichrist, the prophet Joel said, "Hasten and come, all you surrounding nations, and gather yourselves there . . . for there I will sit to judge all the surrounding

THE ISLAMIC EMPIRE | 83

nations" (Joel 3:11–12). Through the prophet Zechariah, the Lord said, "Behold, I am about to make Jerusalem a cup of staggering to all the surrounding peoples. The siege of Jerusalem will also be against Judah. . . . . On that day I will make the clans of Judah like a blazing pot in the midst of wood, like a flaming torch among sheaves. And they shall devour to the right and to the left all the surrounding peoples" (Zech. 12:2, 6, 16 ESV).

Ezekiel also could not have been more clear as he wrote of the day when the people of Israel will no longer be surrounded by people who despise them: "And for the house of Israel there shall be no more a brier to prick or a thorn to hurt them among all their neighbors who have treated them with contempt. Then they will know that I am the Lord God" (Eze. 28:23–24 ESV). The phrase translated here as "all their neighbors" is the same word used in both Joel and Zechariah. It is the Hebrew word *cabiyb*, which refers to those nations that are around Israel, her neighbors.

So, are Israel's "neighbors" the nations of Europe, or are they the nations of the Middle East and North Africa?

THE NATIONS OF THE ANTICHRIST

Throughout the Scriptures, whenever the nations of the Antichrist are mentioned, those that will attack Israel in the last days, they are all Middle Eastern and North African nations—Muslim-majority nations. Conversely, there is not a single mention of a European or any other non-Muslim-majority nation being judged in the Day of the Lord for attacking Israel. Now, that isn't to say that none will. But overwhelmingly, the Bible repeatedly and consistently names and emphasizes nations from the Middle East and North Africa. We should also emphasize those nations. It is where the Bible is silent that we must be extremely careful not to add our own assumptions. When Bible teachers tell you that we should not look to the Middle East as potentially producing the Antichrist and his system, they are simply not being true to the Scriptures. We should focus on that which the Bible focuses on. I hope we are in agreement on this point.

THE MESSIAH WILL CRUSH HIS ENEMIES

Now let's get more specific. We all know the story of Adam and Eve's disobedience. No sooner did the fall of humankind take place than the Lord began pointing to His solution. God described how He would eventually come to crush His adversary. Speaking directly to the serpent, the Lord said, "I will put enmity between you and the woman, and between your offspring and her offspring; he shall bruise your head, and you shall bruise his heel" (Gen. 3:15 ESV). According to this prophecy, throughout history, Satan's seed would be at war with the "seed," which is the Messiah, as well as those who follow Him. In the end, however, Jesus the Messiah, Eve's seed, will crush Satan's head—as well as all of Satan's followers. He will make right all of the damage done on that very dark day in the Garden. It is appropriate, then, that this prophecy is sometimes referred to as "the mother prophecy."[2]

Picking up on the theme of the Messiah someday crushing Satan and his followers, in the book of Numbers, we find another critical prophecy about Jesus. In Numbers 24, Balak, king of Moab, and the prophet Balaam are standing on a high overlook, gazing down over the Hebrews encamped in a vast valley plain below. God's people had completed their exodus from Egypt and were making their way toward the promised land. But Balak was greatly disturbed at having such a vast people group encroaching the borders of his kingdom, so he had hired Balaam to pronounce a curse on the Hebrew people. Rather than cursing them, however, under the inspiration of the Holy Spirit, Balaam began to utter a profound end-time prophecy. "Come," he said to Balak, "I will let you know what this people will do to your people in the latter days" (v. 14 ESV). This phrase "latter days" in the Hebrew is *acharyith yawm*, literally meaning "the last days." He then gave one of the most important messianic prophecies in the whole Torah:

I see him, but not now; I behold him, but not near: a star shall come out of Jacob, and a scepter shall rise out of Israel; it shall crush the forehead of Moab and break down all the sons of Sheth. Edom shall be dispossessed; Seir also, his enemies, shall be dispossessed. (Num. 24:17–19 ESV)

Balaam declared that in the end times, a king would arise from out of Israel. From very early on, Jewish interpreters understood this passage to be a prophecy concerning the Messiah. What does the passage say the Messiah will carry out when He returns? What did the Holy Spirit emphasize would be the primary accomplishment of the Messiah on that day? Expanding on "the mother prophecy" of Genesis 3, the Messiah is once again described as crushing the head of Satan's followers, or "seed." This time, however, these followers are actually named. The Messiah will come back and crush the heads of Moab, Edom, Seir, the sons of Sheth, and the Amalekites. Who do these names refer to? The Moabites and the Edomites lived to the east of modern-day Israel in what is today the nation of Jordan. Mount Seir was the most prominent mountain within the territory of Edom. Thus, the references to Moab, Edom, and Seir all point to the same general region. Likewise, the Amalekites were a people group who lived throughout the greater region to the east of Israel. All of these peoples, throughout biblical history, often carried a deep hatred and enmity toward the Hebrew people. The "sons of Sheth," as translated in the Jerusalem Targum, are "all the sons of the East."[3]

Now, if we take this passage at face value, is it more reasonable to interpret these references to Edom, Moab, and the Amalekites, as pointing us to the Middle East, or to Germany, Italy, and England, as so many teachers of prophecy today teach?

CRUSHING MOAB INTO THE DUNG

A verse frequently read at funerals is Revelation 21:4, "There will be no more death or mourning or crying or pain, for the old order of things has passed away." Few are aware, however, that the book of

Revelation actually borrowed this passage directly from the prophet Isaiah. In Isaiah 25, we are told that the Lord will not only wipe away tears and destroy death, but He will also remove the disgrace of His people Israel from the earth. How will He do this? By destroying Israel's enemies. Let's look at the passage.

> He will swallow up death forever; and the Lord God will wipe away tears from all faces, and the reproach of his people he will take away from all the earth, for the Lord has spoken. It will be said on that day, "Behold, this is our God; we have waited for him, that he might save us. This is the Lord; we have waited for him; let us be glad and rejoice in his salvation." For the hand of the Lord will rest on this mountain [Zion], and Moab shall be trampled down in his place, as straw is trampled down in a dunghill. And he will spread out his hands in the midst of it as a swimmer spreads his hands out to swim, but the Lord will lay low his pompous pride together with the skill of his hands. (vv. 8–11 ESV)

Now, obviously, God has not yet wiped away every tear, and death certainly still exists. This prophecy is clearly yet to be fulfilled. Like the passages we have already looked at, the context is the future, after the return of Jesus. Thus, the Lord says, at the end of the age, His hand of blessing and protection will rest on the head of Zion, His people, while his victorious foot will crush the head of Moab, His enemy, facedown into a pile of dung. It is not a vague or universal enemy of God's people that is specified here. As in Numbers 24, it is "Moab" whom Jesus, the returning Messiah, will judge.

And so once again I ask, according to this passage, at the time of the Lord's return, are the primary recipients of His judgment from Europe, or is the text once again pointing us to the anti-Semitic sons of the East? Common sense clearly tells us that it is the latter.

THE NATIONS OF THE ANTICHRIST IN EZEKIEL

In Ezekiel 25, another clear prophecy speaks of the Lord's divine judgment directed against Ammon, Moab, and Edom because of how they treated "the house of Judah" (v. 12 ESV). Again, these three kingdoms inhabited what is modern-day Jordan. The prophet said that by executing undue "vengeance" against His chosen people, He Himself is "greatly offended" (v. 12 KJV). For this reason, the Lord will judge them with "wrathful rebukes" (v. 17 ESV).

But the text speaks of much more than just Ammon, Moab, and Edom. It also mentions Dedan (v. 13), which is a city located in central Saudi Arabia, known in modern times as Al-'Ula. The prophecy also goes on to mention the Philistines and the Cherethites (vv. 15–16), pointing to regions that are today associated with the Gaza Strip. A few chapters later, many other nations are marked for judgment at the Day of the Lord:

> The word of the Lord came to me: "Son of man, prophesy, and say, Thus says the Lord God: "Wail, 'Alas for the day!' For the day is near, the day of the Lord is near; it will be a day of clouds, a time of doom for the nations. A sword shall come upon Egypt, and anguish shall be in Cush, when the slain fall in Egypt, and her wealth is carried away, and her foundations are torn down. Cush, and Put, and Lud, and all Arabia, and Libya, and the people of the land that is in league, shall fall with them by the sword." (Eze. 30:1–5 ESV)

The ultimate context of the passage is the Day of the Lord and Christ's return. Here, as in so many other passages, the Messiah comes to execute judgment against the enemies of His people, Israel. Included in the list of those marked for judgment are Egypt, Cush (Sudan), Put (North Africa), Lud (Turkey), Arabia, and Libya.

THE NATIONS OF THE ANTICHRIST IN ZEPHANIAH

Following in the footsteps of all the other prophets, Zephaniah prophesied that on "the day of the Lord's anger" (2:3) Gaza, Ashkelon, Ashdod, Ekron, the Cherethites, Canaan, and the land of the

Philistines will all be utterly ruined (vv. 4–5). Together, these names point us to the whole region around the Gaza Strip. But beyond judgment against Gaza, the prophecy warns:

> "I have heard the taunts of Moab and the revilings of the Ammonites, how they have taunted my people and made boasts against their territory. Therefore, as I live," declares the Lord of hosts, the God of Israel, "Moab shall become like Sodom, and the Ammonites like Gomorrah, a land possessed by nettles and salt pits, and a waste forever. The remnant of my people shall plunder them, and the survivors of my nation shall possess them . . . You also, O Cushites [Sudan], shall be slain by my sword. And he will stretch out his hand against the north and destroy Assyria, and he will make Nineveh a desolation, a dry waste like the desert." (Zeph. 2:8–9, 12–13 ESV)

During Zephaniah's day, Assyria straddled the borders of modern-day Turkey, Syria, Lebanon, and Iraq. The ancient city of Nineveh is now called Mosul in northern Iraq.

Of course, it goes without saying that all of these nations and regions are dominated by Islam. So again, if the Lord repeatedly and consistently emphasizes Muslim areas as being singled out for judgment at the Day of the Lord, then why do so many resist the idea that the Antichrist will come from that part of the world?

TREADING THE WINEPRESS OF THE WRATH OF GOD ALMIGHTY

Finally, we come to the book of Revelation. It is there that we find arguably the most well-known passage concerning Christ's return in the entire Bible. In dramatic imagery, Jesus bursts forth from heaven with eyes of fire, riding upon a white horse, with "the armies of heaven" following Him:

> Then I saw heaven opened, and behold, a white horse! The one sitting on it is called Faithful and True, and in righteousness he

judges and makes war. His eyes are like a flame of fire, and on his head are many diadems, and he has a name written that no one knows but himself. He is clothed in a robe dipped in blood, and the name by which he is called is The Word of God. And the armies of heaven, arrayed in fine linen, white and pure, were following him on white horses. From his mouth comes a sharp sword with which to strike down the nations, and he will rule them with a rod of iron. He will tread the winepress of the fury of the wrath of God the Almighty. On his robe and on his thigh he has a name written, King of kings and Lord of lords. (Rev. 19:11–16 ESV)

Most Christians are familiar with this passage. Yet few are aware whose blood is soaking Jesus' robes. Many think it's His own blood, or the blood of the martyrs. The real answer, however, is found in Isaiah 63:

Who is this who comes from Edom, in crimsoned garments from Bozrah, he who is splendid in his apparel, marching in the greatness of his strength? "It is I, speaking in righteousness, mighty to save." Why is your apparel red, and your garments like his who treads in the winepress? "I have trodden the winepress alone, and from the peoples no one was with me; I trod them in my anger and trampled them in my wrath; their lifeblood spattered on my garments, and stained all my apparel. For the day of vengeance was in my heart, and my year of redemption had come." (vv. 1–4 ESV)

In this dramatic passage, Isaiah the prophet is looking eastward from Jerusalem. He sees the majestic and determined Jesus marching victoriously toward His throne in Jerusalem. He is coming out from Bozrah, the capital city of ancient Edom. Today it is called Petra, in modern-day Jordan. It is this passage from which the concept of Jesus treading "the winepress of the fury of the wrath of God the Almighty" comes (Rev. 19:15 ESV). Here, Isaiah informs us that Jesus, the victorious warrior—the Lion of the tribe of Judah—will actually crush God's enemies like grapes, soaking His robes with their blood.

Do you truly grasp what is being conveyed here? When Jesus returns, the "mother prophecy" of Genesis 3 will come full circle and find its ultimate fulfillment. Though Satan has struck the heels of God's people throughout history, when Jesus returns, He will crush not only Satan, but his followers as well. He will tread the winepress of the wrath of God Almighty, and it will specifically be in Edom—again, southern Jordan and northwest Saudi Arabia today—that God's enemies will be crushed.

So to summarize, whenever specific nations are named and highlighted for God's judgment when Jesus returns, they are always regions or nations that are today vastly dominated by Islam. This is the part of the world that the Bible is screaming at us to look toward. It is no surprise, then, that today this part of the world is where hatred of the Jewish people and a lust to possess the promised land most thrive.

THE PILLARS OF THE EUROPEAN ANTICHRIST THEORY

Moving on, let us now consider a few other truly critical passages. If we search through the many works over the years that present a European Antichrist, we will find the same passages cited over and over again. These are the pillars upon which the entire theory is supported:

1. Daniel 2: Nebuchadnezzar's dream of a giant metallic statue

2. Daniel 7: Daniel's vision of four beasts

3. Daniel 9:26: "the people of the prince . . . to come"

Amazingly, although these three passages comprise the primary pillars of the European Antichrist perspective, none of them actually offers any real support. In fact, any careful examination of these passages will lead us not to Europe at all, but rather, to the Middle East. Let's take a look.

THE FOURTH KINGDOM

Together, both Daniel 2 and Daniel 7 prophesy concerning the kingdom or empire that will eventually produce the Antichrist. This kingdom, referred to in both chapters as a "fourth kingdom" (2:40; 7:12), is never actually named. Most commentators, however, have assumed this fourth kingdom to be the historical Roman Empire, which will be revived in the last days. From this assumption many have concluded that the Antichrist will come from Europe. In fact, ever since the birth of the European Union, most of the prophecy-watching world has been looking exclusively to Europe. However, the idea that the Roman Empire and Europe are synonymous is only partially true. As any map will show, the Roman Empire also included portions of the Middle East and North Africa.

So do the prophecies of Daniel 2 and 7 really point to the Roman Empire, as is commonly assumed? A more careful examination of the texts will reveal just the opposite.

DANIEL 2 AND 7

As the story of Daniel 2 begins, we find Nebuchadnezzar, king of the Babylonian Empire, deeply disturbed by what he had seen in a dream. He was shown a towering statue divided into four (or arguably, five) distinct sections. Each section was composed of a different metal. Determined to understand the dream's meaning, the king consulted all of his "magicians, the conjurers, the sorcerers and the Chaldeans [astrologers]" (v. 2), but none were able to offer him any understanding. Daniel, however, having sought the God of Israel in prayer, was able to do what none of the other wise men could do. The Lord revealed Nebuchadnezzar's dream to Daniel, so Daniel stood before the king and described the statue that Nebuchadnezzar had seen. Then, having the king's full attention, he went on to explain what it meant.

The top section of the statue, the head of gold, represented Nebuchadnezzar's Babylonian kingdom (vv. 36–38), explained Daniel. The sections that followed represented three other kingdoms that would succeed Babylon, each possessing its former dominion. The first two kingdoms beneath the head are understood to be Medo-Persia and then Greece. In fact, both are later mentioned by name in Daniel (8:20–21; 10:20). Christian commentators agree that the fourth kingdom, represented by the legs of iron and the feet of mixed iron and clay, represents the kingdom of the Antichrist. But again, this fourth kingdom is never actually named. Nonetheless, many Bibles, so confident of the Roman identity of this fourth kingdom, actually add the name "Rome" into the subheadings. Yet as surprising as this claim may be to many, the various criteria contained within the text, as well as the clear testimony of history, make it impossible to identify the fourth kingdom as the Roman Empire. On the other hand, the Islamic Caliphate, the only other possible candidate, meets all the scriptural criteria perfectly. The Caliphate, the historical Islamic empire, began in AD 632, shortly after the death of Muhammad, the founder of Islam, and culminated in the Ottoman Empire, which officially came to an end in 1923.

THE RISE OF THE FOURTH KINGDOM

The first problem with the Roman identification of the fourth kingdom is that the Roman Empire does not meet the requirements of Daniel 2:40. This verse, speaking of the nature of the rise of the fourth kingdom, says that when it arose, it would crush all three of the other kingdoms: "And the fourth kingdom shall be as strong as iron . . . and like iron that crushes, that kingdom will break in pieces and crush all the others" (NKJV, cf., NIV, NASB, ESV, HCSB, NET).

Later, in Daniel 7, we find an almost identical statement: "[There] will be a fourth kingdom on the earth, which will be different from all the other kingdoms and will devour the whole earth and tread it down and crush it" (v. 23).

Again, this fourth kingdom will specifically trample and crush Babylon, Medo-Persia, and Greece. Since, these three empires never existed at the same time, the crushing must refer to a conquering of their territories. But the Roman Empire conquered only about one-third of the regions controlled by these other three empires. Roughly two-thirds of the regions controlled by these empires was left entirely untouched by Rome. In fact, the Roman Empire never even reached the two Persian capital cities of Ecbatana and Persepolis.

Consider the following modern equivalence: If an invading nation conquered Boston, but never came close to reaching New York or Washington, D.C., it would hardly be accurate to say that such a nation "crushed" all of the United States. Neither would it be correct to say that the Roman Empire crushed all of the Babylonian, Medo-Persian, or Grecian empires. Yet the text is clear; to fulfill Daniel 2:40, an empire must crush all three of these. The Roman Empire simply does not fulfill this requirement. The historical Islamic Caliphate on the other hand, absolutely, completely conquered all their territories.

BORDERS, LANGUAGE, CULTURE

What if we expand the definition of "crush" to include more than mere geography? Consider the description of the fourth kingdom in Daniel 7: "It had great iron teeth; it devoured and broke in pieces and stamped what was left with its feet" (v. 7 ESV). This description certainly seems to point to much more than merely gaining control over territories. I believe it points us to the fourth kingdom actually devouring and crushing the culture, religion, and languages of those it conquers. With this expanded definition in mind, what happens when we compare the Roman Empire to the Islamic Caliphate?

There is no question that the Roman military was a powerful fighting force. When we consider the nature of the Roman Empire, however, and the manner in which it exerted dominance over the people it conquered, once again it is very difficult to make it fit the descriptions of the prophecy. The Roman Empire is actually quite well known for being a nation-building force of the ancient world. When Rome conquered a people, rather than destroying their culture, abolishing their religion, and imposing a new language, it generally tolerated these things, while adding law, building roads and infrastructure, and creating order. The famous Roman roads reached every corner of the Roman Empire. These were well-built, stone-covered roads laid on very solid foundations. Through the famous Roman roads, trade prospered, which in turn brought in more taxes. Eventually every town and city of the empire was connected by an elaborate highway system. This led to the famous phrase "All roads lead to Rome." Rome's law and the protection of its military also created a peace and stability that came to be famously known as the *pax Romana*. Rather than being a crushing and devouring force, the Roman Empire was often quite the opposite. Even John Walvoord recognized and wrestled with this problem, stating, "There is apparently little that is constructive of this empire in spite of Roman law and Roman roads and civilization."[4]

By ancient standards the Romans were also often a tolerant empire compared to many other ancient empires. Under Roman authority, during Jesus' day the Jewish temple stood prominently in Jerusalem, and the Jews openly practiced their own religion. Roman law actually protected their right to do so. While there were certainly exceptions, such as under Emperor Caligula, throughout much of its reign, the Roman Empire was relatively forbearing. That the fourth kingdom is a culturally destructive entity presents a problem when associating the Roman Empire with Daniel's fourth kingdom. Consider for example the relationship of the Roman Empire to Greek culture. Rather than crushing Greek culture, as the text demands, much of the Roman Empire was overwhelmed by Greek ways. Under Roman rule, during Jesus' day in the first century, Greek was the dominant language throughout much of the empire. What's more, Rome also adopted the pagan Greek pantheon of gods. While the names were changed, the basic pantheon remained the same. Zeus became Jupiter, Artemis became Diana, and so on. It would seem apparent that the Roman Empire was not the crushing power referenced in Daniel 2:40.

THE ISLAMIC CALIPHATE

On the other hand, the Islamic Caliphate from its very inception was an Arab-Islamic-supremacist force that crushed and erased the cultures and religions of the peoples it conquered. This is due to the deeply intolerant nature of Islam. It is the very epitome of a totalitarian ideology. The word *Islam* actually means "submission." Consider what life is like under the Taliban or ISIS. Wherever Islam spreads, it brings this oppressive ideology. Not only did Islam conquer all the territories of Babylon, Medo-Persia, and Greece, but it also imposed the Arabic language onto many of the peoples it conquered. Today, in Jordan, Iraq, Syria, Lebanon, and throughout much of North Africa, the people speak Arabic. As an imperial force, Islam imposed Arab religion and culture onto all of its dominated peoples, while erasing previous religions and cultures. An entire book could be written listing the endless examples of Islam crushing and erasing the cultures it conquered. Today in the ancient heartland of the early church, the Christian community is but a struggling minority, often fighting for its very survival. While the cities of Antioch, Alexandria, and Jerusalem were once the thriving missionary-sending capitals of the church, today the indigenous Christian communities there are a shadow of what they once were. Under the control of the Islamic State (ISIS), hundreds of churches throughout the region were destroyed. Where crosses once adorned the roofs of churches, the flag of ISIS was placed, declaring, "There is no god but Allah, and Muhammad is his messenger." Ancient shrines and museums have literally been blown up or smashed with sledgehammers. Similarly, the Muslim waqf in Jerusalem have sought to deny and erase any historical Jewish connection or presence on the Temple Mount.

A list of such examples could literally fill volumes. Wherever Islam has spread, the conquered culture is gradually erased, its symbols destroyed. The religion of the subjugated peoples is most particularly targeted. This is Islam's heritage, the perfect fulfillment of Daniel's predictions (cf. 2:40; 7:7, 19). The fourth beast would crush and devour whatever it conquered. While the Roman Empire has a very difficult time fitting these descriptions, the Islamic Caliphate fulfills them perfectly.

THE "MIXED" FOURTH KINGDOM

Another very interesting hint regarding the ethnic base of the final kingdom is found in Daniel 2:43: "As you saw iron mixed with ceramic clay, they will mingle with the seed of men; but they will not adhere to one another, just as iron does not mix with clay" (NKJV).

Three times, this verse uses the same word translated as "mixed," "mingle," and "mix." Few are aware that this is the Aramaic word `arab (Heb. ereb). In the ancient Middle East, the Arabs were viewed as the mixed desert peoples. Because the descendants of Ishmael and Esau had so intermarried among the various desert pagan tribes, they had become known collectively as "the mixed ones."

The first reference in the Bible to these "mixed ones" is found in the book of Nehemiah. After the Book of the Law had been rediscovered, all of Israel gathered together to hear the Word read publicly: "On that day they read from the Book of Moses in the hearing of the people, and in it was found written that no Ammonite or Moabite should ever come into the assembly of God . . . So it was, when they had heard the Law, that they separated all *the mixed multitude* from Israel" (13:1–3 ESV, emphasis added).

After reading the Law, the Jews realized that it was forbidden for them to take wives from the pagan peoples of the desert, specifically, the Ammonites and the Moabites, who lived in what is today the Hashemite Kingdom of Jordan. So, they excluded from Israel all who were mixed, or 'arab. The very name Arab in its etymological origins refers to the mixed people that lived primarily to the east of Israel. A literal translation of Daniel 2:43, then, is "As you saw iron mixed with ceramic clay, they will be arab, and will thus not remain united, just as iron does not mix with clay."

The riddle-like nature of this verse, pointing to the primary peoples from which the fourth empire would arise, is very reminiscent of an episode in Daniel 5, where Daniel interpreted the writing on the wall as pointing to the fall of the Babylonian Empire to the Medes and the Persians. Daniel read the word *peres*, which means "divided," and interpreted it as reference to the Paras, or the Persians.

To be clear, this possible hint within the text should not be seen as a negative statement in any way regarding Arabs. It may however, be pointing to the nature and origins of this particular kingdom. As any serious analysis of the historical Islamic conquests will show, the early Muslims indeed imposed the language, culture, and religious practices of seventh-century Arabia onto all those they conquered.

CRUMBLING PILLARS

Having examined Daniel 2 and 7, two of the most important pillars of the European Antichrist perspective, this is where we begin to recognize that the case for a European or Roman Antichrist is built on a truly weak foundation. What about the final pillar of Daniel 9:26? Let's turn now to that passage.

THE PEOPLE OF THE PRINCE TO COME

Over the past several years, as I have attempted to explain the scriptural basis for the Islamic Antichrist theory, I've had the opportunity to discuss these things with various internationally known prophecy teachers who espouse the European Antichrist theory. Universally, the passage that every teacher has cited as the basis for rejecting the Islamic Antichrist theory is Daniel 9:26, which speaks of "the people of the prince who is to come."

While varying interpretations have been offered for this verse, most hold that this prophecy means that the specific people who destroyed Jerusalem and the temple in AD 70 are the ancestors of the "people" who will follow the Antichrist ("the prince who is to come").[5] According to this position, then, the verse should be understood as follows:

> The people—that is, the primary followers—of the prince (the
> Antichrist) to come in the last days shall destroy the city (Jeru-
> salem) and the sanctuary (the Jewish temple of the first century).

Though this is only one verse, the weight it carries in the minds
of many as proving a Roman Antichrist is profound. However, after
having examined this passage inside and out for years and having
consulted numerous commentaries and considered all options, I
can say with confidence that the traditional European- or Roman-
centric interpretation of Daniel 9:26 is in error. Please bear with
me as I explain.

Most scholars believe the destruction of "the city and the
sanctuary" in this verse is a reference to AD 70, when the Roman
legions under General Titus destroyed both the Jewish capital city of
Jerusalem and its temple. Because the soldiers were Roman citizens,
many conclude that the primary followers of the Antichrist in the
last days will be Europeans in general or Italians specifically. The
problem, however, is that very few of the soldiers who destroyed
the temple and Jerusalem in AD 70 were actually Italians, or even
Europeans. In fact, history reveals a dramatically different picture.

Before the Roman Empire became an empire, it was called the
Roman Republic. In the early days of the Republic, as it was evolving
into the empire, the majority of the soldiers recruited to serve in the
Roman legions were Italians from the city of Rome and the outlying
suburbs. However, as the empire vastly expanded, it became next to
impossible to man the entire empire with soldiers only from Italy.
There were just not enough Italian men to spread all over Europe,
Northern Africa, and the Middle East. Thus, at the beginning of the
first century, Emperor Augustus made a series of sweeping reforms
that led to significant changes in the ethnic makeup of the Roman
armies. By AD 15, the only portion of the Roman army that continued to consist largely of Italians was the Praetorian Guard, an
elite military unit that protected the emperor. The remainder of
the army was increasingly composed of "provincials," citizens who

lived in the provinces—the outer fringes of the empire, away from the capital of Rome. The "provincialization" of the army was true for all of the Roman legions of this time period, but it was most markedly the case for the Eastern legions that were used to attack Jerusalem. Both ancient historical records and modern scholarship clearly confirm this.

According to Publius Cornelius Tacitus, a senator and Roman historian, "Titus Caesar . . . found in Judaea three legions, the 5th, the 10th, and the 15th [to attack Jerusalem] . . . To these he added the 12th from Syria, and some men belonging to the 18th and 3rd, whom he had withdrawn from Alexandria. This force was accompanied . . . by a strong contingent of Arabs, who hated the Jews with the usual hatred of neighbors."[6]

There are several important bits of information that we can gain from this reference. First, we learn that the Roman legions had been stationed in Judea, Syria, and Egypt. Beyond the Roman legions, "a strong contingent of Arabs, who hated the Jews," accompanied the soldiers. Needless to say, little has changed since the first century regarding the regional hatred for the Jewish people.

Later, Flavius Josephus, another irreplaceable historian from this period, confirmed Tacitus's report: "So Vespasian sent his son Titus . . . [who] came by land into Syria, where he gathered together the Roman forces, with a considerable number of auxiliaries [or, volunteers] from the kings in that neighborhood."[7] Elsewhere, Josephus described an even greater number of Arab soldiers who joined forces with the invading armies: "Malchus also, the king of Arabia, sent a thousand horsemen, besides five thousand footmen."[8] Mind you, six thousand men is the size of an entire legion. Malchus, who was only one of three Arab kings to have sent volunteers, sent enough soldiers to compose a full legion. As I detail in my book *Mideast Beast*, modern scholars of Roman history are in full agreement that the majority of the "Roman" soldiers were ethnically Syrians and Arabs—not the ancestors of modern Europeans, but of the modern-day inhabitants of the Middle East.

Although we can certainly understand how a hasty reading of Daniel 9:26 might lead one to conclude that the Antichrist's followers will be Europeans, doing just a little bit more homework and examining the evidence reveals something quite different from what has been commonly and popularly believed.

SUMMARY

Let us recap this chapter. First, we discussed the Israel-centricity of the Bible. We zeroed in on the actual geographic context of the great end-time wars and showed that they all center around Jerusalem. Then we examined several passages that specifically refer to the invading armies of the Antichrist as "the surrounding nations" or "neighbors," of Israel. Next we explored the fact that throughout the Prophets, the Bible repeatedly names the nations that will follow the Antichrist. They are all Middle Eastern and North African, Islamic nations. Finally, we examined the three primary supporting pillars of the European Antichrist theory. Despite the fact that most throughout church history have assumed the kingdom of the Antichrist to be a latter-day revived Roman Empire, we saw that a far more solid case exists for a revived Islamic Caliphate. When we understand that not only the prophet Daniel, but also all of the other prophets were speaking of the Islamic Caliphate and not the Roman Empire, then suddenly numerous tensions within the Bible disappear. All the major prophecies of the Bible suddenly flow together seamlessly. When we insert the key of Islam into the often puzzling world of biblical prophecy, everything comes into alignment and makes great sense.

CONCLUSION

If the final beast empire is indeed a revival of the Islamic empire, then this sheds tremendous light on the identity of harlot Babylon. This eschatological city is one that will be intimately related to the final beast empire. As we continue to narrow down the various candidates that might be considered, the Islamic identity of the seventh and eighth heads is certainly one of the most important clues. In the next chapter, we will see that not only is the final Babylon a city that is integrally connected to the final beast empire; it is, in fact, the actual religious and financial capital of that empire.

9

THE CITY OF SATAN

AS WE'VE ALREADY SHOWN, the seven-headed beast represents seven historical empires. As soon as the Hebrews had grown to become a great people, Satan hatched what would become the first of many plots to destroy them. Egypt, under Pharaoh, was the first empire that sought to destroy God's covenant people, roughly thirty-five hundred years ago. Since then, Egypt has fallen and several other pagan empires have arisen and fallen. Yet, while the empires may have changed, Satan's goal throughout history has remained consistent: destroy God's people and thwart His plans. As we emphasized in chapter 7, Satan has always worked through pagan empires, governments, and their militaries to effect his own plans and purposes. Whether Egypt, Assyria, Babylon, Persia, Greece, Rome, or the Islamic Caliphate, all of these entities were used like puppets by the devil to vent his rage against the Lord and His people. In the mysterious apocalyptic imagery of a seven-headed monster in Revelation 17, we have, as it were, a pan-historical, spiritual picture of the primary empires that Satan has used.

When we consider the meaning of the woman portrayed as being in partnership with the beast and specifically referred to as a city called "Babylon," we are given yet another critical clue. Very simply, the city of Babylon was the capital city of the Babylonian Empire, the third head of the beast. After Babylon fell, however, the locus of satanic power in the earth moved to another location. No sooner would one empire fall and another arise than Satan would set up shop in a new capital city. This is why the first-century Jews and the early Christians looked at the city of Rome (the capital of the sixth empire) as "Babylon." The ancient pagan city of Babylon was used as the archetype for all the other satanic cities that would follow. Rome was, as it were, the spiritual Babylon of the day. Thus, the apostle Peter was referring to Rome when he wrote, "The church that is at Babylon, elected together with you, saluteth you; and so doth Marcus my son" (1 Peter 5:13 KJV). This verse contains one of the most important keys to help us properly interpret and understand Mystery Babylon.

REACTIONARY OBJECTIONS

Before we can discuss the implications of Peter's comment, we need to briefly discuss the objections of those who deny that Peter was ever even in the city of Rome. Over the years, some Protestants have claimed that Peter was never in Rome. If that could be proven, it would put a solid nail in the coffin of the Roman Catholic teaching that Peter was the first pope. As is most often the case in matters of theological disputes, some will take every opportunity to "stick it" to their opponents any chance they can. As a Protestant, I understand that there are certainly various theological issues that Catholics and Protestants disagree on, but as lovers of truth, we must avoid reactionary theology. The primary goal of reactionary theology is to refute one's theological opponents, not to attain truth. We should never form any theological position simply because it is the opposite of what a rival group believes. If we were to make an honest assessment of the history of the interaction between various religions, sects, and denominations, we would be shocked at how many history-changing doctrines were the result of reactionary theology. The passionate efforts of some to deny Peter's presence in Rome, despite the overwhelming evidence, is a perfect example of this wrong approach. Let's discuss why these objections are unacceptable.

WAS PETER IN LITERAL BABYLON?

Some have argued that Peter was writing his first epistle from the literal, historical city of Babylon on the Euphrates. The first problem with this is that when Peter's epistle was written, in the second half of the first century, Babylon was not exactly a big-ticket destination.

The first significant destruction of Babylon occurred roughly four hundred years before Peter, when, in 309 BC, Antigonis I of Macedonia completely leveled the city. Twenty-four years later, Antiochus I removed and deported the remaining civilian population. Fifteen years after this, in 160 BC, Babylon was refounded by Antiochus IV Epiphanes. Later, the Roman geographer Strabo, writing about the time of Christ, said, "The greater part of Babylon is so deserted that one would not hesitate to say with one of the comic poets . . . 'The Great City' is a great desert."[1] Strabo went on to describe small settlements of Chaldean astronomers who lived among the ruins of the city. It was also during this period that the Euphrates River dried up and what was already a wilderness became even more desolate. Roughly eighty years later, in AD 116, the Roman emperor Trajan arrived at the site of the former great city and "saw nothing but mounds and stones and ruins."[2] Nevertheless, some would still have us believe that it was during this time, when Babylon was all but a virtual wasteland with only a few inhabitants, that the apostle Peter moved there and led a thriving church.

The second problem with the idea that Peter was in literal Mesopotamian Babylon is the fact that he had to use coded language to speak of the church there. Peter sent the greetings of "she who is in Babylon" (1 Peter 5:13). While the King James Version uses the word *church*, the original text simply says "she." The NIV, NASB, ESV, and several other translations read similarly: "She who is in Babylon . . . sends her greetings." But all of the early Syriac, Arabic, and Latin manuscripts inserted the word church in place of "she." Why? Because the early translators understood that Peter was attempting to mask the fact that he was writing on behalf of a church. Coded language would have been necessary only if he were writing from a city where the church was functioning underground due to persecution. If Peter had been in Babylon on the Euphrates, there would have been absolutely no need for him to be secretive or cautious. Even if there had been a tiny Jewish population that Peter was evangelizing, it would have been impossible for him to conceal his purposes for being there. However, if Peter was in Rome, where persecution of the Christians during this period is well documented, then it would make complete sense that he would need to be secretive.

The third problem with the view that Peter was in literal Babylon on the Euphrates is that every single reference from the early church writers places Peter in the city of Rome during this time. There is literally not a single shred of historical evidence that Peter ever went to Babylon on the Euphrates.

BABYLON OF EGYPT

Others still have argued that Peter was in a small town called Babylon, outside of Cairo. The broad consensus of scholarship rejects this idea outright. Apart from the name Babylon, there is simply no evidence for this claim. The little Egyptian town of Babylon was so insignificant that it would have merited an explanation from Peter if he were in fact writing from there. To simply make reference to "Babylon" in the ancient Near East while speaking of the little town of Egypt would be similar to a someone stating today that he was in "Paris" while he was actually in Paris, Texas, rather than the city in France. Failing to clarify this would be outright confusing, if not misleading.

Beyond this, as with literal Babylon, there would have been no reason for Peter to use code words to refer to the believers there if he was in such a small village, where persecution would have been unlikely and where hiding his purposes would have been impossible. In the end, this is simply another option that has absolutely no historical support.

BABYLON AS ROME

Unlike the previous two suggestions, all historical evidence points to the fact that Peter was in Rome when he wrote his first epistle. Peter is believed to have arrived in Rome in roughly AD 47 and remained there until his death around twenty years later. The first epistle of Peter was likely written shortly before his martyrdom under the reign of Nero.

Writing to the Roman Christians in AD 110, a mere forty years after Peter's death, Ignatius of Antioch said, "I do not, like Peter and Paul, issue orders unto you. They are apostles, but I am one condemned; they indeed are free."[3] The inference, of course, is that both Peter and Paul once presided as apostles over the believers in Rome. Ignatius's testimony is important because he was actually alive while Peter and Paul were serving the church.

Ninety years later, Tertullian, in his *Prescription against Heretics*, noted of Rome, "How happy is its church, on which apostles poured forth all their doctrine along with their blood! where Peter endures a passion like his Lord's! where Paul wins his crown in a death like John's."[4] Of course, everyone acknowledges that Paul was martyred in Rome, and here Tertullian spoke of both Peter and Paul as having been martyred in the same city. About the same time, Irenaeus of Lyon wrote of "the great and glorious Church at Rome, which was there founded by the two apostles Peter and Paul."[5] Other early sources and voices, such as the Didache, Polycarp, Clement, Lactantius, Cyril, Eusebius, Jerome, and several others, also made comments that support Peter's time in Rome. In his three-volume work, *The Faith of the Early Fathers*, William A. Jurgens actually lists thirty references from the early Christian writers and other early church documents establishing Peter's presence in Rome. So consistent is the early church's testimony that Peter was in Rome when he penned 1 Peter that *Unger's Bible Dictionary* states unequivocally, "The evidence for his martyrdom there is complete, while there is a total absence of any contrary statement in the writings of the early fathers."[6]

Few are aware that the archaeological and scientific evidence for Peter's burial under St. Peter's Basilica in Rome is also rather compelling. Investigator John Evangelist Walsh, in his book *The Bones of St. Peter*, recalls the fascinating account of the scientific and archaeological inquiry into the validity of what Christian tradition had long held. Walsh's book scientifically and impartially untangles the various threads of the excavation, leaving the objective reader with few doubts that what were discovered under the Basilica are in fact the remains of the apostle Peter. While it would be too much to detail here how the conclusions were arrived at with scientific accuracy, suffice it to say, anyone willing to look at the facts objectively will conclude that Peter was most likely buried in Rome.

In light of the overwhelming weight of evidence, then, we should not be surprised to discover that Eusebius Pamphilius, the great early church historian, referred to this specific verse in AD 303, stating, "Peter makes mention of Mark in his first epistle which they say that he wrote in Rome itself, as is indicated by him, when he calls the city, by a figure, Babylon."[7] The evidence that Peter was using Babylon as a code word is amplified by the fact that, rather than using the word *church*, he said "she" again, most likely to veil his location and purpose while working under heavy persecution.

APOCRYPHAL AND PSEUDEPIGRAPHAL TESTIMONY

Peter's use of the name Babylon to refer to Rome appears to have been the common practice among both Christians and Jews during this period. A few apocryphal and pseudepigraphal works also use the name Babylon to refer to the city of Rome.[8] In *The Sibylline Oracles*, book 5, generally dated about AD 80, the writer foretells a great star falling from heaven and burning Babylon, which it refers to as "the land of Italy . . . city of the Latin land, unclean in all things . . . in widowhood you will sit beside your banks, and the Tiber River will weep for you."[9] *The Apocalypse of Baruch* and *2 Esdras* also use Babylon similarly.

Because "Babylon" was a commonly used code word for Rome during this period, Peter's audience would have likely understood immediately that he was referring to Rome. There was a reason that Jews and Christians alike saw a connection between Babylon and Rome. Both cities were the capitals of the great pagan power of their respective ages. They were glamorous, seductive, pagan, wealthy, and powerful beyond measure. So in AD 70, when the Roman armies destroyed Jerusalem and the Jewish temple, Rome was simply Babylon all over again to the Jews.

BABYLON: THE MIGRATING CITY OF SATAN

Understanding that the apostolic church viewed Rome as a latter-day "Babylon" is vital in any attempt to establish the identity of the final Babylon—the great harlot. To the early believers, Babylon was more than just the literal ancient city of Babylon. Everything that Babylon embodied and represented had migrated. As a spiritual concept, Babylon was not static, not locked into a single location. "Babylon" represents the great stronghold of Satan in the earth at any given time. After Babylon fell, the satanic spirit that once found a home on the Euphrates simply moved to another city and set up its throne there. Each successive reigning empire shared the same characteristics: These empires revolved around some form of pagan religion that carried a hatred of the Jewish people and a demonic lust to possess the promised land of God. After Babylon, the Medo-Persian Empire was followed by the Greek and then the Roman Empire. As Beale stated, "In John's time 'the great city' would refer primarily to Rome, and any of its allies, since it was the center of the ungodly empire that persecuted God's people at that time."[10] With each empire, "Babylon" migrated. As such, Tyconius, a fourth-century Christian theologian, bluntly characterized Babylon as follows: "By it, the city of the people of the devil are signified."[11] Thus, in our quest to understand and identify Mystery Babylon, we now have the following working definition:

> A symbolic term used to identify the capital of the final great satanic empire. It is the final capital of global idolatry and the last great demonic stronghold of the earth, from which Satan will wage his war against Jerusalem and God's redemptive purposes.

Various commentators share this view. For example, Kendall Easley, in his commentary on Revelation, stated:

> In his day—the time of the sixth head of the monster—the form of the woman was Rome. During the days of the seventh head of the monster, another great and wicked city will rise. As Antichrist's splendid capital, she will have no rival.[12]

After listing the capital cities of the Egyptian (Memphis), Assyrian (Nineveh), Babylonian (Babylon), Persian (Persepolis), and Roman (Rome) empires, Easley continued:

> Each was the Babel of its own day. Each rose as an expression of engineering ingenuity, supported by military might and political scheming. Each was a commercial, religious, and cultural center. Each proudly opposed God and the people of God. Roll them all together, and they become the perfect forerunner for one future final great city and civilization opposed to God—"Babylon the Great," mistress of the world. As with the world's first great city Babel, so with the last Babel: God will judge her directly and dramatically.[13]

Easley certainly gets it. Throughout history, it has always been Jerusalem versus "Babylon." In the first century, it was Jerusalem versus Rome. Today, however, Rome is no longer the primary seat of satanic power in the earth. After the sixth empire fell, another arose.

THE CAPITAL OF THE SEVENTH EMPIRE

Having established the definition of Mystery Babylon as Satan's migrating stronghold and the capital of the reigning beast empire, the next step is to simply look to the seventh head of the beast of Revelation 17. Which empire does this represent? As we have already argued, it is the historical Islamic Caliphate, the only candidate in world history that fulfills all of the relevant prophetic passages and the clear pattern established by the previous six empires. Unlike any other entity in human history, the historical Islamic Caliphate has been a champion of anti-Semitism, anti-Judaism, anti-Zionism, anti-Yahwehism, and an anti-Christ spirit. This is true in both doctrine and practice. Though the Caliphate has been officially dissolved for more than ninety years now, it lives on in the hearts and imaginations of much of the Muslim world as multitudes continue to call for its restoration. The efforts of the Islamic State of Iraq and Syria are simply the most recent example of an Islamic endeavor to reestablish a caliphate. That which is coming under Antichrist, however, will far supersede ISIS in size, power, and global impact. In our day, the eighth kingdom of the beast is beginning to arise right before our eyes. I believe it is just a matter of time before the eighth kingdom is fully revived.

Having identified the seventh empire, we must now simply ask, what "city" is the spiritual capital and heart of the Islamic world? This would most certainly seem to be the city of Mecca, and the Kingdom of Saudi Arabia. No doubt, Saudi Arabia is the spiritual epicenter of the Islamic world. While Rome was the Babylon of the first century, for the past fourteen hundred years a new Babylon has reigned over the hearts of multitudes throughout the Middle East.

That city is Mecca, the single greatest city of idolatry that humanity has ever known.[14]

10

THE QUEEN OF LUXURY

IN THIS CHAPTER WE WILL DISCUSS a few final descriptions and characteristics of the harlot found within the prophecy of Revelation 17. Each of these characteristics is critical in identifying the great harlot, defining the very essence of who the woman is, what she represents, and finally, the nature of her final judgment.

DRUNK ON THE BLOOD OF THE SAINTS

Among the first observations the apostle John made was that the harlot was "drunk with the blood of the saints, and with the blood of the witnesses of Jesus" (Rev. 17:6). We must not miss the gravity of what is being described here. The last days will bring about the culmination of the church's testimony to the world, much of which will be accomplished through the martyrdom of the saints on a level unparalleled in history. In the same way that Jesus Himself overcame the world through being mutilated and crushed, the last-days saints will imitate their Master and overcome the world through martyrdom within the context of the proclamation of the gospel. It is for this reason that a loud voice from heaven declares the coming victory of the saints: "They overcame him [Satan] because of the blood of the Lamb and because of the word of their testimony, and they did not love their life even when faced with death" (Rev. 12:11). According to this prophecy, the primary entity responsible for the slaughter of God's people in the last days will be the great harlot. This city and the system she represents will slaughter so many holy ones that she is pictured as actually being drunk on their blood.

We've already emphasized the fact that down through history, each of the seven empires has persecuted and sought to destroy the Jewish people. Later, after Christianity arose, Christians were also persecuted, both under the Roman Empire and under Islam. In the last days, however, the rage of Satan will find its culmination and fullest expression. Revelation 12 describes this final and unparalleled assault:

> And there was war in heaven, Michael and his angels waging war with the dragon. The dragon and his angels waged war, and they were not strong enough, and there was no longer a place found for them in heaven. And the great dragon was thrown down, the serpent of old who is called the devil and Satan, who deceives the whole world; he was thrown down to the earth, and his angels were thrown down with him. Then I heard a loud voice in heaven, saying, "Now the salvation, and the power, and the kingdom of our God and the authority of His Christ have come, for the accuser of our brethren has been thrown down, he who accuses them before our God day and night. And they overcame him because of the blood of the Lamb and because of the word of their

testimony, and they did not love their life even when faced with death. For this reason, rejoice, O heavens and you who dwell in them. Woe to the earth and the sea, because the devil has come down to you, having great wrath, knowing that he has only a short time." And when the dragon saw that he was thrown down to the earth, he persecuted the woman [Israel] who gave birth to the male child. But the two wings of the great eagle were given to the woman, so that she could fly into the wilderness to her place, where she was nourished for a time and times and half a time, from the presence of the serpent. And the serpent poured water like a river out of his mouth after the woman, so that he might cause her to be swept away with the flood. But the earth helped the woman, and the earth opened its mouth and drank up the river which the dragon poured out of his mouth. So the dragon was enraged with the woman, and went off to make war with the rest of her children, who keep the commandments of God and hold to the testimony of Jesus (vv. 7–17).

We must note that whether we are speaking of the Antichrist himself, his followers, or the bloodthirsty harlot, they all function together to fulfill Satan's rage. Lenski rightly stated, "In a sense Babylon, the whore, the kings, the earth dwellers, are one and the same."[1] Christians often think of the persecution of the Antichrist, but rarely consider the great last-days persecution as coming from the harlot. In truth, the two are essentially one and the same. Thus we understand the call for the slain saints, apostles, and prophets in heaven to "rejoice over her, . . . because God has pronounced judgment for you against her" (Rev. 18:20). The blood shed under the shadow of the great harlot will be so great that it is as if she is personally responsible for all of the holy blood shed down through history. This is why the prophecy concludes with such a strong note: "And in her was found the blood of prophets and of saints and of all who have been slain on the earth" (Rev. 18:24). Babylon is not literally responsible for the shed blood of every single last saint in all of history. The persecution that is coming under her influence, how-ever, is vast enough to justify such hyperbolic, all-inclusive language.

QUEEN OF KINGS

It's a perplexing and disturbing picture that the woman is at once a bloodthirsty murderess and a global influencer and power broker over kings, world rulers, and peoples throughout the earth. The prophecy actually begins by highlighting the kings of the earth as her primary patrons. She is described as the one "with whom the kings of the earth committed acts of immorality, and those who dwell on the earth were made drunk with the wine of her immorality" (Rev. 17:2). While the peoples of the earth are drunk on her false religion and the slaughter of God's holy people, she enjoys the support of earthly rulers. This is terrifying.

The harlot's influence is pictured as extending to the ends of the earth. We see this clearly as the angel explains that the waters upon which the harlot sits "are peoples and multitudes and nations and tongues. . . . The woman whom you saw . . . reigns over the kings of the earth" (17:15, 18). To what length the harlot's influence will reach is certainly up for debate. Should we conclude that she literally "rules" over every last "king" or ruler in the earth, or that she simply exerts a truly vast measure of control and influence over a great number of world rulers? Based on other passages that speak of resistor nations, militaries, and peoples, I would suggest it is more reasonable to assume the latter. What we do know is that the harlot exerts such a vast degree of influence and control over kings and peoples that the Scriptures are justified in using such strong language.

A GREAT ECONOMIC INFLUENCE

We've already discussed the harlot's great religious influence. We must also acknowledge the great emphasis the prophecy places on her economic power and influence. Of course, prostitution has always been an economically driven reality. Throughout the prophecy, the woman is portrayed as being seductive, not simply because of her sensuality, but also through her wealth. We are told that "the kings of the earth have committed acts of immorality with her, and the merchants of the earth have become rich by the wealth of her sensuality" (Rev. 18:3). Elsewhere, the text states that "the kings of the earth . . . shared her luxury" (18:9 NIV). The King James Version refers to the relationship of the kings rather interestingly as those who "lived deliciously with her." Quite simply, both the merchants and the kings have grown rich through their relationship with this queen, who herself lives in lavish luxury. As Beale stated, "The description of the woman confirms that she represents worldly economic forces . . . She is the symbol of a culture that maintains the prosperity of economic commerce . . . [She] tries to seduce through her economic attractiveness."[2]

In the most overt ways, spiritual adultery refers to any form of worship or devotion that is given to anyone other than the God of the Bible. However, it need not be restricted only to blatant acts of worship. In this particular prophecy, "immorality" refers variously to any form of support; in fact, it seems as though economic compromise is most emphasized. This is seen in 18:3, where "the kings of the earth have committed acts of immorality with her," is equivalent to "the merchants of the earth have become rich by the wealth of her sensuality." Beyond this, 18:9 speaks of "the kings of the earth, who committed acts of immorality and lived sensuously with her." Instead of "lived sensuously with her," the ESV more accurately uses "lived in luxury with her." Some may object that mere financial "support" does not merit the label of adultery (NIV) or fornication (KJV). Imagine if you would, however, a husband who was secretly supporting a woman financially other than his wife. While financial involvement does not technically involve the act of adultery, very few would deny that this could rightly be described as unfaithfulness and infidelity. So it is portrayed here in Revelation, where the harlot's seduction is both religiously and economically motivated. The guilt of offering support to this woman, however, is greatly amplified by the fact that she is guilty for the shed blood of God's holy people. We've often heard the phrase, "The enemy of my enemy is my friend." Likewise, this passage is informing us that the friends and supporters of this woman, who is herself a supreme enemy of God, are also positioning themselves as God's enemies. Though many nations will commit overt spiritual adultery with the harlot—literally join with her in her false religion—many other nations will no doubt show her support through economic or even military relationships. Some acts of unfaithfulness are less overt and brazen than others, but God views them all as deserving of His condemnation.

ROYALTY

Another important description concerns the prostitute's fine apparel: "The woman was clothed in purple and scarlet, and adorned with gold and precious stones and pearls" (Rev. 17:4). These colors may be interpreted two different ways. First, they are the colors of royalty. When Jesus was taken prisoner, the Roman centurions dressed Him in a robe that is described as scarlet in one gospel (Matt. 27:28) and purple in another (Mark 15:17). The robe was in essence a mock royal garment. Likewise, they fashioned for Him "a crown of thorns . . . and a reed [a mock scepter] . . . and they knelt down before Him and mocked Him, saying, 'Hail, King of the Jews!'" (Matt. 27: 29)

The harlot's purple and scarlet clothes are also an allusion to her as a royal pretender. And because her clothes are literally glittering with gold, jewels, and pearls, she is also portrayed as being rich beyond measure. She is fabulously wealthy and dressed in royal attire.

We should also understand the colors of her clothes as representing sinfulness: "Though your sins are as scarlet," God once told Israel, "they will be as white as snow. Though they are red like crimson, they will be like wool" (Isa. 1:18). This interpretation is supported by the remainder of the Revelation 17 passage—she is, after all, a corrupt and murderous prostitute. In all likelihood, we would be right to understand her appearance as pointing to both realities. She is a queen, but also a sin-stained prostitute and blood-soaked murderess. As bizarre as this may seem, she is all of these things at once.

HIDDEN FROM PLAIN SIGHT

There is another description of the woman that is often missed. In chapter 18, we are told that "she says in her heart, 'I sit as a queen and I am not a widow, and will never see mourning'" (v. 7). This portion of the prophecy is a direct quotation of an earlier prophecy about Babylon made by the prophet Isaiah. It is important that we go back and read the fuller context of that passage:

> Yet you said, "I will be a queen forever." These things you did not consider nor remember the outcome of them. Now, then, hear this, you sensual one, who dwells securely, who says in your heart, "I am, and there is no one besides me. I will not sit as a widow, nor know loss of children." But these two things will come on you suddenly in one day: loss of children and widowhood. They will come on you in full measure in spite of your many sorceries, in spite of the great power of your spells. You felt secure in your wickedness and said, "No one sees me," Your wisdom and your knowledge, they have deluded you; for you have said in your heart, "I am, and there is no one besides me." (Isa. 47:7–10)

The picture is of one who is entirely arrogant, fully deceived by her exalted status. She is convinced that her reign will never be extinguished. From her vantage point, she is beyond displacement, beyond ever being dethroned—she will never mourn. Instead, however, the text goes on to emphasize the speed and power with which she will meet her end as God's judgment falls upon her: "For this reason in one day her plagues will come, pestilence and mourning and famine, and she will be burned up with fire; for the Lord God who judges her is strong" (Rev. 18:8).

Another important element here is the harlot's belief that "no one sees me" (Isa. 47:10). This is rather striking. In the midst of her excessive luxury, debauchery, murders, and prostitution, she believes that no one is aware of her sins. Of course, nothing escapes God's notice, and what is done in secret will be fully revealed. In this case, the whole world will look on as the harlot is exposed, judged, and utterly destroyed.

HER JUDGMENT WILL BE SUDDEN, SHOCKING, COMPLETE, AND ETERNAL

This leads us to our final observation. Much emphasis within the prophecy is placed on the destruction and judgment of the great harlot. There has been some debate among commentators concerning the judgment of the harlot. On one hand we are told that "the ten horns . . . and the beast, these will hate the harlot and will make her desolate and naked, and will eat her flesh and will burn her up with fire" (Rev. 17:16). On the other hand, later we are told that the Lord is the one who judges her: "In one day her plagues will come . . . and she will be burned up with fire; for the Lord God who judges her is strong . . . A strong angel took up a stone like a great millstone and threw it into the sea, saying, 'So will Babylon, the great city, be thrown down with violence, and will not be found any longer'" (18:8, 21). So which is it? Does the beast destroy the harlot or does God destroy the harlot? This possible tension is easily resolved when we understand that the Lord will simply use the beast and his kings to accomplish His purposes: "For God has put it in their hearts to execute His purpose by having a common purpose, and by giving their kingdom to the beast, until the words of God will be fulfilled" (17:17).

Not only does the prophecy emphasize the sudden nature of her judgment: "for in one hour she has been laid waste!" (v. 19), but also its complete and everlasting effects:

The sound of harpists and musicians and flute-players and trum-peters will not be heard in you any longer; and no craftsman of any craft will be found in you any longer; and the sound of a mill will not be heard in you any longer; and the light of a lamp will not shine in you any longer; and the voice of the bridegroom and bride will not be heard in you any longer. (Rev. 18:21–23)

After she is destroyed so violently and swiftly—in a day, with "violence," having been consumed by fire—her judgment is described as being permanent and absolute. Never again will there be heard in this city the sound of music. Workers will never rebuild the city. Tradesmen will never be active in her again. All agriculture will cease. There will be no marriage, no weddings. Human life there will not return. This description of her condition in the age to come, after Jesus' return, is an important factor as we move on to assess the various interpretations of this prophecy.

11

SUMMARIZING WHAT
WE'VE LEARNED

HAVING WORKED THROUGH THE PROPHECY of Revelation 17–18 and observed the various identifying descriptions, actions, and characteristics of the great harlot, let us now summarize what we've noted. As we move forward to consider the strengths and weaknesses of the various interpretations, it is to this list of criteria that we must refer. As we will see, some of the candidates for the Harlot Babylon can be made to align quite well with some of the descriptions, but don't align at all with some of the other criteria. For any interpretation to be seriously considered, it is not sufficient that it align with only some of the items on this list. It must align with them all. Ultimately, whatever our view of Mystery Babylon may be, it must be both formed and informed by the text itself, and not simply because it confirms our previously held assumptions or traditions. Let's consider these various requirements.

A LITERAL CITY

Throughout Revelation 17 and 18, the last-days Babylon is referred to eight times as a "city" (17:18; 18:10, 16, 18–19, 21). Further, the prophecy goes on to detail what must be understood as a very literal list of many of her primary imports (18:11–13). Other portions of the prophecy describe her in ways that can only be ascribed to a literal geographical location (17:3; 18:17, 19).

A GREAT CITY

The city is repeatedly described as "the great city" (17:18; 18:10, 18, 19, 21). While the "greatness" of this city could rest in her vast size, the emphasis seems to focus more on her far-reaching and vast influence over earthly kings, leaders, and various peoples. It is also quite likely that this city's greatness is found in the fact that it is more than just a city alone, but is part of a larger geopolitical sphere of influence. During the biblical period, any great city of renown was the heart of a larger city-state that reigned over large portions of the ancient world. This was true of ancient Babylon as well as ancient Rome. Likewise, our understanding of the last-days Babylon could also very well refer more broadly to a larger city-state or nation.

A DESERT CITY

At the beginning of chapter 17, the apostle John is shown the city in a desert (Gk. *erēmos*). That the last-days Babylon, just like ancient Babylon, is pictured in a desert is likely an important clue as to the natural surroundings and location of the city.

A PORT OR COASTAL CITY

The Bible strongly indicates that she is a port city, or at least close to the sea. After the destruction of the city, those who lament and mourn her loss are specifically the shipmasters, the passengers, and sailors. Further emphasized are those who "make their living by the sea," as they stood at a distance and cried out as they saw the "smoke of her burning . . . [for] all who had ships at sea became rich by her" (Rev. 18:17–19).

A CONSUMER, NOT A PRODUCER CITY

Many of the city's imports (Rev. 18:11–13) indicate that she is not a city of great production, either in terms of manufacturing or agriculture. The city seems to import both her luxury items and basic necessities. The merchants of the earth have grown rich from all of the goods that she purchases. Consequently, this further adds to the likelihood of her being a desert city.

THE GREATEST CITY OF IDOLATRY

The repeated references throughout the prophecy to the harlotry and immorality of the city are metaphorical references to false religion and idolatry. The specific description, literally written across her forehead, of "Babylon the Great, the mother of harlots" (Rev. 17:5) indicates that this city is not simply a city of false religion, but the most significant city of idolatry and false religion that has ever existed.

A RELIGIOUS CAPITAL AND MISSIONARY CENTER

Beyond being the greatest city of idolatry and false worship that has ever existed, she is also a missionary city that spreads her false religion all over the world. She specifically holds sway over, "kings, . . . peoples and multitudes and nations and tongues" (Rev. 17:2, 15). Repeatedly, we are told the kings of the earth sin with her and participate in her idolatrous false religion. Emphatic language indicating that "all the nations have drunk of the wine of the passion of her immorality, and the kings of the earth have committed acts of immorality with her" (18:3) confirms that the religious influence of this city is indeed global.

A CITY OF EXCESS LUXURY

Among the unique descriptions ascribed to this city, she is consistently portrayed as a city of luxury and material excess. Beyond being "adorned with gold and precious stones and pearls" (17:4), she also "glorified herself and lived sensuously" (or "luxuriously," NKJV) (18:7). Upon her destruction, we read that "all things that were luxurious and splendid have passed away" from her (18:14). This results in the lament that "in one hour such great wealth has been laid waste!" (18:17). Many of the specific items she imports are things that require wealth and speak of luxury.

AN ECONOMIC SEDUCER

The material excess and luxury of this city serve to greatly amplify her seduction and influence far beyond that effected through her religion alone. Both the "merchants" (18:3) and the "shipmaster[s]" (18:17) have "become rich through the abundance of her luxury" (18:3 NKJV). Even more important, all of this material wealth is directly responsible for the kings of the earth joining in with her spiritual corruption and bloodshed (17:2; 18:3).

A CITY OF SLAVERY

Concluding the list of the city's imports are, specifically, "slaves and human lives" (Rev. 18:11–13). While every major city globally today is involved to some degree in human trafficking, the fact that the import of "slaves" is emphasized here likely speaks of something more extraordinary than in other cities.

A CITY THAT PROMOTES THE MURDER OF BOTH JEWS AND CHRISTIANS

The city is "drunk with the blood of the saints, and with the blood of the witnesses of Jesus" (Rev. 17:6). Earlier, the beast, with whom the woman is in partnership, is seen seeking to "devour" Israel, as well as "her children, who keep the commandments of God and hold to the testimony of Jesus" (Rev. 12:17). When she is finally judged, the "saints and apostles and prophets" are told to rejoice "because God has pronounced judgment for you against her" (Rev. 18:20). The bloodshed this city brings to the Jewish people and to Christians is so great that we are told, "And in her was found the blood of prophets and of God's holy people, of all who have been slaughtered on the earth" (Rev. 18:24 NIV).

REPRESENTS ROYALTY

The portrayal of the city as a woman "clothed in purple and scarlet, and adorned with gold and precious stones and pearls" (Rev. 17:4) indicates that she represents royalty.

HIDDEN IN PLAIN SIGHT

We are told that this city "says in her heart, 'I sit as a queen and I am not a widow, and will never see mourning'" (Rev. 18:7). This is a picture of a city governed by arrogance, convinced that despite her brazenness, she will never be dethroned. Her declaration that, "no one sees me" (Isa. 47), also points to the belief that her shamelessness goes unnoticed by most. She is hidden, as it were, in plain sight. This is rather striking. In the midst of her debauchery, murders, and corruption, she believes that most are unaware of her sins.

THE SPIRITUAL AND FINANCIAL CAPITAL OF THE ISLAMIC WORLD

The relationship of this last-days city to the seventh and eighth beast empires is as their very heart or capital. As the ancient cities of Babylon and Rome serve as the prototypes of the last-days Babylon, and were themselves the hearts and capitals of their respective empires, so also is the last-days Babylon the capital of the final satanic kingdom.

THIS CITY WILL BE UTTERLY DESTROYED FOREVER

Finally, when this city is destroyed, she will be destroyed suddenly, speedily, and completely. Her destruction will be "in one hour . . . with violence. . . . She will be burned up with fire" (Rev. 18:19, 21, 8). Further, her judgment is permanent and eternal: "Babylon . . . will not be found any longer" (18:21).

CONCLUSION

Whatever our view of the harlot Babylon may be, it must conform to all of the criteria in this chapter. Now that we have reviewed these requirements, let's move on and begin weighing the various options to determine which seem to best fulfill this ancient and mysterious prophecy.

PART TWO

WEIGHING THE OPTIONS

12

ROME

FOR THE FIRST FEW CENTURIES OF THE CHURCH, most Bible
students believed that Rome was the great harlot of Revelation 17–18.
Early writers, including Lactantius, Tertullian, Irenaeus, and Jerome
all referred to Rome as "Babylon."[1] With the gradual decline and
eventual fall of pagan Rome, however, this view was abandoned. By
the sixth century, Andrew of Caesarea openly rejected the old interpretation and expressed his doubts that Rome would ever regain its
"ancient status." Instead, he believed that Revelation 17–18 points to a
city that would arise in the last days.[2] Roughly a thousand years later,
the Protestant Reformers circled back to Rome, but this time, they
pointed specifically to the Roman Catholic Church. Many Protestants
still do today. But do either of these two views hold any water?

PAGAN ROME

With regard to pagan Rome of old, on the surface this city meets several of the criteria established within the prophecy quite well. Of course, Rome was indeed a very literal, real, and "great" city. It was an economic hub and a city of extraordinary luxury and material excess. It was also a city of tremendous idolatry and a source of heavy persecution for the early believers. Many of the early Christians themselves viewed Rome as Babylon, including the apostle Peter, who actually called Rome by this name in 1 Peter 5:13. There are also many very strong parallels between Rome and ancient Babylon. The rulers and people of both cities destroyed Jerusalem and caused the exile of the Jewish people. Further, the imagery of the "seven mountains on which the woman sits" (Rev. 17:9) would have no doubt been recognized by the early believers as a reference to the city of Rome. Coins from the first century even portray the goddess Roma, a personification of the city, as lounging on seven hills and sitting on the Tiber River.

Despite these initial strengths, however, this position must hold that the prophecy was entirely fulfilled in the first century and doesn't actually have any actual last-days application. While the many fatal problems with a first-century fulfillment of the book of Revelation are simply too numerous to address here, various Bible scholars have very ably done so already.[3] We will, however, discuss just a few of the more obvious flaws of this position.

PROBLEMS WITH HISTORICAL PAGAN ROME AS THE HARLOT

The most conspicuous problem is the fact that the city of Rome never fell suddenly, dramatically, or completely, as the prophecy so clearly describes. Instead, after many years of gradual decline and decay, the city of Rome finally "fell" in AD 476, when the Germanic hordes overthrew the last of the Roman emperors. New Testament scholar Grant R. Osbourne correctly articulated this problem when he pointed out that one would actually have to believe "that the prophecy never came true, since Rome lasted another four centuries. One would have to say that the Germanic and Gothic tribes who much later attacked and sacked Rome were part of the ten kings [of Revelation 17:12]."[4] The fall of Rome was such a slow and protracted collapse, in fact, that many claim Rome never actually even fell, but lives on through Western civilization. This is not what the prophecy says. It very clearly states that "in one hour . . . will Babylon, the great city, be thrown down with violence, and will not be found any longer" (18:19, 21). The fall of the great harlot city is plainly described as being sudden, swift, complete, and permanent. There is simply no amount of squeezing, shoving, or shoehorning that will allow us to force the very long, slow, historical decline and eventual fall of Rome into this prophecy. On this point alone, the historical (preterist) interpretation fails miserably.

Another obvious problem with painting Rome as the great harlot is the fact that, although it was indeed the satanic stronghold capital of the first century, the Roman Empire is no longer a reigning beast empire. Rome was the sixth empire, but the prophecy is clear that another empire would come after Rome. In chapters 7–9, I argued that the seventh/eighth empire is the Islamic empire, or Caliphate, and as such, we should look to its capital. Looking to Rome today is no more relevant than looking to ancient Nineveh. These were the capitals of their respective empires and the satanic stronghold cities of their days—but they are no longer. In identifying the fulfillment of the Revelation prophecy, we must look to the capital of the seventh beast empire, not to the previous empires that ruled the region thousands of years ago.

To sidestep this problem, preterists must claim that, rather than pointing to seven historical empires, the seven heads of the beast in Revelation 17 point to seven historical Roman emperors. It is slightly humorous to note that none who hold this position can ever agree on which emperors the text has in mind. Below is a chart of five different lists demonstrating the range of interpretations that preterists have offered.

DATE OF REIGN	EMPEROR	POSSIBLE ENUMERATIONS OF THE REIGN IN REV. 17:10				
49-44 B.C.	CAESAR	1	1			
31 B.C.—A.D. 14	AUGUSTUS	2	2	1	1	
14-37	TIBERIUS	3	3	2	2	
37-41	CALIGULA	4	4	3	3	1
41-54	CLAUDIUS	5	5	4	4	2
54-68	NERO	6	6	5	5	3
68-69	GALBA	7		6		
69	OTHO	8		7		
69	VITELLIUS			8		
69-79	VESPASIAN		7		6	4
79-81	TITUS		8		7	5
81-96	DOMITIAN				8	6

Obviously preterists have failed to come to any kind of consensus on this issue. Assessing the rather hopeless efforts to reconcile the prophecy with history, Beale concluded:

The attempt to identify the seven kings with particular respective world empires may be more successful, since it is more in keeping with the "seven heads" in Dan. 7:3–7, which represent four specific empires. The first five kings, who "have fallen," are identified with Egypt, Assyria, Babylon, Persia, and Greece; Rome is the one who "is," followed by a yet unknown kingdom to come.[5]

Other problems for this view include the fact that Rome does not sit in a desert. In the end, the facts that the prophecy concerns the last days and not ancient history, and that the historical fall of Rome simply does not align whatsoever with the abrupt and eternal annihilation of Babylon as described in the prophecy, make the historical city of Rome an unacceptable option.

THE ROMAN CATHOLIC CHURCH

What then of the second view, that the city of Rome is yet to fulfill the prophecy in the last days? This view must inherently see the Vatican and the Roman Catholic Church as integrally tied to the city and its final judgment. Like the previous view, this view also has some strengths, but also some fatal flaws.

Of course, today the Vatican, or Rome, is indeed a very real city of extraordinary luxury, and it obviously enjoys a tremendous measure of religious influence over many peoples, kings, and nations. Depending on how one views the various Roman Catholic doctrines and worship practices, such as veneration of the saints, the Immaculate Conception, and intercession through Mary, a large number of Protestants no doubt will see Rome as a city of great idolatry. And once again, we may appeal to the fact that the early believers, including Peter, looked to Rome as Babylon (cf. 1 Peter 5:13). Many have also correctly pointed out that since the Reformation, the Catholic Church has been responsible for the death of tens of millions of Protestants. Moreover, today, the Roman Catholic Church tends to take a cold and, at times, adversarial stance toward the State of Israel. In some parts of the world, Catholicism continues to be a source of persecution toward Protestants.[6]

Numerous other more questionable points are often raised to identify the Roman Catholic Church as the great harlot. Dave Hunt, for example, in his book *A Woman Rides the Beast*, declares, "The colors of purple and scarlet once again identify the woman with both pagan and Christian Rome . . . The woman's colors are still literally the colors of the Catholic clergy!"[7]

PROBLEMS WITH THE ROMAN CATHOLIC CHURCH AS THE HARLOT

Some of the same problems that exist for ancient pagan Rome also exist for the idea of a last-days Rome. The city of Rome was indeed the satanic stronghold of the first century, but the Roman Empire, the sixth beast/empire, is simply no longer a reigning beast. As stated earlier, Rome today is no more relevant than Memphis, Nineveh, Babylon, Persepolis, or Antioch. These were all the capital stronghold cities of the earlier beast empires, but no longer. "Babylon" migrates—and the seventh beast has already come. As such, we must look to the capital of the seventh/eighth empire.

So what are some of the most significant problems with viewing the Catholic Church as the last-days Babylon? First, it is difficult to see it as the economic powerhouse that controls the kings of the earth. This isn't to say the Catholic Church has no economic power or sway whatsoever. Certainly it does, but it doesn't seem to wield the level of power that is described in Revelation. If the Vatican were to be destroyed today, it is doubtful that merchants and manufacturers throughout the earth would lament the end of some great source of commerce. It's also rather difficult to say that the city of Rome is a great importer of slaves and human lives (see Rev. 18:11–13). Finally, Vatican City is not a desert city.

ROMAN CATHOLIC BLOODGUILT

While it is certainly true that a vast multitude of Protestants have been killed by the Roman Catholic Church, consider what has transpired over the past twenty years. On March 1, 2000, during a press conference in Paris, representatives of the Roman Catholic Church released a new document entitled "Memory and Reconciliation: The Church and the Faults of the Past." The document quotes Pope John Paul II's 1994 apostolic letter Tertio Millennio Adveniente:

> Hence it is appropriate that as the second millennium of Christianity draws to a close the Church should become ever more fully conscious of the sinfulness of her children, recalling all those times in history when they departed from the spirit of Christ and His Gospel and, instead of offering to the world the witness of a life inspired by the values of her faith, indulged in ways of thinking and acting which were truly forms of counter-witness and scandal. Although she is holy because of her incorporation into Christ, the Church does not tire of doing penance. Before God and man, she always acknowledges as her own her sinful sons and daughters.[8]

Eleven days later, on Sunday, March 12, 2000, Pope John Paul II delivered a homily in the St. Peter's Basilica entitled "Universal prayer: Confession of Sins and Asking for Forgiveness." In the homily, the pope expressed both regret and repentance over the historical sins of those Catholics who persecuted or sinned against "Jews, Gypsies, other Christians."[9] During the homily, the pope apologized on behalf of the Roman Catholic Church and asked for forgiveness:

> We are asking pardon for the divisions among Christians, for the use of violence that some have committed in the service of truth and for attitudes of mistrust and hostility assumed towards followers of other religions.[10]

Sixteen years later, in January 2016, Pope Francis mirrored John Paul II's sentiments, also apologizing to Protestants on behalf of the Roman Catholic Church, stating, "As the bishop of Rome and pastor of the Catholic Church, I would like to invoke mercy and forgiveness for the non-evangelical behavior of Catholics toward Christians of other churches . . . We cannot cancel what has happened, but we don't want to let the weight of past harm continue to pollute our relations."[11]

These public acts and statements of repentance are important as we consider the identity of the great harlot. While the Catholic Church has admitted to sinning against "other Christians," much of the violence and bloodshed that occurred in the days of the Protestant Reformation was not the exclusive sin of Roman Catholicism. Protestants are also guilty of their own share of bloodshed. This side of the equation, however, is rarely discussed. Despite the fact that sin and bloodguilt exist on both sides, many Protestants believe that judgment is due only to the Catholic Church, exempting themselves from any such punishments. But regardless of which side one may take regarding the Catholic/Protestant division, we all agree that God does not punish anyone for sins that have been publicly confessed and repented of. If that were not the case, we would all be in very big trouble.

While the Roman Catholic Church of history is certainly guilty of shedding the blood of many saints, is there any Christian or Jewish blood being shed in Rome today? Whatever religious prejudices and even hostilities do continue to exist in various parts of the world, when we look to the Vatican itself, we do not see calls for violence. Instead, we see apologies and public repentance. This is a far cry from what is described in the book of Revelation, where we read of a city that is actually drunk on the blood of God's holy people. Quite to the contrary, when we look to the Middle East today, in the nations of Iraq and Syria, where ISIS has set up their temporary Caliphate, the majority of those who are being killed for the name of Jesus are indeed Assyrian and Chaldean Catholics.

CONCLUSION

Whether we are considering the historical pagan city of Rome or modern-day Rome/Vatican City, both cities have several characteristics that align well with the prophecy, yet on other critical points simply cannot be made to fit. In the end, neither view is a satisfactory interpretation of Revelation 17–18. Some may ask, "Then how is it that some of the language in the text seems to point so clearly to Rome if it is not the intended subject of the prophecy?" The same could be asked of Babylon. If literal Babylon is not the subject of the prophecy, then why use the actual name "Babylon"? The answer in both cases is simple: the ancient cities of Babylon and Rome were historical prototypes of that which is to come, a much greater, last-days harlot city.

13

JERUSALEM

THERE ARE TWO DISTINCT VIEWS CONCERNING JERUSALEM, just as there are with Rome. First, there is the preterist view: that historical Jerusalem of the first century is the Babylon of Revelation 17–18. Second, there is the futurist view: that the last-days Jerusalem will fulfill the prophecy. While some arguments are unique to one view or the other, most of the same arguments are recycled by both the preterists and futurists. We will thus examine most of the arguments for and against both views together.

THE PRETERIST VIEW

A number of well-known voices espouse the preterist view, that historical Jerusalem is the Babylon of Revelation. These include

New Testament scholar N. T. Wright; well-known and beloved pastor, author, and radio personality R. C. Sproul; the "Bible Answer Man," Hank Hanegraaff; dominionist author David Chilton; hyper-preterist Don Preston; and Roman Catholic theologian Scott Hahn.

This view is largely rooted in the wrong presumption that the Lord rejected Israel and replaced them with "the new Israel" or the church in the first century. So, those who hold this view do so because of their previously held commitment to replacement theology. The danger of this view is that casting historical Jerusalem (representing the larger Jewish nation) as the very embodiment of Satan results in, not only potentially harsh expressions of anti-Semitism, but also some very serious indictments of the very character of God Himself. Consider the language, for example, of Joel McDurmon, president of the ministry American Vision, from his book *Jesus versus Jerusalem*:

> The Old Jewish people were not merely exiled from their kingdom someday to return. No. This time, the Kingdom was taken from them and given to the true nation bearing the fruits thereof. Christ created a new bride. Why would Christ desire to return to the whore He has cast aside and divorced when He has a pristine bride descending from heaven, clothed in righteouness [sic], and uncorrupted by idolatry? He doesn't. He left that whore riding her patron, the beast of Rome. And the great mother of harlots suffered the judgment of her whoredom. She was divorced and disinherited.[1]

Now let me ask you a question; What kind of picture does this paint of God? Does this sound more like the eternally faithful, covenant-keeping God of the Scriptures, or the stereotypically selfish man blaming a midlife crisis for his divorcing his "old" wife and exchanging her for a younger "new" bride?

None will argue of course that the covenant judgments of Deuteronomy fell on Israel in the first century. The suggestion, however, that the Lord has forever rejected Israel, that He has eternally reneged on His "everlasting covenant" to Abraham, Isaac, Jacob, and David (see Gen. 17:7, 13, 19, et al.), is not only fundamentally unbiblical, but it is also a gross indictment of the very integrity and character of God. While preterists such as Mr. McDurmon may say that Israel's exiles are permanent, and "Christ created a new bride," Paul the apostle says, "God has not rejected His people, has He? May it never be! . . . God has not rejected His people whom He foreknew . . . They did not stumble so as to fall, did they? May it never be!" (Rom. 11:1, 2, 11).

This view also logically casts the modern State of Israel and the Jewish people as the descendants and modern representatives of the harlot that the Lord sought to eliminate. Logically, this would also infer that the Lord's efforts to forever destroy Israel as a nation failed. After all, Israel has been reestablished as a nation for well over sixty years now.

Using the standard language of other replacement theologians, N. T. Wright stated, "Instead of seeing Jerusalem as the victim of pagan aggression or corruption," Jesus' reinterpretation of various Old Testament passages "designate Jerusalem herself as Babylon, the enemy of the true people of the covenant god," and thus, "Jerusalem has become Babylon; Jesus and His disciples have become Jerusalem."[2]

Please consider what is being said here. Throughout the prophecies of Isaiah, Jeremiah, Ezekiel, Zechariah, and Joel, the Lord speaks of judging the pagan nations after they engage in a unified military attack of Jerusalem. After a period of being trampled by the nations (Luke 21:24; Rev. 11:2), the Lord will return to deliver the struggling remnant of Israel (cf. Isa. 10:20–22; 37:31–32; Jer. 23:3; Mic. 5:7-8; Zech. 9:14-15; Matt. 24:30). Wright, however, actually understands the many prophecies about the Lord judging Israel's pagan invaders and attackers as needing to be reinterpreted to mean that the Lord will judge and destroy Jerusalem itself. It would be impossible to more perfectly twist the biblical narrative to convey precisely the opposite of what it actually states. Wright reads prophecies about the deliverance of Jerusalem and says it is about the destruction of Jerusalem. Thus, in his view, when Rome destroyed Jerusalem in AD 70, it was not Rome but rather the Jewish nation itself that was the embodiment of Satan and most deserving of God's wrath. While there is no question that the events of AD 70 were the result of the Lord faithfully chastising His backslidden people, in no way whatsoever should we view those events as indicating that the Lord reneged on His covenant promises to them or that they were the very embodiment of evil. *God forbid!* Quite to the contrary, the Lord's chastisements on Israel down through history are the result of His honoring His covenant promises. At the Day of the Lord, despite their repeated backsliding, Jesus will bring the surviving remnant back to Him and redeem His people, specifically as a demonstration of His faithfulness before all the earth.

Preterists are quick to quote Revelation 11:8, where Jerusalem is referred to as "Sodom and Egypt," but they consistently ignore, just six verses earlier, where Jerusalem is called "the holy city" (v. 2). Whatever negative view of backslidden, rebellious Israel we have, we must also acknowledge the Lord's plans and promises to someday restore her. Despite her shortcomings, in the eyes of God she is still "holy." To cast Jerusalem not as a backslidden but deeply loved child, but instead as the fullness of evil deserving the fullness of God's perpetual wrath, is to fundamentally pervert the larger unfolding story of God's faithfulness to His people. If for no other reason, this is sufficient to reject this view.

THE FALL OF BABYLON VERSUS THE FALL OF JERUSALEM

Another fatal problem for the preterist view is that Jerusalem simply did not meet its end as described in the prophecy. According to the biblical description, when Babylon falls, it is drastic, sudden, and complete (see Rev. 18:10, 21). As a simple matter of history, however, Jerusalem's fall was part of a long process—a prolonged siege that lasted close to five years (AD 66–70). Furthermore, Jerusalem was rebuilt multiple times throughout history. Today, not only has

Jerusalem been restored; it is a bustling metropolis. This is a far cry from the language used through the final verses in chapter 18 of a city that would be forever desolate, void of all human life. Try as they might, preterist interpreters cannot account for the drastic discontinuity between what is described in Revelation and what actually took place in history.

BABYLON

Another significant problem for the preterist interpretation, as we have already discussed, is that the term *Babylon* was clearly understood by the early Christians and Jews as referring not to Jerusalem, but to Rome. Every Jewish or Christian document from this period, including the New Testament (1 Peter 5:13), uses the term *Babylon* to refer to Rome. To see Revelation as a complete anomaly on this matter, without any solid basis to do so, may border on irresponsible.

THE CALL TO FLEE BABYLON

Another argument made by preterists is that the command to flee Babylon, "Come out of her, my people" (Rev. 18:4), is noticeably similar to Jesus' call, in His Olivet Discourse, to flee Jerusalem just before its destruction (Matt. 24:15–18; Luke 21:20–21). Preterists claim this call to flee was heard, obeyed, and thus fulfilled when the Christians of Jerusalem fled to safety to Pella some years before the city's destruction in the first century. However, Eusebius wrote that the Christians fled Jerusalem before the Jewish war began[3] in AD 66, whereas the preterists say the book of Revelation was written in AD 65. This would mean the book of Revelation was "prophesying" and calling Christians to leave after they had already done so. Simply stated, "prophecy" written after the fact is no prophecy at all.

JERUSALEM AS AN ECONOMIC POWERHOUSE

This next problem is huge. Both preterists and futurists run into a wall trying to explain away the fact that Babylon is portrayed as a city of tremendous economic wealth and global influence, something that simply cannot be said of Jerusalem either in the first century or today. While it could certainly be said that Jerusalem was famous in the first century, the suggestion that she reigned over the kings and peoples of the earth is beyond an exaggeration. Far from ruling over the earth, first-century Jerusalem was occupied, dominated by, and eventually trampled down by Gentile powers. During the first century, Jerusalem was at its lowest level of regional influence in two centuries, whereas the fall of Babylon in Revelation is portrayed as a dramatic plummet from the peak of power and prosperity.[4] The same is true concerning Jerusalem's religious influence. In the first century, Judaism did not control the earth. So also today, the very suggestion that the whole world is being seduced by Judaism, or that the excessive wealth of Jerusalem controls the earth, is just plain ridiculous.

THE GREAT CITY

Both preterists and futurists argue that the phrase "the great city" in Revelation 17–18 must refer to Jerusalem. In Revelation 11, after the two witnesses are killed, the Scriptures say "their dead bodies will lie in the street of the great city which mystically is called Sodom and Egypt, where also their Lord was crucified" (v. 10). Jerusalem, of course, is the city where Jesus was crucified. Since it is called "the great city" in chapter 11, preterists and futurists believe it must also be the "great city" of chapters 17–18; after all, there can be only one "great city." Jerusalem must be mystical Babylon!

The simple answer to this argument is that throughout the book of Revelation, there are two great cities intended to be contrasted. One is the great city of God and the other is the great city of Satan. As we have shown, there have always been other "great cities" at enmity with Jerusalem. At one time it was Babylon; at another time it was Nineveh. The Lord told Jonah, "Arise, go to Nineveh the great city and proclaim to it the proclamation which I am going to tell you" (Jon. 3:2). A fuller understanding of the narrative of Revelation reveals that these two cities are represented by two different women, two different mothers. As far back as the eighth century, the Venerable Bede, in commenting on the Apocalypse, observed: "For there are two cities in the world, the one proceeding from the abyss, the other from heaven."[5] Expanding on Bede's observations, in the late 1800s J. A. Seiss contrasted the two women of Revelation:

> The first thing which strikes me in the study of this subject, is one which I have nowhere seen duly noticed, namely: the evident correlation and contrast between the Woman here pictured and another Woman described in the twelfth chapter. There, "a great sign was seen in the heaven, a Woman;" here, it is remarked, "he bore me away in spirit into a wilderness, and I saw a Woman." Both these Women are mothers; the first brought forth a son, a male, who is to rule all the nations;" the second "is the mother of harlots and of the abominations of the earth." Both are splendidly dressed; the first is "clothed with the sun." Her raiment is light from heaven. The second is "clothed in purple and scarlet, decked with gold, and precious stone, and pearls." All hers are from below, made up of things out of the earth and the sea.[6]

Finally, Beale offers seven points of contrast between the two women:

> (1) One is a pure bride and a mother of legitimate children, while the other is an impure whore. (2) Parallel introductory phraseology is used in 17:1 and 21:9–10 to introduce respectively the whore and the Lamb's bride. (3) Babylon is dressed in bejeweled attire and "clothed in linen" (so 17:4; 18:16), which hides her corruption, in contrast to the Lamb's bride, who is adorned in costly jewels (21:2, 9–23) and "clothes herself in bright, pure linen," which respectively reveals the glorious reflection of God's presence and "the righteous deeds of the saints" (19:8; cf. especially 17:4 and 21:19: "gilded" or "adorned with precious stone"). (4) Both are persecuted mothers (17:5, 16; ch. 12). (5) The woman

of ch. 12 is delivered, but the woman in ch. 17 is destroyed. (6) One woman has her security "in heaven" (12:1) and the other in the multitudes and the "kings of the earth" (17:15, 18). (7) Babylon is seen in a "desert" and referred to as a "city," which is likewise true of the woman in ch. 12 and the Lamb's bride (19:7–8; 21:2, 10).[7]

Although Jerusalem of both past and present is neither pure nor perfectly holy, the Lord is the one who "calls into being that which does not exist" (Rom. 4:17) and thus often relates to Israel according to what she will become after He has finished His redemptive work with her, rather than according to her present condition. This is why the Lord could refer to Jerusalem, even in its state of sinfulness, as "the holy city" (Rev. 11:2). This is no different from the manner in which He relates to you and me: a weak, broken, struggling Christians now, but unimaginably glorious in the age to come.

SPIRITUAL HARLOTRY

Another argument holds that because the Lord repeatedly charged unfaithful Jerusalem or Israel with spiritual harlotry throughout the Scriptures, Revelation 17–18 must obviously refer to Jerusalem. Indeed, Jerusalem is personified as a harlot on several occasions throughout the Old Testament. The most well-known example is Ezekiel 16:

> Thus says the Lord God to Jerusalem . . . "You trusted in your beauty and *played the harlot* because of your fame, and *you poured out your harlotries* on every passer-by who might be willing. You took some of your clothes, made for yourself high places of various colors and *played the harlot on them*, which should never come about nor happen. You also took your beautiful jewels made of My gold and of My silver, which I had given you, and made for yourself male images *that you might play the harlot with them*." (vv. 3, 15–17; emphasis added)[8]

Because of the unfaithfulness of Jerusalem and for playing the harlot, the Lord then explained that He would judge Jerusalem and allow her sins to come back upon her. Many read passages like this and assume that Jerusalem must surely be the great harlot of Revelation who will also be so severely judged. There is, however, one huge caveat. If we would just read the rest of this prophecy, we would see that the Lord qualified His promises of judgment with promises to remember His covenant with Jerusalem. For despite her (or our) unfaithfulness, the Lord is always faithful. This part of the equation is absolutely critical:

> "Nevertheless, I will remember My covenant with you in the days of your youth, and I will establish an everlasting covenant with you. Then you will remember your ways and be ashamed when you receive your sisters, both your older and your younger; and I will give them to you as daughters, but not because of your covenant. Thus I will establish My covenant with you, and you shall know that I am the Lord, so that you may remember and be ashamed and never open your mouth anymore because of your humiliation, when I have forgiven you for all that you have done," the Lord God declares. (Eze. 16:60–63)

So a more careful reading of this passage shows that the harlot Jerusalem and the harlot Babylon have very different futures. One is restored, while the other is destroyed forever. The two are simply not the same.

TYRE AND NINEVEH

Although this motif of harlot is used somewhat frequently of Jerusalem throughout the Old Testament, we also find that the term is used to refer to the very pagan cities of Tyre and Nineveh. Of Tyre, for example, is it said:

> "Take your harp, walk about the city, O forgotten harlot. Pluck the strings skillfully, sing many songs, that you may be remem-

bered." It will come about at the end of seventy years that the Lord will visit Tyre. Then she will go back to her harlot's wages and will play the harlot with all the kingdoms on the face of the earth. (Isa. 23:15–17)

Of Nineveh, it is said, "Woe to the bloody city, completely full of lies and pillage . . . because of the many harlotries of the harlot, the charming one, the mistress of sorceries, who sells nations by her harlotries and families by her sorceries" (Nah. 3:1, 4).

Likewise, in Exodus 34, God uses the motif of harlotry to refer to the idol worship of the pagan non-Jewish peoples who inhabited the land of Canaan:

You shall tear down their altars . . . lest you make a covenant with the inhabitants of the land, and they play the harlot with their gods and make sacrifice to their gods, and one of them invites you and you eat of his sacrifice, and you take of his daughters for your sons, and his daughters play the harlot with their gods and make your sons play the harlot with their gods. (Ex. 34:13, 15–16 NKJV)

Obviously, the motif of harlot is applied to various cities throughout the Old Testament, not only Jerusalem.

PORNĒ VERSUS MOICHEIA

Some also wrongly argue that the word for harlot (*pornē*) must be understood as referring to apostate Israel, which has turned away from a preexisting covenant relationship. If such were the case, however, the much more specific Greek word for adultery (*moicheia*) would have likely been used. It is a far more precise term for an unfaithful, adulterous covenant breaker. By understanding harlotry in accordance with its broader biblical meaning, the great harlot should instead be understood as an entity that seduces the inhabitants of the world into idolatry in general. She lures many peoples into worshipping a god other than Yahweh, the one true God of the Bible.

Another important point is that because the great harlot's sin is seducing others into idolatry, we can conclude that she represents some form of nonbiblical religion. As Beale has written, "Since the female figures of these chapters all represent purely religious realities, Babylon must also be essentially religious."[9] In fact, since the woman is a religious seductress, luring the world into worshipping false gods, this clearly does not point to Jerusalem, but instead to a Gentile religious system.

THE CITY OF BLOODSHED

Yet another argument for Jerusalem as Mystery Babylon is that because in Babylon "was found the blood of prophets and of saints and of all who have been slain on the earth" (Revelation 18:24) can only be a reference to Jerusalem, of which Jesus Himself declared, "Upon you may fall the guilt of all the righteous blood shed on earth" (see Matt. 23:34–37; cf. Luke 13:34).

It is true that in AD 70, Jerusalem suffered the Lord's judgments for her mounting sins and for rejecting those sent to her. From about the middle of the first century, however, the responsibility for the bloodshed of the saints and prophets has largely shifted to the Gentile world. Rome certainly spilled an abundance of Christian blood in the first few of centuries of the church. None would protest calling Paul and Peter apostles or prophets; they were not martyred in Jerusalem, but in Rome. Likewise, John the apostle was killed in Asia Minor, or modern-day Turkey. Jesus was simply generalizing what was true until that point, that most prophets had died in Jerusalem. When we look out at the world today, it is not Jerusalem that is guilty for the slain Syrian, Iraqi, and Turkish Christians throughout the northern Middle East, or for the Christians being killed daily throughout North Africa, in the nations of Nigeria, Sudan, Somalia, and Kenya. Certainly Jerusalem is not responsible for the Christians who are being regularly attacked and killed throughout Pakistan. While Jerusalem did indeed suffer for its history of persecuting many of the prophets sent to it, this is no longer the case. We must not confuse Jesus' indictment of first-century Jerusalem with the Lord's absolute condemnation of the last-days Babylon.

HEAVEN REJOICES

Another significant problem with seeing Jerusalem as the Harlot of Babylon is the stark contrast between the positive reaction in heaven after Babylon is destroyed and what we find elsewhere throughout Scripture concerning judgment on earthly Jerusalem. In Revelation 19:1–6 we find a multitude in heaven celebrating and expressing jubilation at the news of Babylon's demise. This reaction is precisely the opposite of what we find elsewhere, for instance, when Jeremiah wept at the fall of Jerusalem (Lam. 2:11), and Jesus Himself wept at the mere expectation of Jerusalem's fall (Luke 19:41). Why would heaven rejoice at something that caused Jesus to weep? This is another example of why the view that Jerusalem is harlot Babylon simply does not work.

THE WOMAN RIDES THE BEAST

The relationship of the woman and the beast is also a factor that excludes Jerusalem from being Babylon. Preterists argue that the leadership of Jerusalem was in an illicit relationship with Rome, and thus fulfilled the description of the prophecy. In making this argument, they overlook a few very serious problems. First, the relationship with Rome that Jerusalem enjoyed had significantly deteriorated by the middle of the AD 50s. Yet preterists claim the book of Revelation was written in the mid 60s, by which time the relationship had soured completely. So even if the preterists' earlier dating of Revelation were accurate, it would still mean that Revelation was predicting something that had already happened. That doesn't make any sense. Second, the relationship the woman is portrayed as enjoying with the beast is a very close partnership, something much more intimate than anything Jerusalem ever experienced with Rome.

A PORT CITY

Another potential problem for Jerusalem as Mystery Babylon is that while Babylon is portrayed as a port city, Jerusalem is anything but a port city. Not only does Revelation depict Babylon as sitting upon many waters (Rev. 17:1), but John used four specific Greek terms to describe those in relationship with Babylon and her waters. There are the shipmasters, passengers, sailors, and those who make their living from the sea (18:17). Jerusalem, however, is landlocked, roughly forty miles inland, and up in the mountains. Only if one viewed Jerusalem as the capital and representative of the larger State of Israel, which is indeed a nation of ports and port cities, would this problem be resolved.

BABYLON IS DESTROYED FOREVER

The final glaring problem for the Jerusalem-as-Babylon view concerns the comprehensive and permanent nature of Babylon's destruction. Remember that after the angel of Revelation 18:21 throws the "great millstone . . . into the sea," he declares, "So will Babylon, the great city, be thrown down with violence, and will not be found *any longer*" (emphasis added).

This picture simply cannot be reconciled with the consistent biblical picture concerning Jerusalem. Jeremiah 17:25 tells us that Jerusalem "will be inhabited forever." Jesus will return to Jerusalem to restore the throne of David (see 2 Sam. 7:11–16; Isa. 9:6–7; Matt. 25:31; Luke 1:30–33). It is specifically from Mount Zion that Jesus will rule the nations (see Ps. 110:2).

Proponents of a last-days Jerusalem as Mystery Babylon—such as Chris White, author of *Mystery Babylon: When Jerusalem Embraces the Antichrist*—are forced to take the extremely awkward view that present-day Jerusalem will become a burning desolation forever, and Jesus will rule from a different location entirely, that will still be called Jerusalem. Considering that the city Jesus will rule will maintain not only the same name but also specific geographical locations, such as Mount Zion, this view becomes an impossibility.

Although the future millennial Jerusalem will be much larger than it presently is, there continues to be some direct geographic correlation. After all, as the Scriptures so clearly state, during the millennium,

> many peoples will come and say, "Come, let us go up to the mountain of the Lord, to the house of the God of Jacob; that He may teach us concerning His ways and that we may walk in His paths." For the law will go forth from Zion and the word of the Lord from Jerusalem. (Isa. 2:3)

Throughout the Scriptures, the blessings of the millennial kingdom are consistently and integrally tied to the future glory of Jerusalem:

> At that time they will call Jerusalem "The Throne of the Lord," and all the nations will be gathered to it, to Jerusalem, for the name of the Lord; nor will they walk anymore after the stubbornness of their evil heart. In those days the house of Judah will walk with the house of Israel, and they will come together from the land of the north to the land that I gave your fathers as an inheritance. (Jer. 3:17–18)

This is the city of which the Psalmist declared, "For the Lord has chosen Zion; He has desired it for His habitation" (Ps. 132:13). Elsewhere he wrote that the stones and very dirt of Jerusalem are sacred to those who understand God's plans for this city: "You will arise and have compassion on Zion . . . Your servants find pleasure in her stones and feel pity for her dust" (Ps. 102:13–14). The very notion that the Lord will complete His plan of redemption, which has been unfolding around Jerusalem for thousands of years, not by redeeming it but by burning it and destroying it forever is unthinkable. God forbid! Instead, He promised that when all is said and done, He will "extend peace to her like a river, and the glory of the nations like an overflowing stream" (Isa. 66:12). Intercessors are called to "give Him no rest until He establishes and makes Jerusalem a praise in the earth" (Isa. 62:7). The Lord declares, "For Zion's sake I will not keep silent, and for Jerusalem's sake I will not keep quiet, until her righteousness goes forth like brightness, and her salvation like a torch that is burning. The nations will see your righteousness, and all kings your glory" (Isa. 62:1–2). Far from becoming a place of desolation forever, Jerusalem

> will be called by a new name which the mouth of the Lord will designate. You will also be a crown of beauty in the hand of the Lord, and a royal diadem in the hand of your God. It will no longer be said to you, "Forsaken," nor to your land will it any longer be said, "Desolate"; but you will be called, "My delight is in her," and your land, "Married"; for the Lord delights in you." (Isa. 62:2–4)

So many other passages could be cited. The theme of Jerusalem literally becoming the very seat of Jesus the King and the capital of the whole earth is repeated over and over again throughout the entire Bible. Unless one ignores these passages altogether (or radically reinterprets them, as the Jerusalem-as-Babylon advocates must do), the mere suggestion that Jerusalem will be destroyed forever is not only inconceivable; it is literally the very antithesis of the plan of God and the burning desire of His heart.

CONCLUSION

All things considered, there are simply far too many contradictions and insurmountable difficulties with this view to consider it a viable interpretation. This is true for both the preterist and the futurist positions. While the use of harlot language in Revelation does remind us of various Old Testament passages that speak of Jerusalem, to view her as the subject of this prophecy is to fundamentally misunderstand its true intent. Therefore, we must cross this view off our list of possible interpretations—and move on to consider the next option.

14

THE ILLUMINATI /
NEW WORLD ORDER

THE BELIEF THAT THE LAST-DAYS BABYLON OF REVELATION represents the New World Order or "the Illuminati" has become increasingly popular among Christians. Although there are numerous variations on this view, generally it holds that Babylon refers to a global cabal of world leaders, power brokers, and bankers who control virtually everything. This group, it is claimed, consists of an assortment of secret societies, clubs, and organizations that span the globe. This shadowy network of global leaders is involved in various forms of occult rituals that underlie their Luciferian religion, which is, simply put, the worship of Satan.

The strength of this view, as it relates to the biblical criteria, is that at least conceptually, the Illuminati/New World Order would be both a religious and an economic system. It would control many of the peoples and kings of the earth. Because of the secretive nature of this group, it would also certainly fit the description of an entity that says, "I will be a queen forever" and "No one sees me" (Isa. 47:7, 10). Apart from these basics, however, this view has some very significant problems in aligning with the scriptural criteria.

RELIANCE ON THE NIMROD MYTH

From a purely scriptural perspective, one of the first problems with the Illuminati-as-Babylon view is its reliance on the Nimrod myth in general, and Alexander Hislop's *The Two Babylons* specifically. According to adherents to this view, a large network of world leaders known as the Illuminati practice a religion that was created by Nimrod at the Tower of Babel. The goal of this secret network is to create a "New World Order," which is simply an attempt to return to the Tower of Babel, as it were. As such, the very foundation of the entire Illuminati/New World Order narrative is the story of Nimrod and the Tower of Babel. From a recent (2016) book, *The Babylon Code*, we read:

> To solve the Bible's greatest riddle, we need to go far back into the distant past to a time not long after Noah's flood in ancient Babylon. Here, in the cradle of civilization along the Euphrates River, are the clues we need to piece together a cosmic jigsaw puzzle that predicts what is happening in our world today.
>
> This prophetic mind-twister has its origins in Babylon . . . In the biblical story, the human race—speaking one language—gathered in the land of Shinar a few generations after the Great Flood.
>
> At the time Nimrod ruled Babylon. . . . Nimrod married an alluring prostitute named Semiramis and built . . . the Tower of Babel.[1]

The very basis of the Illuminati/New World Order theory, then, is built upon the need to understand the story of Nimrod's tower.

Without this foundation, the entire narrative falls apart. The Nimrod narrative is also heavily relied upon to support some other very unusual ideas, to say the least:

> The Tower of Babel likely involved advanced technologies. The Tower of Babel and the word Babel, or Barb-ili, means "gate of the gods." Often the only way to truly understand the Bible is to study the root meaning of words in the original biblical language. Thus, the purpose of the Tower of Babel may have been to act as a kind of portal for interdimensional beings to enter the earthly realm. It was there in ancient Babylon that all the ancient mystery religions and secret occult societies were birthed. Ancient code is weaved into the interdimensional fabric of ancient Babylon that is connected to a dimension outside of time and space that we are only now beginning to understand.[2]

"Interdimensional beings" and portals aside, I showed in chapters 4 and 5 that even the most basic elements of the Nimrod story popularly employed by most Illuminati/New World Order theorists have absolutely no basis in the Scriptures, history, or even reality. There isn't a shred of evidence that Nimrod married a woman named Semiramis or that he started a religion. And the information we have in the Bible about Nimrod is scant at best. All of these ideas come from extrabiblical myths and traditions that began no earlier than the first century, having blossomed and swelled up to this present day. Proponents of this view simply have no genuine basis to tie their theory back into the biblical story.

Remember: responsible biblical interpretation should never revolve around or rely upon traditions, myths, or just plain speculation. Besides, there is no need to focus on extrabiblical information about ancient Babel to understand the identity of the great harlot/Mystery Babylon. The Bible already provides us with all we need to properly understand Babylon and how it would have been viewed and understood by the early believers.

WHICH CITY?

Another major clash this view has with the Scriptures involves the fact that the New World Order is a concept, not a city, and particularly not a specific, identifiable city. Yet the Bible describes Babylon in very literal terms. The fact that the Illuminati/New World Order theory does not name a clear capital city as its base is deeply problematic. Of course, many who hold this view often combine it with one of the other views, seeking to tie the Illuminati to, say, New York City, Brussels, Rome, or literal Babylon (now Hillah) in Iraq. In other words, they piggyback on other interpretations, combining the strengths of two theories, as it were. The problem in doing so is that it is not only the strengths of two theories that are combined, but also the weaknesses.

THE ILLUMINATI IS NOT A GLOBAL RELIGION

Another problem with claiming Illuminati satanism to be the religion of the Antichrist is that it does not represent a religion openly practiced by the masses. There are always going to be a few juvenile, attention-seeking flakes who do practice overt satanism, but it is simply never going to become a popular global religion. Adding to the difficulty, according to this view, the Illuminist cabal worships Satan specifically in secret. If such a cabal even exists, they are certainly not open about their religion, engaging in open-air evangelistic campaigns. The harlot of Revelation, on the other hand, waves her golden chalice high. She is brazen in her evangelistic efforts to seduce and lure the kings and peoples of the earth to join her.

As a general rule, Satan tends to be a counterfeiter who sugarcoats his poison. It is rather doubtful, therefore, that any group will seek to seduce the peoples of the world to openly worship Satan in the last days. It is much more reasonable to assert that Satan will deceive the world into worshipping him under the guise of some other well-known religion. This is, after all, how Satan has always functioned. During the first century, most Romans worshipped Zeus. Yet in referring to the Temple of Zeus in Pergamum (also spelled Pergamon), Jesus called it "Satan's throne" (Rev. 2:13). Needless to say, this was far from politically correct.

I am reminded of an illustrative moment I had some years ago when I was still in college. For years, every Tuesday night I used to put on a free cookout for the homeless in a vacant lot in the inner city. One evening, as I was talking to a homeless friend (whom I knew only by the nickname of "Sugar Bear"), a couple of young satanists walked up to get some hot dogs and soup. (It was apparent that they were satanists by the way they were dressed.) Sugar Bear leaned over to me and quietly said, "You know," he said, "I really don't get these guys. I mean, either you believe in the Bible or you don't believe in the Bible. But you don't claim to not believe in the Bible, and then go and worship the biggest loser in the Bible." Sugar Bear was right! It is dubious to believe that the world will ever willingly embrace overt Satan worship, as this is counterintuitive. In keeping with his standard modus operandi throughout history, Satan will more likely seduce an uncountable number of people through, for example, the worship of Allah, the god of the Quran, who is simply Satan masquerading as the God of the Bible. As I said, Satan candy-coats his poison.

THE ILLUMINATI ARE NOT RELATED TO ISLAM

This of course leads us to another potential problem with the notion that the Illuminati/New World Order represents the Babylon of Revelation. Specifically, the Illuminati have no identifiable connection to Islam, the seventh and eighth head of the beast. Of course, one may certainly take a different view concerning the seventh/eighth kingdoms. If this is the case, however, one must be able to cogently and convincingly identify the seventh and eighth beast kingdoms in a way that can be clearly reconciled with Daniel 2 and 7, and still explain how the Illuminati relate to this final kingdom.

THE ENDURANCE OF ILLUMINATI CONSPIRACY THEORY

Although the Illuminati/New World Order theory runs into significant problems scripturally, it truly is a grand narrative whose primary strength is that it seems to explain why virtually everything throughout the world happens. In this sense, it is a superconspiracy, a conspiratorial construct in which an array of lesser conspiracies are all nested together into one vast hierarchical structure. At the top of it all is the devil himself, overseeing, orchestrating, and controlling nearly everything that happens throughout the earth. Because this view is such an all-encompassing narrative, it is able to essentially absorb nearly any of the other views under its umbrella. Thus, if a number of Christians were to be killed by a group of violent Islamists, adherents to this view would simply claim that the Islamists are secretly being controlled by the Illuminati. If an evil Islamist dictator were to emerge from some nation in the Middle East, it could be claimed that he is a mere Illuminati puppet. If the pope were to issue some arguably satanic edict, then obviously he, too, is a pawn of the Illuminati.

The hitch, of course, is that none of this can ever be proven. As I playfully discussed in the opening chapter of this book, I myself have been accused by random Illuminati conspiracy theorists on the Internet of being a secret agent of the shadowy cabal. When no evidence could actually be brought forth, one such theorist claimed to have witnessed me "shapeshift." Of course, there are perhaps a dozen easy jokes I could make here, and it would be equally easy to simply disregard such individuals as delusional and unstable cranks, but it is a serious matter that this kind of thinking is actually not at all uncommon even among widely received Christian leaders, pastors, and teachers.

Again, the notion of a global organization of world leaders who all secretly worship Satan and seek to do his bidding is obviously not something that can be proven. It is, by its very definition, a secret. The strength of this view to convince some is, therefore, also one of its biggest weaknesses. At least it should be. While this view does provide answers to nearly everything, it requires no verification. This should be a massive red flag. Does it make sense that the Lord would, on one hand, command us to "examine everything carefully" (1 Thess. 5:21), as the noble Bereans did (see Acts 17:10–11), to verify what is true and what is not, while on the other hand expect us to simply accept something which by its very nature is impossible to verify? Would He really place His people in such a hopeless position?

To put it bluntly, this view is simply not believable. Every man-made organization is going to be rife with internal divisions, conflicts, and breakdowns. How much more would this be true of an organization composed entirely of devil worshippers? How is it that a global cabal of Satan worshippers has managed to create a vast network that is so disciplined that it can control nearly everything in the world, when even the godliest and most committed Christian organizations tend to fracture and decay within just a few short decades? When we consider the level of power, discipline, and organization often portrayed by those who espouse Illuminati conspiracy theories, it is as if the group were godlike in its omnipresence, omniscience, and omnipotence. Yet, knowing the nature of mankind, I would suggest that thinking believers should find the basic narrative of Illuminati conspiracy theory to be downright dubious from the very start.

If I may go one step further, not only do many Christian teachers who hold to Illuminati conspiracy theories engage in tremendous improvisation, fluidly morphing and adjusting their views according to the need of the moment, but they also tend to deviate far outside of the Bible into all sorts of bizarre ideas. My desire is not to criticize any particular teacher, author, or minister, as I believe many who espouse these ideas are entirely sincere. But understanding the biblical narrative concerning the end times, and even more important, how we as followers of Jesus are to live in these days, is not going to be accomplished by discussing pyramids, UFOs, interdimensional portals, and Nephilim, but through a committed life of prayer and careful Bible study.

CONCLUSION

The merging of Illuminati conspiracy theories with biblical escha-
tology far too often represents a fundamental departure from careful
biblical exegesis and relies instead on scouring for proof texts and
extrabiblical support to prove a previously existing theory. Considering the weight of evidence against the New World Order as
the last-days Babylon, not only in terms of simple common sense
but also in terms of its ability to fulfill the criteria laid out in the
Scriptures, this view is not tenable.

15

NEW YORK CITY / USA

IN RECENT YEARS, an increasing number of books have sprung up casting New York City specifically, or the United States more generally, as the final Babylon. In their book *The Final Babylon: America and the Coming of Antichrist*, coauthors Kreiger, McGriff, and Woodward unapologetically assert that "only the United States of America . . . can muster the money and the might to be THE FINAL BABYLON of Revelation 18."[1] They go on to state, "We have met the enemy and he is us."[2] In his book *America, The Babylon: America's Destiny Foretold in Biblical Prophecy*, author R. A. Coombes claims to set forth thirty-three specific identifying characteristics of Babylon that align with the United States. Several other books, such as *The End of America* by John Price and *America Will Burn* by Nathan Ford, argue similarly that the United States is the great harlot and that Christians should follow the biblical instructions to "come out of her" and flee to foreign lands (see Rev. 18:4). Books such as *Getting Out: Your Guide to Leaving America* by Mark Ehrman actually offer suggestions for how Christians can "flee" the United States. If the United States is the last-days Babylon, the implications are profound. This is one more reason why a proper understanding of Revelation 17–18 is such a genuinely important pastoral and practical matter for our day.

WHY THE UNITED STATES?

The strengths of this view are that New York City is indeed a very literal and "great city" (see Rev. 17:18; 18:10; et al.). As the home of Wall Street, it is also the very heart of the global economy. As Steve Cioccolanti, senior pastor of Discover Church, Melbourne, Australia, stated in a recent sermon:

> Whoever controls the money controls the world. And guess what? It's not the UN; it's not the Euro. It's the U.S. dollar that has been the world's reserve currency since 1944. That gives me another pause to think, Wait a minute. Babylon might be referring to America . . . America is literally the center of the physical, material world . . . America did not exist at the time of the Bible, so it's understandable that an alternative had to be used, and maybe the code was Babylon.[3]

New York City is also a port city planted solidly "on many waters" (Rev. 17:1). If we consider the broader interpretation of the United States, however, then whether through Washington, Hollywood, Las Vegas, or Wall Street, we indeed have an entity that is both profoundly influential and corrupt in perhaps too many ways to count. It's certainly not difficult to see the many parallels between the United States and ancient Rome. At this moment in history, like Rome, the United States is the pinnacle of global power. Like Rome, its influence is vast, and its military—until recently, at least—has been feared far and wide. Unfortunately, also like Rome, our moral underpinnings are rapidly decaying as Americans increasingly pursue all manner of self-indulgence, sexual impurity, gluttony, and you name it. Despite any of these things, however, like the other interpretations we've already considered, this one has several fatal problems.

THE UNITED STATES IS NOT A FALSE RELIGION

While it is certainly fair to highlight the financial and corrupt moral influence of the United States across the globe, the United States fails to satisfy the most significant part of the equation; she does not have a genuine religious component. Neither New York City nor the United States represents a religion, a religious system, the global capital of idolatry, or more specifically, the single greatest false religion that has ever existed. As we have already shown, the great harlot of Revelation represents all of these things. Babylon, as "the mother of harlots and of the abomination of the earth" (Rev. 17:5), does not merely represent some general form of idolatry, such as "materialism" or "consumerism." No, she represents the biggest, the greatest, the vilest and most bloodthirsty religious system the world has ever known. For all of America's faults, there is simply no way that New York City or the United States can be criticized and twisted sufficiently to match the requirements of the prophecy.

Despite any negative influence the United States may have abroad, the other side of the coin seems to be missing from all the books I have read that argue for America as Babylon. Whatever shortcomings the United States may be guilty of, no one can deny that she is also a tremendous source of good in the world. The United States provides an inordinate amount of humanitarian aid to the world. When a massive earthquake devastated the Iranian city of Bam in 2003, for example, the United States spent tens of millions of dollars and rushed in teams of rescue and aid workers to bring relief. This one example could literally be repeated thousands of times. Far more important, however, the United States is the heart of the global missions movement. Beyond providing a high percentage of the world's missionaries to minister and proclaim the gospel throughout the world, the Christian church in the United States is also by far the world's leading source of funding for foreign missions. This is not insignificant. How can the single greatest source of gospel evangelization to the nations, in terms of both funding and actual sending of missionaries, also be "the mother of . . . the abominations of the earth"? This dichotomy alone, I would suggest, rules out the United States as the fulfillment of the last-days Babylon.

How do supporters of this view circumvent this glaring problem? Author R. A. Coombes suggests that the United States does indeed represent a religion, one that worships "Lady Liberty." While idolatry often manifests in various and very subtle ways, to compare the values of freedom, equality, and civil liberties that underscore the Constitution of the United States with the descriptions of the drunk, seductive, bloodthirsty harlot of Revelation is just ridiculous. Can someone idolize concepts such as liberty? Of course, but "Lady Liberty" is not the great end-time persecutor of Christians throughout the world. Nor do Americans bow down before the Statue of Liberty or offer her worship. This kind of stretching of the clear intentions and meaning of the text in order to blacken the United States to satisfy the requirements of the prophecy is far from convincing and, I would argue, is a glaring Achilles' heel of this position.

DRUNK ON THE BLOOD OF THE SAINTS

In Revelation 17, the harlot Babylon is specifically emphasized as being drunk on the blood of the saints (v. 5). Babylon is not simply responsible for the wholesale slaughter of God's holy martyrs; she celebrates and revels in it.

Revelation 12 details Satan's efforts in the last days not only to devour the woman Israel, but also "to make war with the rest of her children, who keep the commandments of God and hold to the testimony of Jesus" (v. 18). Thus, the harlot joyously indulges herself on the shed blood of all of God's people, both Jews and Christians—and seeks to lure the world into joining in on her sick obsession. While it is easy to see the parallels between the United States and the Roman Empire in terms of global prominence economically and militarily, how anyone can say the imagery of the bloodthirsty, saint-killing harlot accurately describes the United States is simply beyond me.

Unfortunately, the only way proponents of this view may support their arguments is to go down the dark and lurid road of endless conspiracy theories that cast the United States in a purely negative light. In *The Final Babylon*, for example, the authors spend much time casting every founding father as either a God-hating neo-pagan or an occultist. From there, they move forward to denigrate nearly every aspect of the American system imaginable. While working through this material, I even found a reference to me—according to these authors, I am possibly a secret "Muslim not wishing to be exposed."[4] Unfortunately this is the kind of mind-set that is required to embrace a scenario where the United States is also secretly the greatest satanic nation in the world.

Recognizing the fairly jarring problem this view poses to the United States-as-Babylon view, Doug Woodward, one of the more vocal champions of this position, argues that the United States fulfills this portion of the prophecy through its support of abortion.[5] The problem, however, is that the harlot's sin is the killing of, not just innocents, but, in particular, "witnesses of Jesus" (Rev. 17:6; see also 12:17; 19:10; 20:4). She is guilty specifically for shedding the blood of "prophets and of saints" (Rev. 18:24). That's why the last-days martyrs are described as having been "beheaded because of their testimony of Jesus and because of the word of God" (Rev. 20:4). Abortion, as gruesome and as horrible as it is, simply is not a matter of biblical martyrdom for the name of Jesus or the Word of God.

With all due respect to Woodward (whom I know and appreciate), efforts to link abortion in America to the great harlot's killing of saints and prophets comes across to me personally as a somewhat desperate effort to explain away one of the most important portions of the prophecy, and the United States' very clear failure to fulfill its descriptions.

To be clear, no one is arguing that the United States is a pure, shining beacon of light without its own sins, flaws, contradictions, excesses, and many dark secrets. To say that the United States is not the last-days Babylon is not to say that it is perfect. Far from it. However, the degree to which some proponents of the United States–as-Babylon view will go to repaint her as the very embodiment of all evil in the last days is not only disturbing, but because it is coming from Christians who have assumed the role of teachers, it is very disappointing. At a time when America's Christian leaders should be rallying the church to cry out and intercede for a revival of repentance to sweep this nation, as it has done in times past, they are instead arguing in favor of her destruction and actually calling other Christians to flee. Playing the role of accuser is the easiest job in the world. Contending for redemption, however, requires the kind of intercessory labor that Jesus Himself modeled for those of us who desire to be His disciples.

We are living in a time when groups such as al-Qaeda, ISIS, and other terrorist organizations are recruiting tens of thousands of kids from all over the world to join the jihad and engage in reckless and brazen acts of mass murder, destruction, rape, enslavement, and outright genocide of various people groups, including the Christians of the Middle East. Numerous nations are endlessly lobbying the UN and working to wipe the State of Israel off the map. To suggest that the United States, of all the nations on earth, is most guilty for the blood of Jews and Christians and most deserving of the full wrath of God, so as to be completely destroyed forever, never to be found again, is ludicrous.

WHERE'S THE DESERT?

Like the other cities we've discussed so far, New York City does not match the topographical description of a city in a "desert" (Rev. 17:3 HCSB). Those who hold to the belief that America is the harlot argue that the word John used, *erémos*, is translated as a "wilderness" in most Bible versions, and therefore it should not be seen as a literal desert. Instead, we are to imagine a forested wilderness—America, as it was when first discovered by the various European explorers. As we have already pointed out, however, the word *erémos* contextually does not refer to a forested land, but specifically to a desert. In Isaiah 21, a passage from which Revelation 17 draws, Babylon is specifically called "the desert of the sea" (Isa. 21:1 KJV). Why? Because ancient Babylon sat in a desert. This is the context of the word in both Isaiah and Revelation. Proponents of the USA view cannot just point to those portions of the biblical prophecies that seem to align with the USA while ignoring others. There is no way around the fact that neither New York City nor the United States at large meets this very simple, yet very important identifying mark of the last-days harlot.

WHERE IS THE CAPITAL OF THE ISLAMIC WORLD?

Another factor that arguably disqualifies both New York City and the greater United States is that neither is the capital of the seventh/eighth beast empire, which I have argued represents the historical Islamic Caliphate and the revived Caliphate of the Antichrist. Quite to the contrary, the United States is most often viewed as "the Great Satan" by most Islamists and jihadists. Together, the United States and Israel are seen as the greatest enemies of Islam in the whole world. Of course, if we are wrong in our identification of the seventh/eighth empire as Islam, then those who espouse the view that the United States is the final Babylon must be able to provide a cogent and scripturally supportable explanation of what those kingdoms are and how they represent the natural progression of the six previous kingdoms.

MISAPPLICATION OF TEXTS

Those who believe that the United States is Mystery Babylon rely heavily on a very selective reading of Isaiah 13–14 and Jeremiah 50–51 to support their view. Woodward, Kreiger, and McGriff, in *The Final Babylon*, draw much from these passages to argue their case for the United States as Babylon. Woodward specifically argues that the destroyer from the north, spoken of in both prophecies, is Russia, who will carry out an attack on the United States. The glaring problem with this idea, however, is that the text directly names the attacker from the north as the Medes (Isa. 13:17; Jer. 51:11). History of course, confirms that it was the Medes, along with the Persians and some other, smaller regional kingdoms, who together conquered Babylon in 539 BC (cf. Dan. 5:31). It is impossible to say that "Medes" is a reference to Russia.

Isaiah 13:20 presents another problem with trying to read the United States into these texts. After Babylon is destroyed, we are told, "it will never be inhabited or lived in from generation to generation; nor will the Arab pitch his tent there." Now, let us honestly ask ourselves, does this sound more like the United States, or the Middle East?

Here's another glaring problem: When the entity described throughout Jeremiah 51 is finally judged, into what body of water is it thrown? The Atlantic Ocean? The Pacific? The Mississippi River? Of course not. Instead, it is cast "into the middle of the Euphrates" (Jer. 51:63). The prophecy concludes with "So shall Babylon sink down and not rise again" (v. 64).

Woodward also sees the term "the daughter of Babylon" as pointing to the United States (see Isa. 47:1; Jer. 50:42, et al.). Again, this is largely due to his reliance on Hislop's fraudulent narrative (see chapter 5). The term actually refers to Babylon itself, or more specifically, her citizens. A similar expression, "daughter of Zion" is used throughout the Scriptures for Jerusalem or her citizens. Zephaniah 3:14, for example says, "Shout for joy, O daughter of Zion! Shout in triumph, O Israel! Rejoice and exult with all your heart, O daughter of Jerusalem!" *The Hexham Bible Dictionary* refers to this expression as "a poetic expression referring to the people of Jerusalem, as well as to the city itself (Psa 9:14; Isa 1:8; 16:1; 52:2; Jer 6:2; Jer 6:23; Lam 1:6; 4:22; Zech 2:10; Zeph 3:14)."[6] *The Baker Encyclopedia of the Bible* similarly states, "Since ancient cities were considered metaphorically to be the mother of their inhabitants, referring to the people of Jerusalem as 'daughters of Zion' was entirely appropriate, particularly in poetic literature."[7] At the conclusion of the great lament in Psalm 137, the psalmist declares, "O daughter of Babylon, you devastated one, how blessed will be the one who repays you with the recompense with which you have repaid us. How blessed will be the one who seizes and dashes your little ones against the rock" (vv. 8–9). Are we really to believe that the Bible is saying that whoever smashes American babies against rocks will be greatly blessed? The basis of this most pained lament is the extremely harsh treatment that the Jews had suffered at the hands of the cruel Babylonians when they were carried away into exile. So, "daughter of Babylon" means Babylon itself; it is not some cryptic reference to the United States.

There are actually several other problems with attempting to apply these Old Testament passages to the United States, but for now, we will allow the weight of these few examples to speak for themselves. We will continue our discussion of Isaiah 13–14 and Jeremiah 50–51 in much greater detail in chapter 16.

CONCLUSION

The United States fails to even come close to fulfilling a few of the most basic requirements of the prophecy of Revelation 17–18. It does not have the kind of genuine religious component that is unarguably so central to the prophecy. The United States is not the primary capital of global idolatry. It is most certainly not the heart of global religious persecution toward Jews and Christians. It does not sit in a desert. The United States simply does not fit the criteria given within the text.

16

LITERAL BABYLON

ALTHOUGH THE RUINS OF THE ONCE-MAGNIFICENT CITY of Babylon are today little more than an infrequently visited tourist attraction, many Christian teachers believe that in the days to come, Babylon will be rebuilt to far surpass its former, ancient glory and fulfill Revelation's prophecy of the last-days harlot city. Among those who espouse this view are classic commentators such as B. W. Newton, E. W. Bullinger, J. A. Seiss, Arthur Pink, and G. H. Lang (one of my absolute personal favorite commentators). More recently, this view has been taught by the late J. Vernon McGee, Arnold Fruchtenbaum, Robert Thomas, John MacArthur, Charles H. Dyer, Andy Woods, Chuck Missler, Mark Hitchcock, and Joel

C. Rosenberg. For years, I also leaned very strongly toward this view.

Not surprisingly, this view gained significant popularity among prophecy teachers after the American invasion of Iraq in 2003. Almost immediately after the fall of Saddam Hussein's government, pastor Mark Hitchcock declared, "I believe that what we see happening before our eyes, in Iraq and the Middle East, is setting the stage for the rapid rise . . . of Babylon."[2] Mirroring such sentiments in 2005, Joel C. Rosenberg predicted that headlines across the world would soon read, "Iraq Emerges from Chaos as Region's Wealthiest Country."[2] To critics of the American invasion of Iraq, he declared:

> Iraq will form a strong, stable, and decisive central government. Iraq's military and internal security forces will be well trained, well equipped, and increasingly effective. The insurgency will be crushed, support for it will evaporate, and foreign terrorists will stop flowing into the country. As the situation stabilizes, Iraqi roads and airports will become safe, and people will finally be able to move freely about the country. Tourists will pour in to visit the country's many ancient archeological sites and national treasures . . . In short order, Iraq will emerge as an oil superpower, rivaling Saudi Arabia. Trillions of petrodollars will flood into the country . . . The ancient city of Babylon will emerge virtually overnight like a phoenix rising from the ashes to become one of the modern wonders of the world . . . The people of Iraq are about to experience a level of personal and national wealth and power they have never dreamed possible. The pundits who have written the country off to failure and chaos will be absolutely stunned by such a dramatic turn of events.[3]

In all fairness to both Hitchcock and Rosenberg, although their timing was wrong, their vision of a revived Babylon is still entirely possible. Iraq may very well eventually find stability and become a global religious hub and economic superpower. At the time of this writing, however, with the nation presently in shambles, at least for the immediate foreseeable future, this is very difficult to imagine. Of course, the future certainly has a way of throwing us all kinds of curveballs, and anything is most certainly possible.

As a side note, this view would work best if the eighth beast kingdom is indeed the Islamic Caliphate. In fact, it is difficult to imagine that it could be fulfilled outside of an Islamic beast scenario. If Babylon were to be revived in Iraq, it seems nearly impossible that it would be the capital of a Western Antichrist power. It is very hard to imagine a major city in Iraq being ruled by a religious system other than Islam.

THE CASE FOR LITERAL BABYLON AS THE GREAT HARLOT

The arguments for the last-days harlot city to be a literal, rebuilt Babylon on the Euphrates are fairly straightforward:

1. The context of Isaiah 13–14 and Jeremiah 50–51 is the end times.

2. Because several events described within these prophecies were not fulfilled in history, they must thus be understood as pertaining to a future judgment of Babylon.

3. Because the prophecy in Revelation 17–18 draws so heavily from Isaiah 13–14 and Jeremiah 50–51, Revelation must simply be a reiteration and expansion of these Old Testament prophecies.

4. In Zechariah 5:5–10, the woman being sent to Babylon (called "Shinar" in the text) so a temple can be built for her is none other than the great harlot, who was sent to Iraq until the last days, when she will be revealed to the world as the final Babylon.

Let us discuss each of these four arguments in order. How well do they hold up under scrutiny?

THE CONTEXT OF ISAIAH AND JEREMIAH

First, does the context of Isaiah 13–14 and Jeremiah 50–51 point to a historical or an end-time fulfillment? Proponents of the literal Babylon view would say it pertains to the end times. The correct answer, however, is it pertains to both. Any honest assessment of these chapters must begin by affirming that both Isaiah and Jeremiah were prophesying concerning the judgment on Babylon that was in their not-too-distant future. Not only is this the clear context of the prophecies in general, but many of the individual details within the text bear this out. In both prophecies, for example, Babylon is said to be conquered by the Medes (Isa. 13:17; Jer. 51:11, 28). As we discussed in the previous chapter, this is exactly what happened. The prophecy of Daniel informs us that it was specifically Darius the Mede who actually took the city (Dan. 5:31).

Despite the historical nature of these prophecies, however, there is also some very clear eschatological language interwoven throughout. Isaiah 13:6, for example, speaks of "the day of the Lord." Although there are occasions within Scripture where this phrase refers simply to a profound divine intervention in history (e.g., Amos 5:18, 20; Eze. 13:5; 30:3), the overwhelming usage of this term refers to the end of this present age. Of course, as legendary commentator J. Alec Motyer reminds us, "the day of the Lord has many interim fulfillments."[4] This is likely the case here as well. Isaiah 14 goes on to give a prophecy directed toward the king of Babylon that essentially bleeds directly into prophesying against the great last-days dictator, also called the Antichrist. Despite the various indicators within the text that point to the end times, however, this does not negate the historical context of the prophecies.

When faced with passages like this, preterist interpreters, who see most prophecy as having being fulfilled in history, and futurist interpreters, who see many prophecies having a last-days fulfillment, simply clash. Many argue that prophecies such as these should be understood as having a rigid either/or fulfillment—either fulfilled in history or awaiting fulfillment in the future—with little to no room for anything in between. I would suggest that such an inflexible approach is entirely unnecessary. Any honest and careful treatment of these prophecies must acknowledge the layering of both historical and future all within the same text. Of course, to modern Western minds, which prefer historical methods to guide them as they strive to neatly dissect even the very Word of God, this can be an extremely frustrating concept. The nature of Hebrew prophecy, so rich in poetry and hyperbole, however, does not always conform to Western categories and rules.

While there is no universal interpretive principle that we can apply to every prophetic passage in the Bible, it is quite common for the prophets to speak about events that were in their near or immediate future, yet in doing so, prophesy through those events to a more distant horizon called the last days. This is also the best approach, I would contend, to understand Isaiah 13–14 and Jeremiah 50–51. Arguably, these prophecies must be understood as speaking of both the historical fall of Babylon and a future judgment of God in the last days. Does this mean that the city of Babylon must be rebuilt on its old foundations? While this is certainly possible, I don't believe the text demands this. But if our reading of these prophecies leads us to conclude that a literal, future city of Babylon must be rebuilt, ultimately we must also demand the same for other kingdoms and peoples who technically no longer exist, such as Edom, Moab, Ammon, and Amalek. Although there were clearly historical judgments on all of these kingdoms/tribes, there are also prophecies that speak of their judgment in the last days. Rarely however does anyone demand that they experience some kind of very literal revival or rebirth. We need not look for a literal rebirth of the kingdom of Edom or of Moab, for example. Most often, the prophecies that speak of an eschatological judgment on these two are simply taken to mean that the regions formerly occupied by these kingdoms will experience some kind of last-days judgment. Alternately, in some cases, these ancient names seem to take on an even broader meaning, representing all of Israel's enemies at the end of the age, with no direct correlation to where they dwell. The prophecy of Obadiah, for example, casts the mountain (or kingdom) of Edom as being judged in the day of the Lord. Most futurists, however, take this to mean much more than a last-days judgment on the region of southern Jordan. Edom in this context is most often seen to represent the whole of Israel's end-time antagonists possessed with what Ezekiel calls "an everlasting hatred" (Eze. 35:5 AMP).

If we are to see Isaiah 13–14 and Jeremiah 50–51 as first and foremost speaking of a historical judgment on ancient Babylon while also speaking more generally to the Lord's end-time judgment of the enemies of God throughout the region of southern Iraq, I believe this would be sufficient to satisfy the meaning of the text. Referring to Jeremiah 50–51, Messianic Jewish professor Dr. Michael Brown accurately comments, "Babylon is given such prominence in the Scriptures . . . because it represents the epitome of human pride and world conquest, it becomes a type of all hostile world powers, serving as the ultimate anti-God symbol in Revelation 17:1–19:5."[5]

THE WALLS OF BABYLON

The next argument made for the futurity of Isaiah 13–14 and Jeremiah 50–51 is that many of their details were not fulfilled in history. Proponents of the literal Babylon view point out, for example, that Jeremiah describes the walls of Babylon being completely razed, when in fact, this did not happen when Babylon fell. Similarly, Jeremiah describes Babylon's physical collapse as very sudden, whereas it was actually long and protracted. Jeremiah also describes Babylon being uninhabited forever, never to be rebuilt, though it has been both rebuilt and inhabited since Jeremiah's day. Upon initial consideration, this seems to make a strong case for the view that this prophecy that has yet to be fulfilled. A more careful consideration of each point, however, reveals some weaknesses in the larger argument.

Let's consider the walls of Babylon. These towering walls were so massive that they were at one time considered to be among the seven wonders of the ancient world. While these descriptions must be exaggerated to some degree, Herodotus wrote that the walls were 56 miles long, 80 feet thick, and 320 feet high![6] So when Jeremiah said that these walls would be "completely razed" (51:58), this was a profound claim. The prophecy also says, "Her high gates will be set on fire." Earlier in the prophecy, Babylon was also predicted to fall "suddenly" and in dramatic fashion (51:8). Yet when Babylon actually did fall, her walls were not razed, her gates were not burnt, and her fall unfolded in a long and protracted fashion. Instead of smashing the great walls, in fact, the armies of the Medes and the Persians actually crept under the walls through the Euphrates River and took the city by surprise. The great walls remained for some centuries, slowly crumbling into disrepair and decay.

Considering the stark contrast between what the prophet described and what actually unfolded in history, we have some interpretive choices to make. First, we might simply understand Jeremiah to have been using dramatic and exaggerated language to describe Babylon's fall. Some interpreters have suggested that Jeremiah used the language of a physical collapse to poetically and forcefully describe what was in fact a devastating, drastic, and sudden political collapse. Second, we may claim that this language of shattered walls and burnt gates must be understood in a very rigidly literal sense and argue that it can only be describing a future fall of Babylon. The problem with this option, however, is that it requires any future Babylon to be surrounded by massive walls and looming gates. If it is not, then even a future destruction of Babylon would not literally satisfy the descriptions of the text. The idea of a modern fortified city, however, would seem to be starkly anachronistic. Though ancient cities often had walls and gates to protect them from invaders, modern cities do not. It is therefore much more likely that the language of walls and gates being shattered was intended to be understood more as hyperbole than as a rigidly literal description. To be clear, I adhere to a more literal hermeneutic. In other words, I interpret Scripture literally whenever possible, but in doing so, I adhere to what I call a "rational literalism," which recognizes that biblical prophecy quite frequently uses poetic exaggeration and hyperbole. Even when reading the Bible literally, we must still take the various kinds of literature we are reading into consideration. Prophetic and apocalyptic literature often use this kind of poetic, exaggerated language.

Consider another detail that demonstrates this quite well. Referring to Babylon's destruction, Jeremiah 51:42 says, "The sea has come up over Babylon. She has been engulfed with its tumultuous waves." Now, obviously, this was not fulfilled literally in history. The sea did not flood the city of Babylon. Rather, the soldiers of the Medes and the Persians flooded her and engulfed her. The hyper-literalist interpreter, who refuses to see this as prophetic language, must claim that a latter-days Babylon will be flooded by the sea. The thing is, Babylon is nearly three hundred miles inland from the Persian Gulf, and the Euphrates River is most certainly not a sea. A rational literalism would acknowledge that this portion of the prophecy is simply using somewhat flamboyant prophetic language to describe Babylon's very drastic historical fall.

Again, the most reasonable approach is to say that although Jeremiah was primarily speaking of the historical fall of Babylon, he was also looking forward, toward a last-days judgment on the Lord's enemies, particularly in the region of southern Iraq.

THE COMPOSITE CITY OF SATAN

The third argument employed by those who take the literal Babylon view is that since Revelation 17–18 draws so heavily from Isaiah 13–14 and Jeremiah 50–51, Revelation itself is simply a reiteration of those Old Testament prophecies. This argument, too, runs into some very significant difficulties. While Revelation 17–18 does, in fact, draw heavily from Isaiah's and Jeremiah's prophecies about Babylon, Revelation also draws from other Old Testament prophecies that point us to several other cities. It actually draws from imagery and prophecies of multiple cities to paint a composite picture of the future, last-days "Babylon," which would not be revealed until the last days. When we carefully analyze the prophecy of Revelation 17–18 and consider all the various citations, allusions, and echoes found there, it points us to Babylon, yes, but also to Rome, Nineveh, Tyre, Edom, Sodom and Gomorrah, and even to Jerusalem. Rather than understanding the last-days Babylon to be any of these ancient cities, though, we should understand it to be a composite of them all. Let's consider some of the passages and symbols that Revelation draws from.

BABYLON

Few can deny that the prophecy of Revelation relies heavily on a few Old Testament prophecies that speak about the judgment of Babylon. The most significant of these prophecies are Isaiah 13–14, 21 and Jeremiah 50–51. When Jeremiah described Babylon's looming judgment, he called God's people to leave Babylon, lest they be caught up in her destruction: "Come forth from her midst, My people, and each of you save yourselves from the fierce anger of the Lord" (Jer. 51:45). In Revelation, we hear an almost identical call: "Come out of her, my people, so that you will not participate in her sins and receive of her plagues" (Rev. 18:4).

In declaring the actual fall of Babylon, Isaiah saw a messenger on horseback shouting, "Fallen, fallen is Babylon; and all the images of her gods are shattered on the ground" (Isa. 21:9). Jeremiah's account contains a similar declaration: "Suddenly Babylon has fallen and been broken. . . . Babylon will become a heap of ruins, a haunt of jackals, an object of horror and hissing, without inhabitants" (51:8, 37). The account in Revelation combines these passages, with the angel crying out, "Fallen, fallen is Babylon the great! She has become a dwelling place of demons and a prison of every unclean spirit, and a prison of every unclean and hateful bird" (18:2).

Further, the Lord's judgment of Babylon is described in Jeremiah with the words, "O you who dwell by many waters, abundant in treasures, your end has come" (51:13). Revelation, on the other hand, says, "Then one of the seven angels . . . came and spoke with me, saying, 'Come here, I will show you the judgment of the great harlot who sits on many waters'" (Rev. 17:1). Similarly, Isaiah 21 is a prophecy against Babylon, called there "the desert of the sea" (v. 1 KJV), whereas in Revelation, John sees Babylon both in a desert and sitting upon many waters (17:1, 3, 15).

BY THE EUPHRATES OR BY THE SEA?

It is important to note here an important distinction between the Babylon of Jeremiah 51 and the Babylon of Revelation 18. As Jeremiah finishes his prophecy, he is told, "As soon as you finish reading this scroll, you will tie a stone to it and throw it into the middle of the Euphrates" (Jer. 51:63). The act of throwing the scroll into the Euphrates is itself a prophetic act representing Babylon being thrown into the river. In Revelation, however, the stone is cast, not into the Euphrates, but into the sea: "Then a strong angel took up a stone like a great millstone and threw it into the sea, saying, 'So will Babylon, the great city, be thrown down with violence, and will not be found any longer'" (18:21). So one city is described as sitting on the Euphrates River, and the other city actually sits by a sea. As we will see later, the "Babylon" of Revelation, in terms of its proximity to the sea, is described in ways much more akin to the ancient seaport of Tyre than the historical city of Babylon, nearly three hundred miles up from the Persian Gulf.

Nevertheless, it is clear that Revelation 17–18 relies heavily on the prophecies in Isaiah and Jeremiah, both of which refer to judgment on literal Babylon. It is because of these clear allusions, in fact, that proponents of the view hold that the last-days Babylon is simply literal Babylon. Their observations, of course, are accurate. It is critical, however, to also consider the numerous other citations and allusions from various Old Testament passages, as well as imagery and symbolism that would have been widely understood by first-century believers.

ROME

As discussed earlier, there can be little doubt that the early Christians would have also understood the prophecy of Revelation 17–18 to be referring, to some degree, to the pagan city of Rome. This would not have been a mistake on their part; it was clearly the Lord's intention when He inspired the prophecy. Not only was the term Babylon commonly used by first-century Christians and Jews to specifically refer to Rome (see chapters 9 and 12), but the Lord specifically chose to use the symbolism of a woman sitting on seven hills. This is fairly specific language. We have shown that Roman coins from this period actually had just such an image on them. Rome was known as the city on seven hills. No one reading this prophecy in the first century would have missed this. Rome was also the primary world economic hub and the center of both idolatry and persecution at the time. There is much about that first-century city that fulfills the descriptions within the prophecy. To suggest that a biblically literate believer in the first century would have seen the prophecy as refer-ring, not to Rome but to literal Babylon, would be to ignore these points. Of course, as we explained in chapter 12, there are other reasons why the city of Rome does not fit or fulfill the prophecy. So on one hand, we must acknowledge that the prophecy draws much from the symbols, characteristics, and spirit of the city of Rome; on the other, we must concede that it is still pointing to something else.

TYRE

Revelation 17–18 also draw heavily from prophecies that speak about the destruction of the city of Tyre. In Isaiah in the prophet's day, Tyre was a renowned economic hub. As a port city just north of Israel, in what is now Lebanon, Tyre was a natural center of regional trade. Merchants from Tyre set out to navigate the Mediterranean waters, and founded various colonies on the coasts of Greece and northern Africa, in Carthage, and as far as Sicily and Corsica, Spain.[7] Interestingly, Tyre was famous for its production of a costly purple dye known as "Tyrian purple," extracted from a type of sea snail.[8]

Remember that in ancient times this color was worn almost exclusively by royalty. That the harlot-queen of Revelation is specifically decked out in scarlet and Tyrian purple is not likely a coincidence. There are also a few other allusions to Tyre in the harlot prophecy.

In Revelation 17:2, we are told, "The kings of the earth committed acts of immorality" with the woman. G. K. Beale and other commentators see here a clear allusion to Isaiah 23, an oracle that is specifically directed against the ancient city of Tyre. There, Tyre is repeatedly referred to as an economic prostitute who "play[s] the harlot with all the kingdoms on the face of the earth" (v. 17). When the angel in Revelation speaks of the judgment against Babylon, he says, "Your merchants were the great men of the earth" (18:23). This language is clearly drawn from Isaiah 23, where we read that Tyre's "merchants were princes" and its "traders were the honored of the earth" (v. 8).

Revelation also draws from a major prophecy in Ezekiel. In Revelation 18, when the merchants, shipmasters, and sailors hear of Babylon's collapse, they break into a lament drawn almost entirely from Ezekiel 27, a prophecy against Tyre. Read through the following two passages and note the numerous similarities between the two.

> Your wealth, your wares, your merchandise . . . will fall into the heart of the seas on the day of your overthrow. At the sound of the cry of your pilots the pasture lands will shake. All who handle the oar, the sailors and all the pilots of the sea will come down from their ships; They will stand on the land, and they will make their voice heard over you and will cry bitterly. They will cast dust on their heads, they will wallow in ashes. Also they will make themselves bald for you and gird themselves with sackcloth; and they will weep for you in bitterness of soul with bitter mourning. Moreover, in their wailing they will take up a lamentation for you and lament over you: "Who is like Tyre, like her who is silent in the midst of the sea? When your wares went out from the seas, you satisfied many peoples; with the abundance of your wealth

and your merchandise you enriched the kings of earth. Now that you are broken by the seas in the depths of the waters, your merchandise and all your company have fallen in the midst of you. All the inhabitants of the coastlands are appalled at you, and their kings are horribly afraid; They are troubled in countenance. The merchants among the peoples hiss at you; you have become terrified and you will cease to be forever. (Eze. 27:27–36)

Now consider just how much of the language and imagery are adapted in Revelation 18:

The merchants of these things, who became rich from her, will stand at a distance because of the fear of her torment, weeping and mourning, saying, "Woe, woe, the great city, she who was clothed in fine linen and purple and scarlet, and adorned with gold and precious stones and pearls; for in one hour such great wealth has been laid waste!" And every shipmaster and every passenger and sailor, and as many as make their living by the sea, stood at a distance, and were crying out as they saw the smoke of her burning, saying, "What city is like the great city?" And they threw dust on their heads and were crying out, weeping and mourning, saying, "Woe, woe, the great city, in which all who had ships at sea became rich by her wealth, for in one hour she has been laid waste!" Rejoice over her, O heaven, and you saints and apostles and prophets, because God has pronounced judgment for you against her. (Rev. 18:15–20)

Of the clear relationship between these two passages, Beale wrote:

Among all the harlot metaphors of the OT, most of which refer to Israel, the one referring to Tyre in Isaiah 23 is the closest verbally to Rev. 17:2. That Tyre is in mind here in the Apocalypse is clear from the repeated reference to the Ezekiel 26–28 pronouncement of Tyre's judgment in Revelation 18 and the specific allusion to Isa. 23:8 in Rev. 18:23.[9]

So not only did the Lord use the ancient cities of Babylon and Rome as historical types of the last-days Babylon; He also drew heavily from prophecies about Tyre.

NINEVEH

Revelation 17–18 also draws from prophecies about Nineveh, another capital city from one of the seven beast kingdoms. Like Babylon and Rome, Nineveh was the great regional power of its day. In Nahum 3, the Lord rebukes this great pagan city of old:

> *Woe to the bloody city*, completely full of lies and pillage; her prey never departs. The noise of the whip, the noise of the rattling of the wheel, galloping horses and bounding chariots! Horsemen charging, swords flashing, spears gleaming, many slain, a mass of corpses, and countless dead bodies—They stumble over the dead bodies! All because of *the many harlotries of the harlot, the charming one, the mistress of sorceries, who sells nations by her harlotries and families by her sorceries.* (Nah. 3:1–4; emphasis added)

Here we see the motif again of a bloodthirsty harlot city, also described as a city of "sorceries." Revelation draws from this oracle when it says of Babylon, "All the nations were deceived by your sorcery" (Rev. 18:23). Thus in Nineveh, the capital of Assyria, we have yet another ancient city to look to as a type of the great harlot city of the last days.

EDOM

In Isaiah 34, we find a prophecy against Edom, which is often used by the prophets to represent Israel's primary end-time adversaries. In describing the Lord's final judgment on Edom, we read: "Its land will become burning pitch. It will not be quenched night or day; *its smoke will go up forever.* From generation to generation it will be desolate; none will pass through it forever and ever (Isa. 34:9–10; emphasis added). Then in Revelation 19, an array of voices from heaven, rejoicing over the fall of Babylon, allude directly to this passage from Isaiah: "He has judged the great harlot who was corrupting the earth with her immorality . . . Hallelujah! *her smoke rises up forever and ever*" (Rev. 19:2; emphasis added). Beale commented, "Here Edom's fall is taken as an anticipatory typological pattern for the fall of [Babylon], which will never rise again after God's judgment."[10] Thus Edom is a fifth city that is also a historical type for the last-days Babylon.

SODOM AND GOMORRAH

In the same way that the destruction of Edom serves as a prefigurement for the judgment on Babylon, so also do Sodom and Gomorrah. As the account from these cities' destruction details:

> Abraham . . . looked down toward Sodom and Gomorrah, and toward all the land of the valley, and he saw, and behold, the smoke of the land ascended like the smoke of a furnace. (Gen. 19:27–28)

The epistle of 2 Peter also speaks specifically of Sodom and Gomorrah's destruction and God's use of it as a warning for future generations. We are told that the Lord "condemned the cities of Sodom and Gomorrah to destruction by reducing them to ashes, having made them an example to those who would live ungodly lives thereafter" (2 Peter 2:6). Thus Sodom and Gomorrah are yet another Old Testament example drawn from in Revelation to paint the composite picture of the great harlot city of the last days.

JERUSALEM

Although we have ruled out Jerusalem, along with Rome, as the primary intended target of the prophecy of Revelation 17–18, we would be remiss if we did not acknowledge that the prophecy clearly draws from language and specific passages throughout the Old Testament that were initially applied to Jerusalem. First, there is the obvious use of the term *harlot*, which, as we have discussed, is often used throughout the Bible to refer to Israel (e.g., 2 Chron. 21:11; Ezek. 16:15; et al.). As Beale noted:

> Indeed, the portrait of the whore throughout Revelation 17 draws also from the depiction of Israel as a harlot in Jer. 2:20–4:30: there Judah is a harlot (2:20) with "a harlot's forehead" (3:3) who causes sin in others (2:33). On her "skirts is found the lifeblood of the innocent" (2:34), her "dress [is] in scarlet," she "decorates herself with ornaments of gold" (4:30), and her lovers will despise her and try to kill her (4:30).[11]

Others commentators have pointed out that the high priest's garments are described in the LXX as being made from "the gold, and the blue, and the scarlet, and the linen" (Ex. 28:5), which is somewhat similar to the harlot of Revelation, who is "clothed in purple and scarlet, and adorned with gold" (Rev. 17:4).[12]

THE COMPOSITE HARLOT CITY

Thus, to respond to those who take the literal Babylon view, while it is true that Revelation 17–18 draws much from Isaiah 13–14 and Jeremiah 50–51, that does not mean that Revelation must therefore be speaking about the literal city Babylon in Iraq. Instead, Revelation points to all of these cities to point us to another mysterious city that did not yet exist. Rather than looking exclusively to Babylon—or any of the other cities, for that matter—we should instead look to all of these wicked cities, which together form one composite picture of the final city of wickedness.

ZECHARIAH 5

The fourth and final argument for a future literal rebuilt Babylon revolves around the prophecy of Zechariah 5:5–10, which we briefly touched on earlier. This prophecy speaks of a woman specifically called "Wickedness" placed into an ephah, or a basket, and being sent to the "land of Shinar," where she will stay until a "pedestal" (probably meaning a shrine) is built for her. This woman, it is argued, represents the great harlot, who is being sent to Babylon until the last days, where she will be revealed to the world as the final Babylon.

Because this prophecy was given in 519 BC (see Zech. 1:7), twenty years after the fall of Babylon, there is no question that it speaks of something future to Zechariah's day for "the land of Shinar." More specifically, it points to a future for this land that involves both wickedness and religion. Specifically, the prophecy never actually mentions the last days. While it certainly could be a last-days reference, it does not actually say this. Also, instead of saying that the woman is being taken to the city of Babylon, Zechariah uses the more general term, "the land of Shinar." While this could identify a specific spot where the ancient city was located, it also allows for the much broader region.

It is interesting that in the eighth century, the city of Kufa, just thirty-five miles south of Babylon on the Euphrates, actually became the home of the Islamic Caliphate and thus the capital of the Islamic world for about twelve years. After this, the Caliphate was moved north to Baghdad, where it resided for roughly 450 years. The fact that the very capital of the seventh beast empire, which dominated the entire Middle East, was actually established so close to Babylon for nearly five hundred years is certainly not insignificant. Could it be that this is what Zechariah was writing about? While I would not be willing to fully commit to this view, it is possible that this is all that is required to see Zechariah's prophecy fulfilled without insisting on a completely restored city of Babylon.

Another less likely possibility is that the city of Mecca, which is today the spiritual heart of the Islamic world, may have actually fulfilled this prophecy. Mecca is indeed the home to a cube-shaped shrine (the Kaaba) where the people in that region literally bow and pray five times a day. This is indeed a city in which a shrine for "Wickedness" has been established for more than fourteen hundred years and which now functions as the spiritual polestar for the majority of the hearts throughout the entire region. We will discuss this shrine and its significance in much greater detail as we move forward. This possibility, of course, hinges entirely on how broadly the term "the land of Shinar" might be understood. While most Bible atlases and dictionaries identify Shinar as the entire region roughly from modern-day Baghdad to the Persian Gulf, there is also some ambiguity, with the *Holman Illustrated Bible Dictionary* acknowledging that the term has an "uncertain meaning used in various ancient Near Eastern documents apparently with somewhat different localities in mind."[13] While I would also hesitate to affirm this view as the most likely meaning of the prophecy, it may be a legitimate option to explain the text.

In the end, Zechariah's prophecy, while certainly stirring up some challenging questions, is not a solid enough foundation to build a case for a rebuilt literal Babylon as the great harlot.

THE REALITY ON THE GROUND

Having considered some of the difficulties with and weaknesses of the primary arguments for a future literal Babylon being rebuilt and subsequently destroyed by the Lord, I'd like to conclude by highlighting just a few more difficulties that exist for this view. For one, although there are some strong scriptural arguments in its favor, in terms of present-day, real-world, on-the-ground realities, it is actually the weakest among all the other views.

At this present time, Babylon, or more specifically, Hillah, in Iraq, is not even close to being worth considering as the subject of Revelation 17–18. Hillah is not a global religious hub or economic powerhouse. It does not rule over the kings of the earth. It is not drunk on the blood of the saints. This view relies entirely on the idea of something that may happen in the future but which, at the present time, has little to no possibility of taking place on the immediate horizon. Does that mean it cannot happen or will never happen? Of course not. At least for now, though, it seems unlikely.

After the American invasion and decade-long occupation of Iraq, and after ISIS took control over many of Iraq's central and northern territories, much of the nation has been functioning in survival mode. With suicide attacks taking place somewhat regularly in the capital of Baghdad, Iraq is hardly ready to build a megacity worthy of being considered a global capital of finance only fifty miles away.

Still, anything is possible. Any number of events may unfold over the next five to thirty years. If I am to be honest, however, I doubt there is that much time before Jesus returns. If we reach the year 2045 and Jesus has not come back yet, I will be a bit surprised. Of course, the years certainly do have a way of rolling right on by, and we must never presume to know with any degree of certainty what the future holds. The whole world was shocked at how fast the Arab Spring and the events that followed on its heels transformed the Middle East and North Africa seemingly overnight. If a major regional war (or even a world war) were to unfold in the years ahead, which I think may very well be the case, then this also would radically alter the geopolitical landscape of the Middle East and the world. So yes, just about anything is possible.

Proponents of this view might also rightly point out how quickly the city of Dubai was built. In 1990, Dubai was barely a city, having only one main strip through a relatively barren desert town with a few tall buildings and an airport. Yet by 2009 it had emerged as a major regional city with dozens of skyscrapers, including the world's tallest building, the Burj Khalifa. Today, with emerging technologies, new building techniques, and enough capital, a major city could be built in as little as ten to fifteen years. If such a project began in the next several years, it could be finished by perhaps 2030. So this scenario is certainly possible. Nevertheless, at least for now, the idea that Hillah, the home of Babylon's ruins, will emerge anytime soon as a major religious and economic hub and fulfill all of the descriptions of the prophecy in Revelation 17–18 seems really difficult to believe.

MYSTERY? WHAT MYSTERY?

Another of the difficulties I have with this interpretation is the profoundly anticlimactic, perhaps even contradictory nature of this view. It would seem strange for an angel to refer to this end-time city as a "mystery" if in actuality it is no mystery whatsoever. Ladies and gentlemen—behold! The solution to this great mystery of the ages, the answer to that which has confounded exegetes, scholars, and Bible students for centuries, is about to be revealed. Drum roll, please. The identity of the great mystery of the last-days Babylon is . . . Babylon.

Wait. What?

If the mystery of the last-days Babylon is simply literal Babylon, how anticlimactic is that?

CONCLUDING THOUGHTS

Although, the idea that the great harlot is simply literal Babylon is perhaps stronger than the previous views we've discussed thus far, it does nevertheless have some flaws, some perhaps fatal. As always, God knows best, and time will soon enough reveal the truth. Until then, we must remain humble and attentive to the signs as they unfold before us.

THE BRIDE OR THE HARLOT?

Before we conclude this chapter, as somewhat of a side note I do find a proposed project for Basra, a city roughly 280 miles south of Hillah/ Babylon, to be rather fascinating. Basra is a port city of Iraq on the Persian Gulf. Its nickname is "the bride of the gulf." Expanding on this theme, plans are presently in the works to build "a vertical city," a massive building, which its planners are simply calling "the Bride."[14] A report in the UK's *Guardian* gives us the fascinating details about what could soon begin to unfold in the city of Basra:

> We're used to the crown of "world's tallest building" following the world's economic centre of gravity: the US for most of the 20th

century, then the Far East (Malaysia's Petronas Towers, Taiwan's Taipei 101), and now Dubai, with the Burj Khalifa due to be superseded by Saudi Arabia's Kingdom Tower in about 2019. But now comes a tower to eclipse them all—in Iraq. Yes, you read that right: the world's tallest building is due to be in Basra, southern Iraq. It is called The Bride of the Gulf, and it will be 230 sto-reys—1,152 metres—high. That's roughly the Burj Khalifa with the Shard on top of it . . . There's also a vast canopy over a public area at the base of the towers, called "The Veil." Bride, veil—see what they did there? . . . If your mental image of Basra is still the war zone it was in 2003, when British and American troops first entered Iraq, it's clearly in need of an update. Basra is a prosperous and relatively peaceful city these days, "more like Kuwait than Baghdad." The tentacles of the Islamic State are at least 600km away. There's oil money sloshing around. There are new cars on all the new roads. Five-star hotels and a new sports stadium recently opened (Basra is football-crazy, apparently). The government is working on a new masterplan for the growing city, of which the publicly funded Bride would be the centrepiece. The Bride of the Gulf is actually a local nickname for the city. Basra was once considered one of the most beautiful and cosmopolitan places in the Gulf—before Saddam Hussein punished its mostly Shia population, then the Iraq war further scarred it. It was also the supposed location of the Garden of Eden.[15]

Is it possible that the biblical descriptions of a last-days Babylon could be fulfilled in a city that is nearly three hundred miles farther south on the Euphrates than the original Babylon? We cannot rule it out entirely. It's difficult not to be struck by the potential prophetic character of this story. Would it not be typical of Satan to call his capital city "the Bride" instead of the harlot, as it is called by the Lord? Even if a city is built, though, the idea of it becoming a major religious capital and economic global hub is still somewhat difficult to imagine. While speculating on these things is quite intriguing, for now it is only theoretical. This city presently exists only in the minds of the planners. No actual construction has begun. Regardless, along with the potential for an actual rebuilt city of Babylon, this is also certainly something to watch in the years ahead.

PART THREE

THE FINAL BABYLON

17

MECCA / SAUDI ARABIA

IN THIS CHAPTER WE WILL CONSIDER THE CASE for the view that the great harlot prophecy is pointing us to Mecca or the Kingdom of Saudi Arabia. If this is the first time you've heard this interpretation, it may sound incredibly novel and even dubious to you. I completely understand. I was also very doubtful when I first began to ponder this interpretation. But after examining the scriptural case for it, I concluded that it has genuine merit. Here's why.

Throughout this book we've sought to stand upon the principle that it is not enough to find an interpretation that fulfills one, a few, or even several of the scriptural criteria, but fails on the others. Only an interpretation that satisfies all of the biblical criteria will suffice. Of all the possible positions, this view is the only one that seems to meet this requirement. In fact, the fit is so good that it's rather stunning.

So let's begin by considering the various criteria and descriptions we've identified from Revelation 17–18 and weigh them against the reality that exists politically, financially, religiously, morally, and even geographically in the city of Mecca and the Kingdom of Saudi Arabia.

A LITERAL CITY

Obviously, Mecca is a very real and tangible city and not merely some vague concept, such as "the world system" or "global apostasy." If we consider the broader kingdom of which Mecca is the spiritual heart, then no doubt, it would be the Kingdom of Saudi Arabia. In an even broader sense, Mecca is the spiritual capital of the entire Muslim world. To be clear, we are not arguing for an overly limited interpretation that sees Mecca alone as Babylon, but a view that allows for the broader Kingdom of Saudi Arabia, including its economic capital cities of Riyadh, Jeddah, and even the emerging King Abdullah Economic City. As we've discussed, during the biblical period any great city of renown would have been the heart of a larger regional city-state, kingdom, or empire. This was most certainly true of ancient Babylon as well as ancient Rome, which are the most significant of the prophetic prototypes that we should look to.

THE GREAT CITY

In the sense that Mecca is the womb, the heart, the very center of spiritual gravity for the entire Islamic world, it fulfills the role of the "great city" of Revelation 17–18. Remember: the greatness of "Babylon the great" doesn't so much rest in how many tall buildings she has or the square miles she covers. Rather, the prophecy seems to focus more on her far-reaching and vast influence over kings, peoples, nations, and tribes. There are several notable ways in which Mecca might be viewed as the great city. Let's begin with the most obvious.

THE WOMB AND HEART OF ISLAM

First, the city of Mecca is the very womb from which the religion of Islam was birthed. Every significant event in the early development of Islam under Muhammad took place either in Mecca or on the Arabian Peninsula. It was in Mecca that Muhammad was born, grew up, launched his early "prophetic" career, and began preaching his new religion, and it is where Islam eventually experienced its greatest success. Saudi Arabia is the home of both Mecca and Medina, the two cities where Muhammad spent most of his life.

Because of Muhammad's connection to both Mecca and Medina, they are unquestionably the two most sacred cities to Muslims worldwide. Non-Muslims are not even allowed into these cities. Thus, not only is Mecca/Saudi Arabia the womb, but also the very heart of Islam and the Muslim world. One of the most critical descriptions of the harlot that we identified is as the most significant center of global idolatry that ever existed. Babylon is specifically referred to as the "mother of harlots," representing the big mamma of false religions. Mecca is actually worthier of the title "spiritual capital" than any other city in the world. Think about this: Whenever someone is describing the archetypal epicenter of anything, he or she calls it the "mecca" of whatever it might happen to be. Hollywood, for example, is the "mecca" of film. Wall Street is the "mecca" of finance and investment. The name Mecca is virtually synonymous with supreme capital. The physical Mecca, however, is not the capital of film or finance, but of the single largest false religion that the world has ever known.

Today Mecca serves as the spiritual center for 1.6 billion Muslims. It is the spiritual capital of the world's second-largest religion, ruling over and controlling every single nation that surrounds Israel. If we understand the deeply Israel-centric narrative of the Scriptures, then this fact is profound. Of course, Islam controls far more than just the nations of the Middle East and North Africa. Its influence is also increasingly being felt in nations all over the earth. In 2016, the city of London saw its first Muslim mayor elected. No doubt, the influence and impact of Islam globally will only continue to be felt in the years to come. Five times daily, multitudes upon multitudes of Muslims from nearly every nation in the world turn their faces in prayer toward Mecca. Islamic supply stores sell a variety of electronic compasses and clocks made specifically to help Muslims always know the time to pray and the direction toward Mecca— no matter where they might find themselves. Furthermore, every Muslim is expected at least once in his or her life to make a spiritual pilgrimage to Mecca. The Masjid al-Haram, or Sacred Mosque, which houses the Kaaba (see chapter 16), is actually the single most visited location in all the earth. There can be no question that Mecca is the geographical and spiritual heart of the entire Islamic world. Of all the cities on earth, what city better fulfills the description of having sway over kings and "peoples and multitudes and nations and tongues" (see Rev. 17:15)?

THE WOMB AND HEART OF RADICAL WAHHABI ISLAM

Saudi Arabia is also the womb of Wahhabism—or Salafism, as they prefer to call it. In the eighteenth century, when Mohammed ibn Saud, the patriarch of the Al-Saud tribe, was fighting for the consolidation of tribal power, he forged an alliance with the patriarch of modern radical Sunni Islam, Mohammed ibn Abdul Wahhab. Since those days, the House of Saud and the House of Wahhab have been inseparable. As one astute observer has commented, it's "Saud and Wahhabi, Wahhabi and Saud, that still rules Saudi Arabia."[1]

Wahhabism/Salafism is essentially a Sunni Muslim reformation movement with the goal of returning to the practices of the earliest Muslims. Salafis strive to purge Islam of any later introductions or innovations (Arabic: *bid'ah*), which they claim compromise the purest expression of the Islam that Muhammad and his closest and earliest disciples preached and practiced. Because of this, Wahhabism produces the most extreme expressions of Islam and is the primary source of so many radical Sunni Muslims worldwide. Al-Qaeda, ISIS, the

Taliban, Boko Haram, and several other radical jihadist movements all were birthed out of and identify with Salafi thought.

In 2016, a British think tank called Integrity UK translated an appearance of Sheikh Adel al-Kalbani, the former imam of the Grand Mosque in Mecca. According to al-Kalbani, the Islam widely practiced and sanctioned by the Saudi government "follow[s] the same thought [as ISIS] but apply it in a refined way. They draw their ideas from what is written in our own books, from our own principles . . . We do not criticise the thought on which it (ISIS) is based."[2]

To make matters worse, Saudi Arabia is not only the primary ideological fountainhead for the radicals, but it is also the main source of funding for radical Wahhabism worldwide. We will discuss this matter in much more detail as we move forward. For now, beyond recognizing that Saudi Arabia is the very womb and the heart of worldwide Islam, we must understand that Saudi Arabia is also the womb and heart of the vilest and most murderous, violent, determined, and dangerous form of radical Islam the world has ever known.

If Mecca and Saudi Arabia indeed represent the great harlot, then it is not at all difficult to see why it is said that much of the world is drunk under her spell and influence. In terms of Mystery Babylon's role as the greatest source of religious influence over the peoples of the earth and of spreading the worst and most bloodthirsty form of false region that humanity has ever known, Mecca/ Saudi Arabia fulfill the description perfectly. Today the addicting and maddening wine of the harlot's sorceries are rapidly spreading all over the world as ISIS and similar groups take over entire nations and have somehow made radical jihadism trendy among multiplied millions of young Muslims throughout the earth. When I consider how ISIS was able to recruit somewhere close to thirty thousand often younger Muslims to leave everything behind and move to Syria to possibly die, it is easy to grasp why the angel spoke of "those who dwell on the earth [being] made drunk with the wine of her immorality" (Rev. 17:2). Understanding that the "immorality" in the prophecy is idolatry or false religion, and that the Kingdom of Saudi Arabia is the entity responsible for the spread of the most wicked and demonic form of radical Islam—surely it is Saudi Arabia that is being described when it is said, "Truly the nations have drunk of the wine of the passion of her immorality" (Rev. 18:3).

THE CLASH OF TWO CITIES

As we discussed in chapter 9, the book of Revelation is largely a tale of two great cities. It is a tale of a clash between the harlot and the bride, the city of Satan and the city of the great King. Since King David took the throne on Mount Zion in Jerusalem more than three thousand years ago, the city of Jerusalem has been both a prophetic city and the epicenter of Jewish religious expectations. It was there that the Jewish temple was built by King Solomon, and then by Herod. And it is there that devout Jews have awaited their Messiah to establish Himself on the restored throne of David—from which the rule and blessing of the Jewish Messiah will extend to the ends of the earth. As the prophet Isaiah declared:

> There will be no end to the increase of His government or of peace, on the throne of David and over his kingdom, to establish it and to uphold it with justice and righteousness, from then on and forevermore. The zeal of the Lord of hosts will accomplish this. (Isa. 9:7)

Likewise, the book of Revelation describes the day when a renewed and heavenly Jerusalem will be ruled by Yeshua (Jesus), the Jewish Messiah. His rule will extend over all the earth and, again quoting Isaiah, "the earth will be full of the knowledge of the Lord as the waters cover the sea" (Isa. 11:9). The prophet Micah perhaps best described this age when the messianic throne in Jerusalem will be over the whole earth. During the nearly two-thousand-year dispersion of the Jews abroad, they have never forgotten these prophecies:

And it will come about in the last days that the mountain of the house of the Lord will be established as the chief of the mountains. It will be raised above the hills, and the peoples will stream to it. Many nations will come and say, "Come and let us go up to the mountain of the Lord and to the house of the God of Jacob, that He may teach us about His ways and that we may walk in His paths." For from Zion will go forth the law, even the word of the Lord from Jerusalem. And He will judge between many peoples and render decisions for mighty, distant nations. Then they will hammer their swords into plowshares and their spears into pruning hooks; nation will not lift up sword against nation, and never again will they train for war. (Mic. 4:1–3)

It is a passage from which many poets and dreamers have found their inspiration. Certainly, it speaks of an age that all who love truth and seek peace yearn for.

The point here is that to both Jews and Christians, Jerusalem is the pinnacle of all religious expectation, longing, and hope. It is the city of peace—the city of Yahweh. On the other hand, Muslims have an entirely different city that they look to as the spiritual center of the world. This city is Mecca—the city of Allah. While Islamic prophecies do indeed look toward a day when Muslims will rule over Jerusalem, it is not to them the ultimate "holy" city. This position is held by Mecca. Jerusalem ranks only as the third holiest city in Islam.

In the book of Ezekiel, we read Yahweh's own declaration regarding Israel and Jerusalem as the center of the earth: "Thus says the Lord God, 'This is Jerusalem; I have set her at the center of the nations, with lands around her'" (Eze. 5:5). Later in Ezekiel, the Lord again calls Jerusalem "the center of the world" (38:12). Perhaps even more emphatically, the Jewish Midrash Tanchuma articulates the place of Jerusalem in Jewish thought as both the beginning and the center of God's creation:

As the navel is set in the centre of the human body,

so is the land of Israel the navel of the world . . .

situated in the centre of the world,

and Jerusalem in the centre of the land of Israel,

and the sanctuary in the centre of Jerusalem,

and the holy place in the centre of the sanctuary,

and the ark in the centre of the holy place,

and the foundation stone before the holy place,

because from it the world was founded.[3]

Not surprisingly, scholars of Jewish and Islamic history indicate that in the early centuries of Islam, Muslims usurped terms such as, "the first of [God's] creation" from Jewish traditions and applied them to Mecca.[4] In the Islamic schema, it is not Jerusalem but Mecca that is the center of the world and the very "navel of the earth." Muslim tradition holds that two thousand years before creation, the city of Mecca was a mere spot floating upon the waters until Allah stretched it out and from it, created the universe.

The spirit of contention that rests on Mecca specifically toward Jerusalem is transparent. To understand the spiritual conflict in the Middle East, one must understand the Muslim mind-set particularly regarding Israel and Jerusalem. We have two important principles working together. One is the unbending, monochromatic fashion in which the more puritanical forms of Islamic thought function—in strict blacks and whites. The second is the incontestable idea that Islam has a divine right to rule the world. As such, it is unbearable to the radical Islamic mind that there exists in the Middle East another city that claims to be the religious or spiritual center of the world. If Israel is the thorn in the side of the Muslim world, then

Jerusalem is the poisoned tip. The Muslim world cannot rest until the throbbing pain caused by Jerusalem is silenced. As the prophet Zechariah made clear, in the last days, Jerusalem will be as a cup of strong drink that causes the surrounding nations to become drunk with a spirit of jealousy and rage (Zech. 12:2). This drunken rage is evident in the endless inflammatory rhetoric such as the following from comments by Hamas: "We are announcing a war against the sons of apes and pigs, which will not end until the flag of Islam is raised in Jerusalem"[5] or when Safwat Hagazy said on Egyptian TV during the height of the first Egyptian Revolution, "Our capital . . . shall be Jerusalem, with Allah's will. Our chant will be 'Millions of martyrs will march towards Jerusalem!'"[6]

What other religion on earth causes its followers to become so drunk with jealousy toward Jerusalem, with such a demonic lust to possess the land of Israel, and a hatred of the Jewish people? There is no other religion in the world that comes even close. Besides Mecca, the spiritual heart of Islam, of what other city can it so perfectly be said, "Those who dwell on the earth were made drunk"? (Rev. 17:2).

Today, an age-ending spiritual clash is unfolding throughout the nations. It is a clash between many peoples, two religions, two books, and ultimately the gods of two very different cities. It is a deadlocked struggle for spiritual primacy over the Middle East—and ultimately over the whole earth. The spiritual clash between the holy and the vile, between Jerusalem and Mecca, cannot be overstated. The story of Jerusalem someday becoming the joy of the whole world, and the city of the great King (Ps. 48:2), is the ultimate focal point of hope and expectation throughout the entire Bible. In terms of a city that represents a deliberate and concerted demonic effort to thwart those very plans, Mecca is unparalleled.

18

THE GREAT PAGAN CITY

IN THIS CHAPTER, we will continue to consider the possibility that the city of Mecca, the Kingdom of Saudi Arabia, and to a larger degree, the very religion of Islam, is in fact the great harlot of Revelation. In pondering this view, we must more carefully examine Mecca, as well as the somewhat mysterious shrine called the Kaaba, or "Cube," that sits in its center. A tremendous amount of mystery and controversy surrounds the Kaaba. Where did it come from and what does it mean today to Muslims?

According to Islamic history, the shrine was initially built by Adam, but later rebuilt by Abraham and Ishmael. The Muslim website Al-Islam.org describes it this way:

Historically when Ibrahim was ordered by Allah to build the Shrine for worship . . . he uncovered the original foundations of the Kaaba built by Adam. Ibrahim with the help of his son Ismael erected the new shrine on the same foundations.[1]

According to the Quran, Abraham built the shrine for the worship of one God:

Behold! We gave the site, to Ibrahim, of the (Sacred) House, (saying): "Associate not anything (in worship) with Me; and sanctify My House for those who compass it round, or stand up, or bow, or prostrate themselves (therein in prayer)." (Quran 22:26, Yusuf Ali translation)

Muslims are taught that shortly after Abraham died, the Kaaba was taken over by pagans, who began to use it as a house of idol worship.[2] When Muhammad was growing up in Mecca, the Kaaba was actually home to 360 different idols! Later, after he conquered Mecca, he is said to have purged the Kaaba of every idol and dedi-

cated it exclusively to the worship of his god, Allah.

Today the Kaaba is sixty feet high, sixty feet wide square. A door is fixed about seven feet above the ground facing northeast. Fixed to its lower eastern corner, five feet high, is a large black stone in a silver encasement.

The Kaaba or "Cube"

THE KAABA'S PAGAN ORIGINS

While Islam's own history acknowledges that the Kaaba was long used as a thoroughly pagan shrine, there is no real evidence that it was once built by Abraham. Quite to the contrary, there are many indicators that the Kaaba was a pagan shrine from its beginning. Let's consider some of the evidence.

To the shock of some, the Kaaba may have actually been a Hindu shrine, filled with 360 idols, but perhaps also dedicated to "Shiva." Some have suggested that the word Kabba may have originated from the Tamil word *Kabaalishwaran*, referring to a temple for Shiva. Tamil, considered one of the most ancient languages, is spoken in southern India and Sri Lanka, just to India's south. Today a large temple dedicated to Shiva (sometimes transliterated into English as the Kapaleeshwarar Temple) towers over the town of Mylapore, Chennai, in the Tamil state.[3]

Shiva is one of the three major gods of Hinduism, often referred to as "the destroyer of the world."[4] Among the primary symbols used in icons and images of Shiva are a third eye on his forehead, a large snake around his neck, and a crescent moon above his head. Could Shiva's crescent moon have some historical connection to the crescent moon that features so prominently in Islamic symbolism

and is affixed on top of mosques throughout the earth? It may be impossible to know for sure, but as we will see, the symbol of the crescent moon has a long history of being associated with various pagan gods throughout the ancient Middle East.

Shiva: The Hindu god of destruction with crescent moon on head

It is also worth mentioning that the most well-known symbol of Hinduism, the Aum, actually represents Shiva, Brahma, and Vishnu, the three main gods of Hinduism. The top portion of the Aum that represents Shiva is none other than a calligraphic representation of the crescent moon and star.

The Hindu Aum. Shiva is represented by the crescent moon on the top portion.

MIDDLE EASTERN ASTRAL AND WAR GODS

Throughout the ancient Middle East, various astral, war, and fertility gods or goddesses used either the sun or the moon as their primary identifying symbols. Archaeological evidence from various temples throughout Turkey and all across the ancient Assyrian Empire has given us numerous idols, coins, and carvings that attest to this. It is not difficult to see the continuity between these ancient astral and war gods and the god of the Quran, whose symbol is the crescent moon and whose call is to jihad or "holy war."

An ancient idol of Astarte, or Aphrodite, with crescent moon about her head.

THE CRESCENT MOON IN THE BIBLE

Many are also surprised to learn that there are even references to the crescent moon in the Bible. One example is found in Judges 8, where Gideon defeated the Midianites. Here's the story (note what was among the spoils):

> Gideon arose and killed Zebah and Zalmunna [the Midianite kings], and took the crescent ornaments which were on their camels' necks. Then the men of Israel said to Gideon, "Rule over us . . . , for you have delivered us from the hand of Midian." But Gideon said to them, "I will not rule over you . . . [but] I would request of you, that each of you give me an earring from his spoil." (For they had gold earrings, because they were Ishmaelites.) And they answered, "We will willingly give them." And they spread a cloak, and every man threw in it the earrings of his spoil. And the weight of the golden earrings that he requested was 1,700 shekels of gold, besides *the crescent ornaments* and the pendants and the purple garments worn by the kings of Midian, and besides the collars that were around the necks of their camels. (Judg. 8:21–26; emphasis added)

It is fascinating to see that as far back as Gideon's day, thousands of years before Muhammad, the Ishmaelite pagans of the desert were already adorning themselves and their camels with the sign of the crescent moon.

The word used for "crescent ornaments" is the Hebrew *saharonim*. This word is closely related to *sahar*, which appears later, in Isaiah 14, a passage wherein the Lord refers to Satan as "Lucifer, son of the morning" (KJV) or, in other translations, as the one who has fallen from heaven, the "star of the morning, son of the dawn" (Heb. *heylal heylal ben sahar*) (v. 12). In Arabic, the name for the crescent ornaments placed atop mosques is *hillal*, equivalent to the Hebrew *heylal*. So quite literally, the very wording used in the Hebrew Scriptures to refer to Satan, the "morning star" (HCSB), is used in Arabic to refer to the crescent moon, which is placed on nearly every Muslim national flag and on top of nearly every mosque throughout the world. That the very symbol of Islam down through the centuries is precisely the symbol the Bible uses to refer to Satan is certainly not irrelevant and should not be ignored.

CIRCUMAMBULATION OF THE KAABA

Another Muslim practice that originates from pagan pre-Islamic history is circumambulation, or walking in circles around the Kaaba. This practice, an integral ritual during the Muslim sacred pilgrimage to Mecca, is called *Tawaf* in Arabic. The Kaaba is the single most circumambulated structure in the world, circled by pilgrims literally twenty-four hours a day, except for the five times a day when the pilgrims stop to bow in prayer.

But ritualistic circumambulation is also a common practice within Hinduism and Buddhism, called *pradakshina*, or *parikrama*. One Hindu website explains its religious purpose:

> Pradakshina (Sanskrit), meaning circumambulation, consists of walking around in a "circle" as a form of worship in Hindu ceremonies in India. The devotees walk around the garbha griha, the innermost chamber of the shrine housing the temple deity. It is done around sacred fire (Agni), trees and plants as well . . . Pradakshina or Parikrama is done in pilgrimage centres also.[5]

An ancient carving of Hindus practicing pradakshina around a temple

There are absolutely no Jewish, Christian, or any biblical roots whatsoever to this practice. It is an entirely pagan tradition. So here we have another example of an Islamic ritual that is not only common among other pagan religions today, but is also derived entirely from ancient paganism.

RAMADAN AND THE HAJJ

Adding to the list of pre-Islamic pagan practices that were simply adopted by Muhammad and his followers is the annual pilgrimage to Mecca, known as the hajj, as well as the month of fasting, known as Ramadan. In Muhammad's day, once a year, during Ramadan, the various pagans who lived throughout Arabia would fast, don a white pilgrim's cloak, and make their way up to Mecca to worship their various gods at the Kaaba. After founding Islam, Muhammad continued this practice. Thus today, making this pilgrimage is one of the five foundational "pillars" of Islam. Every Muslim believer who is able to raise the necessary funds should at least once make a religious pilgrimage to Mecca during Ramadan. The Quran mentions Ramadan and claims that it was given to mankind by Allah (Quran 2:185). To convey how powerful the experience of the hajj can be, one Saudi Arabian minister of the hajj said it was like "twenty Super Bowls in one stadium, when two million will come, and . . . these two million people will actually be taking part in playing the game."[6]

Some have even suggested that the very name Ramadan is derived from the Hindu god Rama or, more precisely, a human manifestation of the god Vishnu. Muslims, however, claim it comes from the Arabic word for "burn," because this month burns away the sins of Muslims. As Imam Al Qurturbi says, "It (this month) was named Ramadan because it burns the sins of people with righteous deeds."[7]

THE MILLENNIAL PILGRIMAGE

Zechariah the prophet, after describing the military gathering of the nations against Jerusalem in the last days, followed by the return of Jesus on the Mount of Olives, continued his prophecy by detailing the magnificent pilgrimage that will take place each year when many nations will travel to Jerusalem to worship Jesus and celebrate the feast of tabernacles or booths (Heb. Sukkot). Multitudes of people will go up annually to Jerusalem for celebration. Consider this profoundly powerful picture of the coming Jewish kingdom:

> Then it will come about that any who are left of all the nations that went against Jerusalem will go up from year to year to worship the King, the Lord of hosts, and to celebrate the Feast of Booths. And it will be that whichever of the families of the earth does not go up to Jerusalem to worship the King, the Lord of hosts, there will be no rain on them. If the family of Egypt does not go up or enter, then no rain will fall on them; it will be the plague with which the Lord smites the nations who do not go up to celebrate the Feast of Booths. (Zech. 14:16–18)

Isaiah also touches on this theme, "Many peoples will come and say, 'Come, let us go up to the mountain of the Lord, to the house of the God of Jacob. He will teach us his ways, so that we may walk in his paths'" (Isa. 2:4).

THE HAJJ: THE GREAT COUNTERFEIT SUKKOT

Of course, it's difficult to consider this picture of peoples from every nation streaming to Jerusalem each year to worship Jesus without our minds turning to the hajj, which in so many ways is the great satanic counterfeit of the great annual Sukkot pilgrimage to come. There are many striking similarities between Sukkot and the hajj, in fact. During the hajj, instead of streaming to Jerusalem, however, as during Sukkot, the Muslim pilgrims from all over the world stream to Mecca. And instead of worshipping Yahweh, the God of the Bible, they come to worship Allah, the god of the Quran.

Each year, tens of thousands of tents are arranged outside the Grand Mosque to accommodate the Muslim pilgrims making hajj.

Millions of Muslim pilgrims flow like rivers toward the Kaaba at the center of the Grand Mosque in Mecca.

THE BLACK STONE

Perhaps the greatest pinnacle of the hajj ritual is the act of kissing or rubbing the black stone that is affixed to the corner of the Kaaba. Numerous historians have observed that black meteorites were commonly used throughout the ancient world in association with the worship of pagan gods and goddesses. Black meteorite rocks most often featured prominently in the various idols of deities such as Venus or Aphrodite at Paphos, Cybele in Rome, Astarte at Byblos, and, of course, the famous Artemis/Diana of Ephesus. This is why Artemis's "image" in the book of Acts was seen as having fallen from heaven:

> "Men of Ephesus, what man is there after all who does not know that the city of the Ephesians is guardian of the temple of the great Artemis and of the image which fell down from heaven?" (Acts 19:35)

So where did the black stone of the Kaaba come from? Not surprisingly, like the black stone used to carve out the head of the great Artemis idol, the black stone revered by Muslims, according to their own tradition, also fell from heaven:

> It was narrated that Ibn 'Abbas said: The Messenger of Allah (peace and blessings of Allah be upon him) said: "The Black Stone came down from Paradise."[8]

Who will deny that this black stone, such a central feature of the Muslim hajj, is actually the residual tie to the ancient pre-Islamic paganism of the Kaaba? Now consider this: Muslims actually believe that this stone has the ability to absorb and forgive the sins of all those who kiss or touch it during hajj:

> It was narrated that Ibn 'Abbas said: The Messenger of Allah (peace and blessings of Allah be upon him) said: "When the Black Stone came down from Paradise, it was whiter than milk, but the sins of the sons of Adam made it black."[9]

Thus according to Islamic doctrine, all of the Muslims' sins committed until that point in their lives are wiped clean. Again, this wiping of the slate clean is the pinnacle and goal of the entire pilgrimage.

It was narrated that Ibn 'Umar said: I heard the Messenger of Allah (peace and blessings of Allah be upon him) say: "Touching [the Black Stone] is an expiation for sins."[10]

It is even said that the black stone will become animated, possessing eyes and a mouth, and actually stand as a witness on the day of judgment, either condemning or acquitting those whose sins it had absorbed:

It was narrated that Ibn 'Abbas said: The Messenger of Allah (peace and blessings of Allah be upon him) said concerning the Stone: "By Allah, Allah will bring it forth on the Day of Resurrection, and it will have two eyes with which it will see and a tongue with which it will speak, and it will testify in favor of those who touched it in sincerity."[11]

The idolatry of this act has not gone unnoticed. As early as thirty years after Islam began, John of Damascus, a Christian Syrian monk, wrote about the obvious idolatry of the black stone:

They furthermore accuse us of being idolaters, because we venerate the cross, which they abominate. And we answer them: "How is it, then, that you rub yourselves against a stone in your Ka'ba and kiss and embrace it?"[12]

Amazingly, John went on to say that the black stone of the Kaaba was a piece from an ancient idol of none other than the goddess of love and fertility!

This stone that they talk about is a head of that Aphrodite whom they used to worship and whom they called Khabár. Even to the present day, traces of the carving are visible on it to careful observers.[13]

Idol of Diana or Artemis, with the head carved from a black meteorite.

John's reference to the head of Aphrodite being made of a black meteorite is well attested to as common throughout the region, where black meteorites were used for the heads of idols to Artemis, or Diana, as well as Aphrodite and other astral, war, and fertility goddesses.

The use of black stones as objects of worship among the pagans of the Middle East is also well attested to. In Paphos, Cyprus, a large black stone was found that is nearly identical to the black stone of the Kaaba. This conical stone is now on display at the Kouklia museum. It was venerated as a representation of Venus, or Aphrodite.

Observers have also noted that the odd silver encasement covering the black rock of Kaaba seems to be designed to resemble a female sexual organ, and may very well confirm its origins in the worship of one of the many pagan fertility goddesses from the region.

The black stone of Paphos

So once again, just to highlight the stark contrast here, while the Bible speaks of a coming day when people of every ethnic group will stream to Jerusalem to worship Jesus, the only

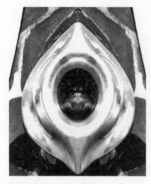

The black rock of the Kaaba, in its silver encasement.

One who can truly forgive sins, today Muslims from every nation make pilgrimage each year to Mecca, to kiss a black stone from the idol of a pagan goddess, believing it brings forgiveness of their sins. Even today, this is no doubt the purest form of ancient idolatry. As the black stone is essentially the great counterfeit of the blood of Christ, so is the Islamic hajj the great satanic counterfeit of the true pilgrimage of Sukkoth that God has ordained for all the nations who will each year go up to Jerusalem.

THE VEIL

It is worth noting that the Kaaba, like a Muslim woman, is covered with a veil. The four outer walls of the Kaaba are covered with what is essentially a giant burqa. Like the full burqas worn by the strictest among Muslim women, the curtain covering the Kaaba is made from black fabric. Like the more ornate head coverings, the veil of the Kaaba also features the Shahada, or Islamic creed (There is no god other than Allah, and Muhammad is the final messenger of Allah), outlined in gold in the weave of the fabric. About two-thirds of the way up runs another gold embroidered band covered with more Quranic text. That the Kaaba is essentially "dressed" like a woman may also be further residual evidence of the ancient pagan roots of the shrine dedicated to some form of ancient Middle Eastern fertility goddess.

MUSLIM COSMOLOGY OF THE KAABA

Today, despite the clearly pagan nature of the Kaaba, Muslims view its role as similar to the tabernacle and Holy of Holies in Judaism. Although the Kaaba actually sits in a small valley, Islamic sacred cosmology holds that the Kaaba is the highest place in the whole world, and nothing is closer to heaven.[14] The Kaaba, it is taught, is an earthly representation of the very throne of Allah, which sits directly above the Kaaba in Mecca and which the angels perpetually circumambulate.[15] As Muslim historian Muhammad Wajid Akhter stated, "Directly above the Kaaba in heaven is an exact replica." Because of its alleged proximity to the throne of Allah, the Kaaba is also called "the gate of heaven," or *bab al-Jannah* in Arabic. This, of course, copycats the biblical account of the tabernacle built by Moses, which was modeled after the tabernacle in heaven. As the author of Hebrews reminds us, the earthly temple and the various associated rituals "serve [as] a copy and shadow of the heavenly things, just as Moses was warned by God when he was about to erect the tabernacle; for, 'See,' He says, 'that you make all things according to the pattern which was shown to you on the mountain'" (Heb. 8:5). This is yet one more way in which the Kaaba serves as Satan's effort to counterfeit the true temple in Jerusalem.

ABRAJ AL-BAIT

In 2012, the Saudi Binladin Group completed construction of the Abraj al-Bait, also known as the Mecca Royal Clock Tower Hotel. The Abraj al-Bait is a massive, seven-building structure featuring the world's tallest clock tower at its center, atop of which is a massive crescent moon and the name Allah in Arabic calligraphy. Construction began in 2002, after the Saudis demolished the Ajyad Fortress, an eighteenth-century Ottoman citadel that stood atop a small hill overlooking the Grand Mosque, sparking a massive outcry from Turkey. Though not quite the tallest building in the world, the Abraj al-Bait is classified as the largest building in the world, covering far more area than any other tower.

In 2014, the Bible prophecy world exploded after an article appeared claiming that the Abraj sat on top of "Mount Babel" and must therefore be the true last-days "Tower of Babel." This is inaccurate, however, as the hill is actually called Bulbul, named after a common songbird found throughout the Middle East. (The bulbul was very close to becoming the national bird of Israel.) Because the Abraj al-Bait is the world's largest building and is adorned so prominently with pagan symbols and the crescent moon, it is certainly a fascinating structure that perhaps might even conjure up thoughts of the Tower of Babel of old. The name of the hill upon which it was built, however, has absolutely no relationship to the names Babel or Babylon.[16]

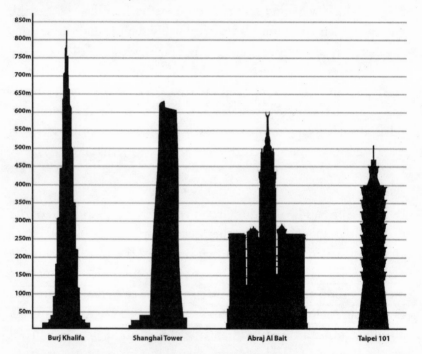

Abraj al-Bait compared to the world's other presently three tallest buildings.

CONCLUSION

Having considered the degree to which nearly all of the practices and symbols associated with the Kaaba are so thoroughly pagan, it is stunning to realize that it is this shrine that 1.6 billion Muslims pray toward five times daily. Wherever they are in the world, Muslims are expected to face the Kaaba when performing prayer. As Akhter stated, "There is no place on Earth as venerated, as central or as holy to as many people as Mecca. Thousands circle the sacred Kaaba at the centre of the Haram sanctuary 24 hours a day . . . The Kaaba is the epicenter of Mecca."[17] This is the pagan shrine of which the Quran says, "So turn your face toward al-Masjid al-Haram (The Sacred Mosque). And wherever you believers are, turn your faces toward it in prayer" (Quran 2:144, Sahih International translation).

For years, many Protestant teachers have looked to Rome and the Catholic Church as the primary hub of global false religion. Comparatively, the amount of attention the city of Mecca has received has been minimal. It is as if it has been off the radar. While most are aware of its centrality and importance to Muslims, they have not fully recognized the profound degree to which it wields control over the kings and peoples that surround Israel on every side. While wrongly claiming that every ritual and practice of the Catholic Church are actually just modern manifestations of ancient "Babylonian" paganism, they've missed the relevance of the city whose very foundations are rooted in the most primal kind of ancient paganism—the evidence of which can clearly be seen to this very day. Distracted by five hundred years of sectarian polemics and pointing to Rome, many Protestants have missed what should be glaringly obvious: nearly all of the various practices associated with the city of Mecca, arguably the most influential religious city on earth, are thoroughly pagan. The great city of harlotry that controls the hearts and minds of the majority of the Middle East is right in front us. Now, as violent jihad and terrorism continue to explode across the Western world, making their increasing relevance felt, the city of Mecca, the very womb and heart of the most anti-Semitic, antichrist, violent, and pagan religion the world has ever known is finally beginning to seize our attention. While it is possible that a different city may emerge in the future that will replace Mecca as the great pagan city of false religion, no one can dispute that Mecca is indeed one of the great harlot cities, a pagan city that until this point, has had no equal in all of human history.

19

THE KINGS OF LUXURY

ANOTHER SIGNIFICANT CHARACTERISTIC of the great harlot defined by the text of Revelation 17–18 is her excessive wealth and the degree to which she lavishes herself with material excess. In Revelation 18:3, we read about "the abundance of her luxury" (NKJV). Just a few verses later, we're told, "she glorified herself and lived luxuriously" (18:7 NKJV). It would be nearly impossible to imagine a better description of the House of Saud, the royal family of Saudi Arabia.

FROM RAGS TO RICHES: THE STORY OF THE SAUDI ROYAL FAMILY
In the early 1930s, after many years of fighting and wrestling for

power on all sides, Muhammad Ibn Saud, an Arabian Desert Bed-
ouin, managed to consolidate his tribal supremacy over the entire
Arabian Peninsula and name it after himself: Saudi Arabia. His
timing was impeccable. In 1933, only one year after the tribe of
Al Saud had come to power, Ibn Saud "granted broad exploration
rights to Standard Oil of California."[1] Three years later, in 1936,
they struck oil in what would become the richest and most produc-
tive string of oil fields the world would ever see. This quickly led to
the formation of a mega oil consortium named Aramco (Arabian
American Oil Company). A series of governmental and corporate
alliances was forged between the United States and the Al Saud
tribe; World War II subsided; and the world became an open market
for the Saudis. There has never been a speedier rise to the top of
the global food chain of wealth and influence. As if overnight, an
obscure Middle Eastern desert was transformed into a growing
industrialized network of oil wells, refineries, and pipelines. Likewise, the long-divided berg of desert tribes was transformed into
a unified and formidable international presence: "the Kingdom of
Saudi Arabia." Suddenly, in just a brief decade, a new royal family
emerged. Since those days, as the late French neoconservative
Laurent Murawiec sarcastically stated, members of the Saudi royal
family "daily hear 'your royal highness' more than anyone since the
Sun King."[2] Former CIA agent and author Robert Baer described
the practical results of the transformation to the House of Saud:

> Ibn Saud's offspring, and their offspring, would become some
> of the world's richest people, famous from the casinos of Monte
> Carlo to the brothels of London for their profligacy; the lords
> of billion-dollar palaces, owners of the best thoroughbreds and
> yachts, donors of university chairs and college laboratories, buyers
> of influence in every capitol of the West, ready to whisk around
> the world at a moment's notice on fleets of private jets.[3]

INCOMPARABLE SAUDI WEALTH

With regard to the wealth of the Saudi royal family, it would be nearly impossible to overstate the degree to which they lavish themselves with luxury. When some Bible students look at this portion of the Mystery Babylon prophecy—the excessive materialism the harlot lavishes onto herself—they immediately see the United States. This is understandable. It is reasoned that America is the most affluent and materialistic society imaginable. Undoubtedly there are many aspects of American society that can quite justifiably be criticized, and materialism is certainly among its most notable problems. Whatever outrageous examples of excess one might be able to find in American society, however, they nearly all pale in comparison to what we find, not as anomalies, but as the rule among the Saudi royal family. In fact, it is an outright, over-the-top excessiveness that has come to define the Saudi elite. Bizarre anecdotes could fill a book. For our purposes, however, we will just consider a few more illustrative examples.

Let's begin with the deceased King Fahd. As far back as 1974, Fahd spent an evening gambling in Monte Carlo. In one night, he gambled away nearly $5 million. This was 1974—$5 million then would be valued at around $25 million today. When was the last time that anyone heard of some member of the Hollywood elite, an eccentric American CEO, a sports figure, a musician, or any American president or senator gambling away $25 million in one evening just for entertainment? Has Bill Gates or Warren Buffett ever been known to do such a thing? Did Ronald Reagan or even Barack Obama ever act like this? Even when compared to the excesses of America's richest, most powerful, and most elite, the overindulgence of the Saudis is in a league all of its own.

A recent article featured in the *Daily Mail* highlighted the lavish lifestyle of twenty-three-year-old Saudi billionaire Turki Bin Abdullah. Turki is known for being best friends with American rap legend Dr. Dre and driving around London with a small fleet of custom, gold-plated cars, all of which were imported to the city. His vehicles include: a custom $500,000 Aventador; a $540,000 six-wheeler Mercedes AMG off-roader; a $500,000 Rolls Phantom Coupe; a $320,000 Bentley Flying Spur; and a $260,000 Lamborghini Huracan.[4] Again, this kid is twenty-three, and this is just what he brings with him when traveling.

Gerald Posner, the author of *Secrets of the Kingdom*, elaborated on the wealth of the Saudi royal family by enumerating just a few of the deceased King Fahd's real estate holdings. Story after story conveys the broad chasm between American wealth and Saudi wealth. King Fahd built for himself "several enormous palaces . . . each one grander than the one it replaced."[5] One palace was actually a near replica of the White House, but after several advisors counseled the king that living in it would convey the wrong message, it simply sat vacant. Posner continued:

> His "official" palace was a throw-back to when the Kingdom's first kings lived behind walled cities. It was essentially a tiny Vatican City, with opulent furnishings and walls that ran several miles around the perimeter. Architects who worked on the palaces estimated that they were worth several billion in the 1980s.[6]

Today that several billion would be valued closer to upwards of $30 billion. This is only the value of one of the king's palaces. The late king had many more homes, including

> a one-hundred-room house in Marbella Spain; a spectacular estate outside of Paris that was initially built for the eighteenth-century French kings; a mansion near London on which he spent nearly $60 million in refurbishments; and a sprawling palacio in Geneva, in which, he was fond of boasting had over 1,500 telephone lines. He flew between cities in a private 747-SP fitted with an enormous pink master bedroom, gold bathroom fixtures, a mahogany elevator, a sauna, and Baccarat crystal chandeliers. Fahd's lavish yacht—the size of a luxury liner—cost $50 million, and he kept over two dozen Rolls-Royces, fitted with gold hood ornaments and grills, in his different homes.[7]

Posner also amusingly pointed out that Fahd actually had a British firm modify a Rolls-Royce Camargue into a super, custom, one-of-a-kind dune buggy. A Rolls-Royce dune buggy! If that is not enough, consider that King Fahd's favorite son, Abdul Aziz, known among the royal family as Azouzi ("Dearie"), built himself a home—more of an Islamic theme park, really—that cost him over $4.6 billion. Not million—billion.[8] Again, this is only one of his homes. Consider the amount of money this is: not many homes anywhere in the world have ever sold for more than $150 million.[9] Azouzi's Islamic version of Michael Jackson's Neverland Ranch cost him more than forty times that amount. Prince Aziz is far from alone among the Saudi princes in surrounding himself with luxury beyond imagination. In March 2005, *Forbes* magazine described the Riyadh palace of Prince Alwaleed bin Talal Alsaud, which has, among other things, 317 rooms. It cost the prince over $130 million to build. "Totaling 400,000 square feet, it has a soccer field, eight elevators and more than 500 television sets."[10] It certainly sounds like a lovely single-family dwelling. This even trumped Donald Trump—a name virtually synonymous with real estate wealth—who got only $95 million for his Palm Beach mansion.[11]

CONCLUSION

One of the most important and defining characteristics of the great harlot is her lavish lifestyle. Of the city Mystery Babylon it is said, "How much she hath glorified herself, and lived in luxury" (Rev. 18:7). Although we could literally go on forever listing examples of Saudi excessiveness, with each anecdote or outlandish figure outdoing the last, the point is, this critical description of the harlot could not be a better fit than with the sultans of opulence, the kings of luxury known collectively as the Saudi royal family.

20

SEDUCER OF NATIONS

BESIDES CHRISTIANITY, Islam is the only other major world religion with a significant evangelistic thrust. And hands down, leading the global charge to spread the message of Islam is the Islamic Affairs Department of Saudi Arabia. In my own personal library several Islamic books and booklets, including a large, bound, hardcover Quran—all of which were sent to me free of charge—compliments of the Saudi embassy. All I had to do was go to the website of the Saudi Arabian Embassy and fill out a basic request form.[1] There was no charge whatsoever. Soon I received in the mail a very nice Quran and literally a box of books and booklets, all declaring the miracles, wonders, and beauty of Islam—and of course, the shortcomings and failings of Christianity, Judaism, and other "corrupted" religions. Can you imagine if America or England or any other Western country provided anyone in the world a free Bible and Christian evangelistic materials?

Not only is Mecca the historical womb from which Islam was birthed, but the modern rulers of Saudi Arabia continue to be the primary source of ideological and financial support for the rapid spread of Islam globally. According to popular Saudi TV host and commentator Dawood al-Shirian, the tens of billions of dollars used by the Saudi royals pay for an estimated 90 percent of the "expenses of the entire faith."[2] Let me rephrase that: 90 percent of the funding for the spread of Sunni Islam globally comes from Saudi Arabia. In the same way that the United States serves as the greatest source of funding for global Christian missions, Saudi Arabia serves as the greatest source of funding for Islam.

The Saudi program to reach the world is simple. First they fund and build the madrassas, Islamic centers, and mosques that exclusively promote the Saudis' own acidic brand of Wahhabi Islam. They build them all over the world. If you have a large mosque in your city, it was most likely paid for by the Saudi Arabian government. Beyond building the mosques, the Saudi government also trains, sends, and funds the ulema (Islamic scholars and teachers)—missionaries of Wahhabism—all across the world. Thousands of these missionaries are funded beyond most Christian missionaries' wildest dreams. Once in the target country, they establish and support the various Saudi Islamic centers and front organizations, such as the World Assembly of Muslim Youth (WAMY) or the World Muslim League (WML). Laurent Murawiec, late author of *Princes of Darkness: The Saudi Assault on the West*, described the nature of Saudi influence on the world,

> Islamic centers financed by Riyadh, mosques, and Koranic schools where only the Wahhabi doctrine is taught, obscurantist universities, missionaries with money to burn and large goals who preach

from Morocco to Indonesia, from Nigeria to Uzbekistan, the international press in Arabic monopolized by rich Saudis, international Arab organizations all converge to produce a single picture.[3]

Finally, the Saudi government actually fills those mosques, Islamic centers, and schools with its own books, tracts, and educational literature. What kind of material specifically are they sending?

THE WAHHABI INDOCTRINATION OF THE WORLD

In a fairly comprehensive 2005 report, titled *Saudi Publications on Hate Ideology Invade American Mosques*, the human rights group Freedom House related that Saudi government–sanctioned literature that promoted the radical brand of Wahhabi Islam was being distributed widely to American mosques. The report followed a yearlong study examining more than two hundred books and tracts found in mosques from Los Angeles, Dallas, and Oakland, to Houston, Chicago, New York, and Washington.[4] In the materials examined, Muslims living in America are encouraged to "behave as if on a mission behind enemy lines."[5] Those who convert to Christianity or Judaism are told, "If you do not repent, you are an apostate and you should be killed because you have denied the Koran."[6] According to Nina Shea, the director of Freedom House:

> A review of a sample of official Saudi textbooks for Islamic studies used during the current academic year reveals that, despite the Saudi government's statements to the contrary, an ideology of hatred toward Christians and Jews and Muslims who do not follow Wahhabi doctrine remains in this area of the public school system.[7]

Some examples of the kind of statements that were found in the Saudi-sanctioned literature included the following:

- From a first grade textbook: "Every religion other than Islam is false."

- From a fourth grade textbook: "True belief means . . . that you hate the polytheists and infidels."

- From a sixth grade textbook: "Just as Muslims were successful in the past when they came together in a sincere endeavor to evict the Christian crusaders from Palestine, so will the Arabs and Muslims emerge victorious, God willing, against the Jews and their allies if they stand together and fight a true jihad for God, for this is within God's power."

- From an eighth grade textbook: "The apes are Jews, the people of the Sabbath; while the swine are the Christians, the infidels of the communion of Jesus."

- From a ninth grade textbook: "The clash between this [Muslim] community (umma) and the Jews and Christians has endured, and it will continue as long as God wills," and again: "It is part of God's wisdom that the struggle between the Muslim and the Jews should continue until the hour [of judgment]."

- From a twelfth grade textbook: "Jihad in the path of God—which consists of battling against unbelief, oppression, injustice, and those who perpetrate it—is the summit of Islam. This religion arose through jihad and through jihad was its banner raised high. It is one of the noblest acts, which brings one closer to God, and one of the most magnificent acts of obedience to God."[8]

The report also states that

involvement by the Saudi government was immediately evident from the seal or name of a government department emblazoned on the cover of the literature. Materials examined were easily identifiable as originating from the Saudi Embassy in Washington, the Education Ministry, the Saudi air force and other branches of the Saudi government.[9]

So we must understand that when Saudi Arabia spreads Islam throughout the earth, it is not merely Islam, but its own unique brand of radical Wahhabi Islam. Worse yet, this kind of material is not merely being sent to the United States. It is actually being sent all over the world. As author Gilles Kepel wrote, "From the African plains to the rice paddies of Indonesia and the Muslim immigrant high-rise housing projects of European cities, the same books could be found, paid for by Saudi Arabian government."[10]

SAUDI SEDUCTION

What we've discussed thus far is only the tip of the iceberg of the great Saudi seduction. Entire books have been written on the subject, and as we will see, the spidery fingers of the lords of petro-Islam have reached every nook and corner of the earth. In 2005, Prince Alwaleed bin Talal, the fabulously wealthy prince mentioned earlier, donated $20 million to Harvard University and another $20 million to Georgetown University to establish two Islamic studies programs in the United States.[11] Four other such centers were established at the University of Cambridge, the University of Edinburgh, the American University in Cairo, and the American University in Beirut. Now let me ask you this: How can these institutions ever criticize the same regime, the same hands, that gave them the largest private donation in the history of the school? This kind of money buys more than just an Islamic Studies center; it also buys compliance.

At the announcement of the donation at Harvard, Alwaleed gave a speech in which he preached, "Bridging the understanding between East and West is important for peace and tolerance."[12] Please stop and ask yourself: Is there more intolerance and misunderstanding of Christianity in Saudi Arabia, or more intolerance and misunderstanding of Islam at Harvard University? A Christian studies program at any university in Saudi Arabia would be illegal. To further demonstrate the absurdity of this, this is the same prince who just the year before donated $27 million to support the families of Islamic suicide bombers in Israel.[13] We will discuss this matter more in chapter 22, but for now, consider the degree of hypocrisy required for a Saudi prince to come to Harvard University to preach about the need for Americans to embrace understanding and religious tolerance, while his own country is one of the most religiously restrictive nations on earth. No religion other than Islam may even be publicly practiced there. It is actually legal to behead apostates. Christians cannot even wear a cross lest they face being sternly punished by Saudi law. Jews were actually banned from even stepping foot onto Saudi soil until at least 2002. To top this off, only one month before Alwaleed's announcement, on November 12, 2005, a female Saudi chemistry teacher was sentenced to 750 lashes for "speaking positively about Jews" in class.[14] *How dare she?* Is this the type of religious tolerance that Prince Alwaleed wishes the West to learn about at Harvard, Georgetown, Cambridge, and Edinburgh?

Despite Harvard's reputation as a bastion of high-mindedness and tolerance, for $20 million they were happy to prostitute themselves to the most religiously restrictive regime in the world. How does the Saudi harlot seduce the world to commit immorality with her and support her harlotry? Everyone has their price, and in most cases, the Saudis can and will pay it.

THE GREAT EVANGELIST HARLOT

So just how much are the Saudis spending to spread the message of Islam? In 2005, former U.S. CIA director James Woolsey testified before the U.S. House of Representatives' Committee on Government Reform that "some $85–90 billion has been spent from sources in Saudi Arabia in the last 30 years, spreading Wahhabi beliefs throughout the world."[15] According to Yousaf Butt, a nuclear physicist and visiting senior research fellow at the Center for Technology and National Security Policy at the National Defense University:

> Exact numbers are not known, but it is thought that more than $100 billion have been spent on exporting fanatical Wahhabism

to various much poorer Muslim nations worldwide over the past three decades. It might well be twice that number. By comparison, the Soviets spent about $7 billion spreading communism worldwide in the 70 years from 1921 and 1991.[16]

Stop and consider the numbers. The Southern Baptist International Missions Board (IMB) is one of the largest Protestant missionary organizations in the world. Their annual budget is roughly $300 million per year.[17] If the Saudis spent $100 billion over a thirty-year period to spread radical Wahhabism globally, that means they spent roughly the equivalent of the IMB's entire annual missions budget every three weeks, continuously for thirty years. The Saudi campaign to reach the nations with the message of Islam is literally the single largest evangelistic or propaganda campaign the world has ever known. Nothing else even comes close. Friends, are we justified in saying that this kingdom fulfills the role of the "great city" that spreads its influence and false religion all over the earth?

CONCLUSION

Saudi Arabia, as the spearhead and the foremost leader of Islamic world evangelization, is indeed seducing the world with its barrels full of money that quite literally bubbles up from the earth. She seduces and evangelizes the world with a false religion that, although painted as "the religion of peace," is in reality fundamentally totalitarian in nature—violent, extreme, and indeed antichrist to its very core. Like the harlot who proudly holds her golden cup high, calling all the world to partake of her maddening brew, Saudi Arabia also calls out to the world to embrace what they call the only true and final religion. In truth, what the Saudis are offering to the world is a cupful of abominable things, the utter filth of a genuinely pagan and unarguably demonically inspired religion.

21

CORRUPTER OF KINGS

IN THIS CHAPTER WE WILL CONSIDER the tremendous amount of influence Saudi Arabia wields globally through its abundant oil wealth. As author Gerald Posner reminds us:

> Saudi Arabia acts much like any other country trying to cultivate U.S. support [and] influence foreign policy on issues it considers important . . . But what makes the Kingdom different from many other countries with similar ambitions is the power of money. It has succeeded on a scale unmatched by other countries.[1]

Simply stated, there is ample evidence that the Saudi royals buy influence, favor, and privilege; live above any law; and then, when all is said and done, buy silence. The Saudi royals—of which there are now well over forty thousand—are the single most privileged family in the world. Because of the truly ridiculous amount of money they have at their disposal, they are also the single greatest source of corruption within the United States government. *And that is saying a lot.*

Some years back, PBS *Frontline* produced a documentary called *Black Mo*ney, in which they interviewed the former Saudi ambassador to the United States, Prince Bandar. When specifically asked about the astronomical amount of Saudi cash lost every year to corruption and bribery, Bandar simply responded, "So what? We did not invent corruption."[2] What needs to be understood is that the Saudi corruption of the U.S. government to the highest levels is not simply a by-product of their tremendous wealth; rather, it is the foundation of their very deliberate and calculated approach to diplomacy. Far from trying to hide any of this, Bandar actually flaunted the Saudi approach: "If the reputation then builds that the Saudis take care of friends after they leave office, you'd be surprised how much better friends you have who are just coming into office."[3] To say it bluntly, the Saudi royals are the sugar daddies of the kings of the earth, and of nearly every high-level American politician you could name. Author Laurent Murawiec spelled it out quite plainly:

> Saudi Arabia . . . buys politicians, government officials, journalists, academics, diplomats, colonels, generals, and intelligence officers. It buys "experts" at bargain prices, and countless propagandists and lobbyists. When it sees fit, it demands the television programs be censored. It has flooded the circles of power with its petrodollars. It demands that American companies accept its political conditions in order to be able to do business even in violation of the U.S. Constitution.[4]

Retired CIA agent Robert Baer gives a very hearty amen to Murawiec's claims:

Any Washington bureaucrat with a room temperature IQ knows that if he stays on the right side of the [Saudi] kingdom, some way or another, he'll be able to finagle his way to feed at the Saudi trough. A consulting contract with Aramco, a chair at the American University, a job with Lockheed—it doesn't matter. There's hardly a living former assistant secretary of state for the Near East; CIA director; White House staffer; or member of Congress who hasn't ended up on the Saudi payroll in one way or another, or so it seems. With this kind of money waiting out there, of course American bureaucrats don't have the backbone to take on Saudi Arabia.[5]

He continues:

At a corporate level, almost every Washington figure worth mentioning has served on the board of at least one company that did a deal with Saudi Arabia, and practically every deal with the Saudis grows opaque, lost in some desert sandstorm back near the well heads where all the money sprang from.[6]

Abundant evidence testifies to the fact that Saudi corruption in the United States is pervasive. Where Baer left off, Posner filled in the blanks:

The Saudi petrodollars that have flooded the United States during the last thirty years have affected American business, politics, and society. That money has bought the House of Saud a coveted seat at the table with America's corporate and political elite, and the Saudis have assiduously courted the clout and access that results from such enormous influxes of cash.[7]

The vast amount of Saudi money has not only corrupted American politicians, however. The problem, quite literally, is global. As Murawiec testified:

The Al-Sauds have used the enormous power and wealth that came from oil to buy countries, consciences, political parties, celebrities and mercenaries. And not only in the Muslim world. The corruption has played a large role, especially in the Middle East. But the Al-Saud has been smart enough to extend its purchases beyond the Muslim world: the rot has also reached Europe and the United States.[8]

In 2011, shortly after the Arab Spring broke out, I appeared as a guest on the Glenn Beck show on Fox News. In an unprecedented move, Beck invited me onto one of the most highly watched programs in the nation, in the prime-time slot, to discuss the role of Islam and the Antichrist in the last days. Just before we went live, I looked at Glenn and said, "I apologize for whatever fallout occurs tomorrow." Not surprisingly, within just a few weeks, it was announced that Beck would be leaving Fox News. While there were various reasons given publicly as to why he finally left Fox, behind the scenes, I was told that it was largely due to the fact that Prince al-Waleed bin Talal owns a large stake in Fox News's parent company, News Corporation,[9] that Beck was forced out. Apparently our show was one of the last straws. Whether or not this is true, I cannot say for sure, but it should greatly alarm all Americans that a man who has donated nearly $30 million to encourage suicide bombing in Israel actually owns the largest stake in such a well-known American news outlet.

In reading several books that expose the relationship between Saudi Arabia and the United States, I was stunned at the degree to which many of the statements made by these secular authors seemed to echo what is described in the book of Revelation. Whereas the Bible speaks of "the great harlot who was corrupting the earth with her immorality" (Rev. 19:2), Baer wrote of "the oil that fed their whoring and corruption."[10] The Bible says, "The nations have drunk of the wine of the passion of her [sexual] immorality" (Rev. 18:3). Baer says, "Washington made us lie down with the devil. It made the bed, pulled back the covers and invited the devil in. We whispered in his ear and told him we loved him."[11]

CORRUPTER OF KINGS

To take the matter even further, consider the impact that Saudi bribery, blackmail, and corruption have had not merely on US corporations, universities, and various politicians, but actual "kings," as the prophecy repeatedly describes. Has the corrupting hand of the House of Saud actually reached to the highest political office in the world, that of the president of the United States?

PRESIDENT JIMMY CARTER

Let's begin with President Jimmy Carter. Several authors and reporters have detailed Carter's deeply compromising financial relationship with the Saudi royal family. Whether it was to secure extremely friendly loans to bail out his failing peanut farm, or to garner the more than $100 million that have been donated to the Carter Center, this president may have literally sold his soul to the Saudis.[12] According to the book *Bearing False Witness: Jimmy Carter's Palestine: Peace Not Apartheid*, published by the Committee for Accuracy in Middle East Reporting in America (CAMERA):

> Jimmy Carter's dependence on Arab funding stretches back to early business connections in the 1970's and continues in the present with multi-million dollar donations to his richly-endowed Carter Center in Atlanta, Georgia. The center's 2006 annual report reveals total net assets of $412,393,757, a strikingly large figure for a nonprofit organization.[13]

Reflecting on such sentiments, in a fairly bold statement, Harvard professor Alan Dershowitz said that Carter

> has been bought off by millions of dollars in donations from Arab governments that refuse to recognize Israel and from Arab rulers who actively promote Jew-hatred in the Middle East and elsewhere. Investigative journalists have revealed the extent to which Carter has been "bought and paid for" by Arab and Islamic money. The Carter Center, a philanthropic founda-

tion that the former president started after leaving office, has received donations in excess of $1 million from Saudi Arabia, the United Arab Emirates, and the Sultanate of Oman; and groups and individuals with close ties to these governments, including OPEC, the Saudi Binladin Group, and the late Saudi king Fahd, a "founder" member of the center.[14]

What is so absolutely critical to understand here is that none of this is done out of the goodness of the Saudis' hearts. It is calculated, and it has a very clearly defined purpose. As former British diplomat John Kelly has so accurately said, "The rulers of the Arab oil states are neither simple philanthropists nor disinterested patrons . . . They expect a return upon their donations."[15] If President Carter has indeed been bought, then what did the Saudis get for their investments? Why, President Carter went on to become a virulently outspoken critic of Israel, of course! Given that they were coming from a former American president and Nobel laureate, his criticisms of Israel carried tremendous weight. His anti-Israel rhetoric reached its crescendo, however, when he wrote the book *Palestine: Peace Not Apartheid.* After its release, the book was widely criticized as "moronic (*Slate* magazine), "anti-historical" (*Washington Post*), and "laughable" (*San Francisco Chronicle*).[16] The book was so egregious, in fact, that after its release, fifteen members of Carter's advisory board actually resigned, including Kenneth Stein, who had been on the board of the Carter Center for over twenty-three years. In an open letter, Stein wrote that Carter's anti-Israel treatise was "replete with factual errors, copied materials not cited, superficialities, glaring omissions, and simply invented segments."[17] What was Carter's response to the resignation of so many board members? He falsely claimed they had all left because they were Jews under pressure from the Jewish lobby. Think of the utter hypocrisy here. Although President Carter himself made numerous accusations and inferences regarding the influence of "Jewish money" in American politics, according to the Committee for Accuracy in Middle East Reporting in America:

The reported hundreds of millions of dollars from Saudi and Gulf contributors that have flowed into the Carter Center as well as the vast sums of Arab money donated to American universities, think tanks, lobbies, religious institutions, and other opinion shaping institutions elicit no concern whatever from Jimmy Carter about Arab influence on American foreign policy.[18]

So much is said by the modern anti-Israel commentators and conspiracy theorists about the all-powerful "Israel lobby," but how often do we hear of the "Saudi lobby"? Yet the Saudi lobby is not only quite real; it is the single most powerful and well-funded lobby, not only in Washington, but in the history of the world!

Beyond Carter's staunch opposition to Israel, repeatedly accusing the Jewish state of every imaginable human rights violation, he remained completely silent regarding the endless, very well-documented cases of the most flagrant forms of human rights violations throughout the Saudi Kingdom. Thus, not only did the House of Saud quite literally buy an American president to serve as a mouthpiece for their anti-Israel campaign; they also paid for that very same mouth to stay shut when they willed it to be shut. As the saying goes, "Dance, monkey, dance."

PRESIDENTS GEORGE HERBERT WALKER BUSH AND GEORGE W. BUSH

At this point, some readers will likely blame Carter's corruption on his liberal political leaning. The Saudis, however, have corrupted both Democrats and Republicans. In fact, whatever measure of wealth President Carter was able to extract from the Saudis, the Bush family left Carter in the dust. In his 2004 book, *House of Bush, House of Saud: The Secret Relationship Between the World's Two Most Powerful Dynasties*, author Craig Unger thoroughly and painstakingly detailed the long history of the Bush and the Saudi royal families. Unger systematically worked through the tangled network of shell companies, businesses, banks, and friendly loans, the end result of which is just shy of one and a half billion dollars having been transferred from Saudi hands to the Bush family. Unger wrote:

In all, at least $1.476 billion had made its way from the Saudis to the House of Bush and its allied companies and institutions. It could safely be said that never before in history had a presidential candidate—much less a presidential candidate and his father, a former president—been so closely tied financially and personally to the ruling family of another foreign power. Never before had a president's personal fortunes and public policies been so deeply entwined with another nation.[19]

Unger actually goes on to say that this figure of $1.47 billion dollars is a conservative estimate. This is only the amount that can positively be identified. Again, please stop and really let the reality of what is being said here sink in. We are not speaking about some random lobbying firm having made some vaguely large donation to some obscure politician. We are talking about one and a half billion dollars being transferred to two American presidents, directly from a foreign government that is unarguably the single greatest source of radical Islamism in the world. How in the world is this not being shouted from the rooftops? How can we think this kind of money has no effect on decision-making and foreign policy? How is it possible not to see the fulfillment here of Revelation 18:9, "The kings of the earth . . . lived luxuriously with her"?

Before I continue, I want to be clear; by no means am I a 9/11 Truther. I believe the 9/11 attacks were carried out by Islamic terrorists. There were, however, some obvious cover-ups by the George W. Bush administration both on 9/11 and in the days, weeks, months, and years that followed. Specifically, I am referring to the relationship of high-ranking Saudi government officials and the attackers. It was not until January 2016, in fact, that news broke that the Bush administration had actually removed twenty-eight pages from the Congressional Report of the Joint Inquiry into the 9/11 attacks. According to the *Foreign Policy Journal*:

There are twenty-eight pages classified secret of a congressional inquiry into 9/11 that allegedly found Saudi financial support for the alleged 9/11 hijackers. Neither the George W. Bush nor the Obama regimes would release the classified pages. Only a few members of Congress have been permitted to read it under guard, and they are not permitted to speak about it.[20]

When news of the redactions broke, the British news website the Guardian interviewed John F. Lehman, who actually sat on the congressional committee from 2003 to 2004:

> "There was an awful lot of participation by Saudi individuals in supporting the hijackers, and some of those people worked in the Saudi government," Lehman said in an interview, suggesting that the commission may have made a mistake by not stating that explicitly in its final report. "Our report should never have been read as an exoneration of Saudi Arabia."[21]

As I said, not only does Saudi money buy influence and privilege; it also buys silence. No other nation in the world would have been able to get away with what the Saudis got away with that day. Remember: fifteen of the eighteen hijackers were Saudi citizens. If there was one nation in the world whose citizens should have been treated with suspicion, it was Saudi Arabia. Yet quite to the contrary, as the skies all across the United States were completely shut down, the only planes allowed in the air were those owned by Saudi princes. The Saudi royals received special privileges that even American government leaders were not afforded! They were the only group completely exempt from the law. This all took place under the Bush administration, and it was no mistake.

> In the measure that she glorified herself and lived luxuriously, in the same measure give her torment and sorrow; for she says in her heart, "I sit as queen, and am no widow, and will not see sorrow." (Rev. 18:7)

You felt secure in your wickedness and said, "No one sees me,"
Your wisdom and your knowledge, they have deluded you; for
you have said in your heart, "I am, and there is no one besides
me" (Isa. 47:10)

BILL AND HILLARY CLINTON

Let's also consider the Saudi influence on Bill and Hillary Clinton.
In the run-up to the 2016 election, the media was abuzz when it
was discovered what vast amounts of money had been donated to
the Clinton Foundation by Saudis and Gulf Arab states. As a report
in the Daily Caller explained:

> Bill and Hillary Clinton received at least $100 million from
> autocratic Persian Gulf states and their leaders, potentially
> undermining Democratic presidential candidate Hillary's claim
> she can carry out independent Middle East policies. As a presi-
> dential candidate, the amount of foreign cash the Clintons have
> amassed from the Persian Gulf states is "simply unprecedented,"
> says national security analyst Patrick Poole.[22]

This $100 million, however, came from a handful of Gulf Arab
states. According to Politifact, Saudi Arabia's donations specifically
amounted to closer to $35 million.[23] This figure does not include
donations given by individuals in the kingdom or groups such as
the Friends of Saudi Arabia or the Islamic World Conference.

Why would the Saudi royals donate tens of millions of dollars
to the Clinton Foundation? Are we to truly believe that the Saudi
royals are this passionately committed to Clinton's various humanitarian projects? Or did those donations have something to do with,
for example, the colossal weapons sales to the kingdom that Clinton
oversaw while serving as secretary of state? According to *Mother Jones*:

> In 2011, the State Department cleared an enormous arms deal:
> Led by Boeing, a consortium of American defense contractors
> would deliver $29 billion worth of advanced fighter jets to Saudi

Arabia, despite concerns over the kingdom's troublesome human rights record. In the years before Hillary Clinton became secretary of state, Saudi Arabia had contributed $10 million to the Clinton Foundation, and just two months before the jet deal was finalized, Boeing donated $900,000 to the Clinton Foundation, according to an International Business Times investigation released Tuesday. The Saudi transaction is just one example of nations and companies that had donated to the Clinton Foundation seeing an increase in arms deals while Hillary Clinton oversaw the State Department.[24]

The Saudis know how the game is played. They know what they want, and they know how to get it. One would hope that the office of the president of the United States would be beyond the reach of lobbying from state sponsors of terror, but as I have demonstrated, the access of the powerful and persuasive House of Saud to every American president is simply unparalleled.

CONCLUSION

Entire books have been written detailing the Saudi corruption of the American political system all the way to the very top. The effects of this corruption range from catering to the Saudis' Islamist anti-Israel agenda, to ignoring their pervasive human rights atrocities, to affording them the privilege of living outside of the law, to greasing the skids of multimillion-dollar weapons deals, to who knows what else? The Saudis have the means and the know-how to get whatever they want. Unfortunately, everyone has their price, including virtually every president of the United States of America for the past few generations. Considering again the great harlot's description as she "with whom the kings of the earth committed fornication" (Rev. 17:2 NKJV), who "reigns over the kings of the earth" (17:18), and with whom they live "luxuriously" (18:9 NKJV), the Saudi royal family fits it to near perfection. In fact, I would argue that no other religious or political entity in the world fits it more perfectly.

22

DRUNK ON THE BLOOD

OF THE SAINTS

ONE OF THE MOST IMPORTANT DEFINING CHARACTERISTICS of the last-days Babylon is that she is the great persecutor of the saints. Among the first observations the apostle John made of the harlot is that she was "drunk with the blood of the saints, and with the blood of the witnesses of Jesus" (Rev. 17:6). Although there is a historical element to this, the prophecy is primarily speaking of last-days martyrdom. The persecution of the great harlot will result in the culmination of Satan's rage against the saints down throughout biblical history. This is why the prophecy concludes with such a strong note: "The blood of prophets and saints, and of all those slaughtered on earth, was found in you" (Rev. 18:24 HCSB). How well do Mecca, Saudi Arabia, and Islam fulfill this description?

EARLY ISLAMIC CONQUESTS

After Muhammad's death in June, AD 632, his best friend, Abu Bakr, became his successor. Under the leadership of Abu Bakr and his general, Khalid ibn al-Walid—known as the Sayf-Allah al-Maslul (the drawn sword of Allah)—the new Muslim movement exploded north out of the Arabian Peninsula and into the Middle East, including the regions of modern-day Jordan, southern Syria, and Iraq. After two years, Abu Bakr died and was succeeded by Umar, another of Muhammad's trusted friends. Umar reigned for ten years. During his rule, Islam expanded at an unprecedented rate, conquering Persia, much of North Africa, and more than two-thirds of the Byzantine Empire.[1] The third Caliphate, under Uthman, brought the Islamic conquest all the way to Afghanistan, and north into Armenia. If one works carefully through the history of all that unfolded during these years—the Christian cities destroyed, the Christians murdered, the women and children who were taken as slaves—the numbers are absolutely devastating.[2] This is a part of history that is rarely taught in the secular universities today that seem so determined to engage in historical revisionism to cast Islam in a favorable light.

Here are the facts: Within four years after Muhammad died, roughly a third of a million Christians were slaughtered. Over the next ten years, another million were killed. After six hundred years of the church expanding through the entire Mediterranean region and the Middle East, in just one generation the ancient heart of the church was crushed. All of the great ancient capitals and missionary-sending cities of Christianity throughout the region came under Islamic domination. Antioch, Jerusalem, Alexandria, as well as Ephesus and the other six churches of Revelation were all reduced to struggling outposts of the Christian world. Within a quick one hundred years, 50 percent of global Christianity had come under Islamic subjugation and rule.[3]

ISLAM'S WAR AGAINST THE JEWS

The Islamic conquests were no less kind to the Jews. Consider the testimony of Maimonides, the great Jewish sage who lived in Spain and Egypt, both of which came under Islamic control during the Middle Ages:

> The nation of Ishmael . . . persecute us severely and devise ways to harm us and to debase us . . . None has matched it in debasing and humiliating us. None has been able to reduce us as they have. We have done as our sages of blessed memory instructed us, bearing the lies and absurdities of Ishmael. We listen, but remain silent . . . In spite of all this, we are not spared from the ferocity of their wickedness, and their outbursts at any time. On the contrary, the more we suffer and choose to conciliate them, the more they choose to act belligerently toward us.[4]

THE SAUDI WAR AGAINST ISRAEL AND THE JEWS

While the West is still just beginning to truly feel the sting of terrorism, the pain has long been felt by Israelis, who have always been the Muslim world's first front. The Saudis most often try to hide their connection to terrorism throughout Europe and in the United States (such as on 9/11), but when it comes to Israel, they have barely attempted to hide their support for the Islamic terrorists. For years, through the Saudi Committee for the Support of the al-Quds Intifada (SCSQI), the Saudis have provided the surviving families of Palestinian suicide bombers with a $25,000 reward.

As far back as 2002, Saudi Arabia held a national telethon to raise funds for SCSQI. Saudi Prince Alwaleed bin Talal pledged $27 million. The telethon was hosted by a prominent Saudi-government cleric, Sheikh Saad al-Buraik, who, during the live television coverage, told the audience:

> I am against America until this life ends, until the Day of Judgment, I am against America even if the stone liquefies. My hatred of America, if part of it was contained in the universe, it would collapse. She is the root of all evils and wickedness on Earth . . .

Muslim Brothers in Palestine, do not have any mercy, neither compassion on the Jews, their blood, their money, their flesh. Their women are yours to take, legitimately. God made them yours. Why don't you enslave their women? Why don't you wage jihad? Why don't you pillage them?[5]

The overall contribution by the Saudi royal family was roughly $50 million. After loud protests from America, another Saudi Prince, Naif bin Abdulaziz, the Saudi minister of interior from 1975 to 2012, defiantly declared in a statement: "The committee will continue to provide direct assistance to the families of Palestinian martyrs and those wounded while resisting the occupation."[6] The Middle East Media Research Institute, in July 2003, published a report on the Saudi royal family's financial support to the Palestinians from 1998 through 2003. The report states:

> For decades the royal family of the Kingdom of Saudi Arabia has been the main financial supporter of Palestinian groups fighting Israel, through the creation of two major committees. The Popular Committee for Assisting Palestinian Mujahideen and The Support Committee for the Al-Quds Intifada and The Al-Aqsa Fund have to date given over 15 billion Saudi Riyals (4 billion $U.S.) and reportedly pledged Palestinians up to 1 billion dollars to finance the continuation of the Intifada, which is also commonly referred to by Saudi officials as "Jihad" and "resistance."[7]

I've often heard it charged that the true problem in the Middle East is Israel: had Israel not been restored in the Middle East, Muslims and Jews would enjoy peaceful relations. This opinion ignores the obvious fact that Islam's anti-Semitic history extends all the way back to Muhammad himself. Anti-Semitism is a foundational part of Islamic doctrine, which is why in 1937, long before Israel was formed as a state, Ibn Saud, the founder of modern Saudi Arabia, told one reporter, "The word of God teaches us—and we implicitly believe this—that for a Muslim to kill a Jew, or for him to be killed by a Jew [in Jihad] ensures him an immediate entry in Heaven and into the august presence of God Almighty."[8]

Of course, the hatred and bloodlust of the harlot is directed not only toward the Jewish people, but also toward Christians, and ultimately, toward the whole world (see Rev. 18:24).

DRUNK ON BLOOD

Today, the most violent jihadist terrorist organizations in the world find their ideological roots in Saudi Arabia. Whether we are speaking of al-Qaeda (global), ISIS (Syria, Iraq, Libya, Sinai), the Taliban (Afghanistan), Abu Sayyaf (Philippines), Lashkar-e-Taiba (Pakistan), Jabhat al-Nusra (Syria), Al-Shabab (Somalia), or Boko Haram (Nigeria), they are all Salafi groups whose ideological roots extend directly to the Kingdom of Saudi Arabia. If there is one nation in the world that is most guilty for the vast number of terrorist attacks that continue to expand throughout the earth over the past few decades, there can be no question it would be Saudi Arabia.[9]

It has been well documented that many of the Saudi royals fund or support radical Wahhabi/Salafi Islam and jihad. In Gerald Posner's exposé of life in Saudi Arabia, *Why America Slept*, Posner details a truly fascinating story. In the very early days of the war in Afghanistan, just after 9/11, American troops had captured Osama bin Laden's number three man (at the time), named Abu Zubaydah. The American military devised a scheme that they believed would make Zubaydah talk. He was taken to a CIA facility in Afghanistan that had been created to resemble the inside of a Saudi Arabian military prison. Zubaydah was led to believe that he had been turned over to the Saudi authorities. Two Arab-American Special Forces soldiers interrogated him. The reasoning was that if Zubaydah believed that he was really in Saudi custody, the fear of harsh torture would cause him to talk or agree to cooperate with the (far less harsh) Americans.

But something very unexpected happened. As soon as Zubaydah "realized" that he was in Saudi custody, he was entirely relieved.

He simply told his interrogators to call one of two cell phone numbers that he rattled off from memory. Call, Zubaydah assured them, and "he will tell you what to do."

"The subterfuge backfired," Posner wrote. The CIA was shocked to find out that the cell numbers belonged to Prince Ahmed bin Salman Abdul Aziz, the nephew of then King Fahd. Prince Ahmed was a Western-educated businessman and one of the wealthiest of the Saudi royals. His father had been the governor of Riyadh, the capital of Saudi Arabia, for more than forty years.[10]

ALMS FOR JIHAD

In 2006, an unprecedented work, *Alms for Jihad: Charity and Terrorism in the Islamic World* by J. Millard Burr and Robert O. Collins, was published by Cambridge University Press. This rather exhaustive book documents numerous examples of terrorism financing from prominent members of the Saudi royal family and government. Not surprisingly, Khalid Salim A. Bin Mahfouz, a Saudi billionaire, banker, and former chairman of the National Commercial Bank, who was identified as a financier of al-Qaeda, sued the publisher to have the book removed from circulation. In an unprecedented move, the publisher agreed and the books were literally pulled from bookstores and libraries. Today the book is nearly impossible to get apart from various pirated files on the Internet. There is a critical lesson here. Not only has Saudi money often gone to support global terrorist organizations, but it has consistently silenced any whistleblowers. In fact, the Saudi royal family's compliance with radical Islamic jihad is perhaps one of the most well-known but least discussed facts in Washington and at the UN. In a 2002 briefing to the Pentagon, the Defense Policy Board Advisory Committee—a federal advisory think tank for the US Department of Defense—referred to Saudi Arabia with perhaps more candor than anyone in Washington had ever dared to speak in public:

Saudi Arabia is the chief vector of the Arab crises and its out-wardly directed aggression. The Saudis are active at every level of the terror chain, from planners to financiers, from cadre to foot-soldier, from ideologist to cheerleader.[11]

While President George W. Bush rightly declared that "money is the lifeblood of terrorist operations," according to one damning report sent to the UN Security Council, "Saudi Arabia transferred half a billion dollars to al Qaeda in the ten years beginning in 1992."[12]

Look out at the world today. Look at the nations of North Africa. Consider Nigeria, where nearly seven thousand people were killed in 2014 alone by Boko Haram. Think about the vast number of churches that have been attacked, the number of women who have been kidnapped. Ponder the horrific carnage effected by ISIS across Syria and Iraq. When we see the suffocating shadow cast across Afghanistan by the Taliban, or the terrorist attacks now multiplying across Europe and the United States, this ultimately can all be tied back to the unique form of Islam that flows out of Saudi Arabia like a gushing fountain. Ask just about anyone what Saudi Arabia's primary export is, and he or she will almost always say it is oil. Their first export, however, is radical Islam.

When we study the picture the Scriptures paint of the great harlot, we discover that, rather than feeling any guilt for the blood she has spilled, instead she is proud, intoxicated, and lusting for more. She flaunts and raises her golden cup high, enticing the inhabitants of the world to partake of her maddening wine and the immorality of her false religion. Who better fits that description than Saudi Arabia and its barbarous national, and now increasingly global, religion: Islam?

END-TIME MARTYRDOM—BY BEHEADING

There is one more chilling detail to consider as we study the biblical descriptions of the great harlot, the beast, and the last days. Not only will God's people be martyred during this period; they will be "beheaded":

And I saw the souls of those who had been beheaded because of their testimony of Jesus and because of the word of God, and those who had not worshiped the beast or his image, and had not received the mark on their forehead and on their hand. (Rev. 20:4)

This is certainly a unique and very telling fact. Shall we expect the Vatican to begin beheading Christians all across the earth, specifically because of "their testimony of Jesus"? Shall we expect the United States to begin doing this? Or would it be more reasonable to expect the Muslim world, so deeply influenced by Saudi Arabian Wahhabism, to be responsible for beheading the saints?

On May 30, 2016, the Saudi government executed its ninety-fifth person that year, prompting many to voice concerns over the high number of executions in Saudi Arabia. In 2015, there were 158 people beheaded for various crimes. Among the crimes punishable by beheading is apostasy.[13] That's right. In Saudi Arabia, if someone leaves Islam to become a Christian, he or she may be legally beheaded by the government.

Why are we so determined to look for some new, undefined religion to emerge and begin beheading believers, when such a religion already exists? Once again, the Kingdom of Saudi Arabia perfectly matches the biblical description of the great harlot Babylon.

23

THE PROSTITUTE OF THE DESERT

BY NOW YOU HAVE LEARNED both from Scripture and from the previous chapters that the harlot city of Revelation 17–18 is described as sitting in a desert. Of course, Saudi Arabia itself sits upon the great Arabian Desert. But what's more interesting is that another, traditional name for the kingdom's holiest city, Mecca, is Faran, a reference to the Old Testament's Desert of Paran (see Gen. 21:21 NIV). This Islamic city could not be a more perfect fit for this prophecy.

Of course, the prophecy also describes Mystery Babylon as a port city, which Mecca itself is not; it sits fifty miles inland from the Red Sea. However, in the same way that both Rome and historical Babylon were much more than just cities, the last-days Babylon is likely also more than a city. No doubt, this prophecy is speaking of a broader geopolitical sphere of influence.

Fifty miles to Mecca's west is the port city of Jeddah. Not only is Jeddah the main religious port of the kingdom, serving multiplied millions of pilgrims each year on their way to Mecca and Medina, but it is also the most important commercial hub. As one of the most developed cities in Saudi Arabia, Jeddah boasts a dazzling array of high-rise buildings and luxury hotels that line the shore of the Red Sea. In 2013, the Saudis also began construction on the great Jeddah Tower, planned to become the world's tallest building by 2020, superseding even the Burj Khalifa in Dubai. The Jeddah Tower is slated to become the centerpiece and first phase of a proposed development known as the "Jeddah Economic City." Part of the larger plan also involves building another major city sixty miles to the north, known as King Abdullah Economic City (KAEC). Under construction since 2005, today KAEC is a spider's web of cranes and dozens of partially completed high-rises. A report from BBC News described the city: "At 70 sq miles, KAEC will eventually be a metropolis slightly larger than Washington DC and at a cost of $100bn (£67bn), mostly from private funding, the King Abdullah Economic City is second to none in the grandeur of its vision."[1] The developer, in describing its plans, called it a "mega-port."[2] The goal is to make both Jeddah Economic City and the King Abdullah Economic City the most technologically advanced series of commercial ports in the world, replacing Dubai as the region's commercial hub on one of the world's busiest shipping routes. KAEC will also be home to "Financial Island," the purpose of which is to become the largest regional financial nerve center for the world's leading banks and investment houses.

Connecting the cities of Jeddah, Mecca, Medina, and KAEC will be the Haramain High Speed Rail, also known as the "Western Railway." This train will travel at 190 miles per hour and allow access to any three of the cities in fewer than thirty minutes.

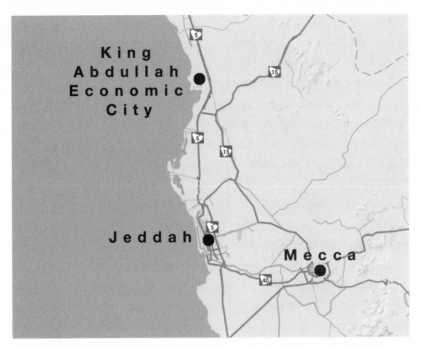

Saudi Arabia's West Coast

It is clear that the cities of Jeddah and KAEC, sitting directly on the shore of the Red Sea, absolutely fulfill Revelation's descriptions of a mighty seaport. In the years ahead, if the Saudis' plans proceed as intended, certainly this will become all the more apparent. While many fine Christian interpreters are presently looking for a powerful economic hub to arise overnight in Babylon, at this very moment such a project is already well under way on the Red Sea. More than $120 billion are being poured into this project. Meanwhile, less than an hour's drive to the east of this emerging financial capital sits the most significant city of religious idolatry that humanity has ever known. All of this will be interconnected by a highly advanced transportation system, essentially making them one unparalleled megacity. Surely all of this must be seen as prophetically significant. In fact, in considering what this regional project will become over the next decade or so, we would seem to have a near perfect fulfillment of the prophecy. While Mecca is no doubt the religious center of gravity of the region, Jeddah, and perhaps KAEC, are the most significant centers of commerce on the Red Sea. Until another megacity emerges in the region that may legitimately contend with Mecca and Jeddah as a religious and financial global capital, there is simply no reason to look elsewhere. For now, the busy coast of the Red Sea and the great harlot city of Mecca would seem to fulfill the biblical descriptions of Mystery Babylon.

A CONSUMER KINGDOM

In chapter 11 I pointed out that Mystery Babylon is primarily a consumer, not a producer of goods. While merchants grow rich from all of the goods that she purchases and imports, it seems the only thing she exports is her false religion. As a desert nation whose wealth comes almost exclusively from the sales of oil, a resource that flows out of the ground, Saudi Arabia imports nearly everything. Laurent Murawiec wrote:

> Since the House of Saud orchestrated soaring oil prices through OPEC, in 1973 and 1974, and again in 1978 and 1979, the Saudi treasury has raked in the almost unimaginable sum of two trillion dollars, that is, an average of nearly $80 billion each year . . . The sums of money fall like manna: fortunes are made without effort, without work, without investment, without scientific research, without technological innovation. All of that is imported.[3]

A KINGDOM OF SLAVERY

In chapter 2, I mentioned that the last-days Babylon will be an importer of, among other things, "slaves and human lives" (Rev. 18:13). Certainly human trafficking could be in view in this passage. But could it be that that's not all? Might there be another, deeper meaning implied by this phrase—something that might further implicate and identify Saudi Arabia as the great harlot city?

There is no other nation in the world where such an incredibly large percentage of its population is made up of noncitizens. Saudi Arabia is a nation filled with foreign nationals and expatriate workers. In fact, one out of every three of those living in the kingdom are not even citizens. Over 90 percent of all nongovernmental jobs are filled by foreign laborers.[4] According to Saudi labor minister Dr. Ghazi al-Ghosaibi, there are roughly 9 million foreign workers in Saudi Arabia.[5] Comparatively, there are fewer than 19 million Saudi citizens living in the kingdom.

The conditions that so many of these foreign workers face have been a constant source of criticism from human rights groups. Everything from torture, to unfair trials, to forced confinement, to physical abuse and rape; all of these things are widely reported. Consider the following statement by Human Rights Watch staffer Sarah Leah Whitson: "We found men and women in conditions resembling slavery . . . Case after case demonstrates that the Saudis are turning a blind eye to systematic abuses against foreign workers."[6] Murawiec wrote of the

> six million immigrants who do the work—Americans, Europeans, Indians, Pakistanis, Filipinos, Egyptians and Palestinians, Yemenites, Koreans, all mercenaries deprived of their basic rights, virtual slaves who keep the machine running, who assemble, repair, manage, and construct. . . . The kingdom consumes. . . . The Saudis . . . despises those who produce.[7]

Leading affluent lives themselves, many Saudi households employ foreign nationals as servants to do household chores, such as cooking and cleaning. Many of these foreign workers come from poorer Asian countries. A large number are hired from Sri Lanka and the Philippines. Their employment is subject to a contract, which allows the "master" to hold their passports throughout the duration of the contract; the workers in turn are paid very low wages. Also, the worker cannot leave the country without the sponsor's permission, and females may not leave the country without a male escort.

There have been many reports of female servants being sexually harassed and raped.

But slavery? Surely this is an exaggeration. Surely actual slavery is not compatible with Saudi culture or laws! Actually, in 2003, prominent Saudi sheikh Saleh Al-Fawzan rather brazenly declared that "slavery is a part of Islam."[8] When we understand who Al-Fawzan is, this becomes all the more stunning. As historian and commentator Daniel Pipes reminds us, "Al-Fawzan is no maverick." He is a member of the Senior Council of Clerics, Saudi Arabia's highest religious body, and of the Council of Religious Edicts and Research; he is the imam of the prominent Prince Miteb Mosque in the Saudi capital city of Riyadh; and he is a professor at Imam Mohamed Bin Saud Islamic University.[9]

To this day, the Saudi Arabian government continues to refuse to sign the United Nations treaties on slavery or other human rights issues because they do not want to be subject to their provisions. They will not sign extradition treaties even with Washington. They constantly declare they are free of slavery yet refuse any international scrutiny that might indicate otherwise.

HAREMS AND SEX SLAVES

There are too many examples of kidnapping and international human trafficking into Saudi Arabia for the purpose of sexual exploitation and slavery to even begin to address here. Some years ago, an organization called Americans against the Sauduction of Washington was formed largely by the parents of those who are convinced their children were taken to Saudi Arabia as sex slaves. A brief account from the Sauduction website tells of the son of the former King Fahd and his involvement in the human trafficking trade:

> King Fahd's sons' control their child sex ring from their Beverly Hills palaces. They learned from the Al-Fassi palace sex scandals in Beverly Hills during the 1980's and rent motels away from their palaces to conduct orgies with children procured for them.

Around these motels they have a cordon of US security guards. An inner cordon is made up of the princes body guards, usually foreign. The younger the child the more desirable. These children are brought up through the sex ring channel to the point of purchase under the modeling or acting ruses of going to a shoot or set in Saudi Arabia. Upon purchase, children are then taken by limousine directly to the Saudi prince's plane at Los Angeles airport. As we mentioned in our prior newsletters, Washington allows Saudi princes and their entourage to circumvent customs and immigration which allows them to ship their child sex slaves out of the US without need of the customary passport. The children are then escorted directly onto the Saudi princes plane and flown to Saudi Arabia never to be seen again.[10]

Endless truly horrid stories can be found on the organization's website describing the free rein the Saudi princes enjoy not only in the United States, but all over the world. In the same way that the Saudis have perverted justice and corrupted the highest levels of political authority in the United States, so also have they looked to the world as their personal marketplace to fulfill their own sexual gratification. It's no wonder the harlot city is referred to as a place that deals in "slaves and human lives," the literal interpretation of which is "the souls of people" (Rev. 18:13).

CONCLUSION

In conclusion, whether we are speaking of the vast number of foreign workers in construction jobs, often abused and living in truly squalid conditions, locked in their trailers at night like property, or the millions of house servants, also treated like slaves, or the uncountable number of concubines and actual sex slaves, the Kingdom of Saudi Arabia is the "poster girl" for the harlot Babylon. Surely, this is why, just before her final judgment, the Lord calls out to His people to flee before His wrath consumes the whole land:

Come out of her, my people, so that you will not share in her sins, so that you will not receive any of her plagues; for her sins are piled up to heaven, and God has remembered her crimes. (Rev. 18:4–5 NIV)

24

THE HATED HARLOT OF
THE MIDDLE EAST

ANOTHER VERY TELLING PORTION of the harlot prophecy of Revelation 17–18 concerns the nature of her destruction. While her judgment clearly comes directly from the throne of God, as you saw earlier, quite shockingly and ironically it is carried out by the very beast that she is riding:

> And the ten horns which you saw, and the beast, these will hate the harlot and will make her desolate and naked, and will eat her flesh and will burn her up with fire. For God has put it in their hearts to execute His purpose (Rev. 17:16–17)

The beast in this passage, as mentioned earlier, is an alliance of ten kings who will submit themselves and their nations to the

Antichrist. This is the revived empire of the Antichrist. If this empire is Islamic, as I have argued, why would such a coalition ever turn on Saudi Arabia? If the Kingdom of Saudi Arabia is the primary ideological and financial source of the global Islamic revival, then why would any coalition of Muslim nations be opposed to her? Although at first glance this may seem a bit unusual, it actually makes perfect sense, as you will see.

WHY THE SAUDI ROYAL FAMILY IS SO HATED

Many Westerners are not aware that the perception of the Saudi royal family throughout the Middle East, and most specifically by more devout Muslims, is very negative. For one, the royals are hated because of their friendly relationship to the United States. According to *Sleeping with the Devil* author Robert Baer:

> There's actually more than enough rage against the West and Riyadh and against the House of Sa'ud. It's in the air in Riyadh and Jeddah's bazaars: the conviction that all the money and oil money has corrupted the ruling family beyond redemption, that the Saudi leaders have defiled the faith by allowing U.S. troops into the kingdom. Getting rid of the American military might help, but the grief against the ruling family runs further than the United States.[1]

There is also the simple matter of class envy. As a general rule, no matter where you go, nearly everyone loves to hate the rich. With the financial chasm between the Saudi ruling class and the average Saudi citizens growing ever wider, so also is the hatred for the royal family expanding. Observers of Saudi society are ever warning of looming revolution and uprisings. Baer describes Saudi Arabia simply as "a powder keg waiting to explode."[2]

Beyond disapproval of the Saudis' relationship with the United States and class envy, everyone hates hypocrites—especially religious hypocrites. In the world of religious hypocrisy, the Saudi royal family are truly the kings. On one hand they promote and fund the global spread of the most radical and puritanical form of Islam known to man, yet on the other hand they live the classic *A Thousand and One Nights* lifestyle of reckless hedonism, absolute perversity, and utter corruption. Rumors, whispers, and anecdotes abound as to how the Saudis really live behind closed doors. Stories of alcoholism (alcohol is illegal in Saudi Arabia), rampant drug abuse, serial rape, orgies, homosexuality, child molestation, and any variety of other profoundly non-Islamic activities that you can imagine seem to flourish within the Saudi royal family. According to well-respected journalist and author Said Aburish, King Saud, who ruled the kingdom from 1953 to 1964, was a notorious alcoholic and a homosexual pedophile.[3] Although the king had more than a hundred wives by the age of fifty-two, this was not enough to quench his lusts.[4] According to investigative journalist Gerald Posner, Saud's father, Ibn Saud, on a rare venture outside of his country into Egypt, actually said to the foreign minister, "This country is full of pretty women and I would like to buy some of them and take them home. How about 100,000 (Egyptian pounds) worth of them?"[5] In equally tacky form, Ibn Saud's grandsons, while traveling to Paris and London, paid prostitutes with solid gold watches that had a picture of their father, King Saud, on the dial.[6]

In 2002, one of the Saudi royals, Nayef bin Sultan bin Fawwaz al Shaalan, was indicted by a Florida grand jury on charges of using his own personal airplane to transport over two tons of cocaine from Caracus to Apris.[7] Baer wrote of the numerous private estates that different Saudi princes have built along the Mediterranean specifically for entertaining prostitutes and having wild parties away from the prying control of the Saudi religious police, or more properly, the Committee for the Promotion of Virtue and the Prevention of Vice. He cited one horrific story out of Morocco that he became aware of while working for the CIA:

[A] Saudi prince with well-placed friends in Washington had bitten off the breast of a young Moroccan girl in a drunken frenzy. King Hassan [of Morocco] swiftly had the incident covered up. The girl's family was paid off, and she was told she would keep her mouth shut or spend the rest of her life in jail.[8]

Just as the stories of excessively lavish lifestyle among the Saudi royals abound, so also do stories of perversion, corruption, and colossal hypocrisy simply roll on and on and on. While presenting themselves as the paragons of Islamic virtue, they live far worse than most infidels.

This leads to another critical reason why so many Islamists wish to see the Saudi government defeated. The Saudi royal family are royalty simply because they say they are. Before the last century, there was no "Kingdom" in Saudi Arabia whatsoever. The concept of a monarchy is viewed as a Western or even a pagan form of government that has no legitimate place within a truly Islamic society. Those who strive to obey the tenets of Islam seek an Islamic government—a caliphate—not a kingdom. Many Islamists would love nothing more than to see an Islamic form of government gain control over the vast amount of oil wealth presently monopolized by the Saudi monarchy.

IRAN

Beyond understanding the deep-seated desire of the Wahhabi radicals to displace the Saudi royal family from power, one also needs to understand the threat from their Shi'a opponents. Today the Middle East is deeply divided. On one side are the Sunni Muslims, (roughly 87 percent of the total Muslim world), and on the other side are the Shi'a (roughly 12 percent of the Muslim world). Presently most would see Saudi Arabia as the alpha dog of the Sunni world, while there is no question that Iran leads the Shi'a world. This rivalry is far deeper than most realize, extending all the way back to Islam's beginnings. Today, many Wahhabi Muslims view Shi'a Muslims as worse than the worst kind of infidels. In the ISIS-controlled portions of Syria and Iraq, one is far safer as a Christian than as a Shi'a Muslim. Most Shi'a Muslims who live in Saudi Arabia work in the eastern provinces among the oil wells that line the coast. In 2016, protests began to grip the eastern province that were reminiscent of similar protests that had gripped the province during the Arab Spring in 2011. Protesters shouted the slogans, "The people want the fall of the regime," as well as, "Down with the al-Saud family."[9] In response, the Saudi government actually executed forty-seven Shi'a Muslims along with a highly respected Shi'a cleric, Sheikh Nimr al-Nimr. In Iran, as soon as the news broke out, protesters stormed the Saudi embassy in Tehran and set it on fire. The Iranian government also renamed the street the Saudi embassy is on after Sheikh Nimr al-Nimr. One Iranian news outlet declared that the execution "has brought the weak foundations of the bloodthirsty government of Saudi Arabia closer to collapse."[10] For many years, Saudi Arabia and Iran have been competing to be the alpha dog of the region. The notion of an attack coming from Iran against the kingdom is not at all out of the question. In fact, with the Middle East increasingly melting down into chaos, such a conflict is probably inevitable.

TURKEY

Arguably, an even larger threat to Saudi Arabia is the nation of Turkey. The Turks, through the Ottoman Empire, ruled much of the Middle East for roughly five hundred years. Until the Ottoman Caliphate was disbanded in 1923, the Turks controlled the Hijaz— the whole west coast of Saudi Arabia, including the cities of Mecca, Medina, and Jeddah. The Turks also have a very long memory, and with the rise of the conservative Islamist AKP party in Turkey, many Turks are turning their attention back to their former dominion. In the same way that Iran would love to take out the Saudis, so also is Turkey yearning for the day when they once again control the Arabian Peninsula.

We shouldn't be surprised to learn that there is also much scriptural evidence that Turkey will rise to become the leader of the coming Islamic Antichrist empire. I detail many of those reasons in my books *Mideast Beast* (WND, 2012) and *Islamic Antichrist* (WND, 2009). In fact, as far back as 2004 (when *Islamic Antichrist* was written), I predicted the rise of Turkey exactly as we've watched it unfold over the past thirteen years. In 2004 I stated:

> While presently, there is not any pressing reason to see Turkey as the leader of an imminent world empire, this is nevertheless, what Ezekiel prophesied . . . The Turkish Empire was the seat of the Islamic Caliphate. It was not until 1923 that the Islamic Caliphate was officially abolished. Today the Islamic world is awaiting the restoration of that Caliphate. The Bible teaches that someday soon the Turkish Empire will be revived.[11]

If this is the case, it also makes perfect sense that once the Antichrist has consolidated his power over the ten kings, he would turn his attention to Saudi Arabia. In fact, a careful reading of Ezekiel 38–39 reveals that this coming Antichrist empire will include Iran, which makes an attack on Saudi Arabia all the more likely. No doubt, this is exactly why the Scriptures declare that "the ten horns . . . and the beast, these will hate the harlot and will make her desolate and naked, and will eat her flesh and will burn her up with fire" (Rev. 17:16).

GEARING UP FOR A SHOWDOWN—THE SAUDI MILITARY

The Saudi royal family is very conscious of their predicament. For this reason, like David Koresh and the Branch Davidians, they have armed themselves to the teeth in preparation for the proverbial day of judgment. For the past few decades, the Saudis have been busy purchasing and stockpiling weapons as fast as the American arms dealers can produce them. The Saudis spend a tremendous percentage of their GDP on military. According to Robert Baer:

The Saudi Government probably spends more per capita than any other country in the world on arms. (It acknowledges only that it spends 13 percent of its gross domestic product, but half of its revenue is earmarked for military.)[12]

The United States in comparison spends only roughly 4 percent of its gross domestic product per year on military.[13] The Saudis seemingly have as many weapons as they have grains of sand. While being so well armed helps them avoid any regional wars, it increases their chances of being hit very fast and very hard should a full war ever erupt with another nation. Is it possible that the kingdom could someday sustain a full-blown nuclear attack? If the oil fields on the eastern shores of the kingdom were taken out, it is reasonable to suggest that the entire Western economy would suffer tremendously, if it survived at all. Interestingly, such a massive and sudden blow is certainly in keeping with the description that we find in the book of Revelation of a city that "in one day . . . will be burned up with fire" (18:8), never to be inhabited again, whose smoke will rise and smolder "forever and ever" (18:21–19:3).

25

SUMMARY AND CONCLUSION

IN THIS CHAPTER I WILL SUMMARIZE all the ways that Mecca/ Saudi Arabia match the scriptural criteria and descriptions of the harlot city in the book of Revelation.

A LITERAL PLACE: The last-days harlot Babylon is a very real and identifiable geopolitical entity. So are both the city of Mecca and the Kingdom of Saudi Arabia.

A DESERT CITY: The harlot city sits specifically in a desert. Mecca/ Saudi Arabia obviously match this description perfectly.

A PORT OR COASTAL CITY: The Bible seems to indicate that the harlot city is a port city, or at least close to the sea. Mecca sits fifty miles inland from Jeddah and the emerging King Abdullah Economic City, which are both presently being built specifically to become the world's most technologically advanced and active seaports. These three cities form a triangle in relative close proximity to one another and will be linked together by a high-speed train system allowing travel from any city to the other in about thirty minutes.

A CONSUMER, NOT A PRODUCER: Harlot Babylon imports everything. She does not appear to be a great producer in terms of manufacturing or agriculture. The earth's merchants have grown rich from all of the goods that she purchases. This is a perfect description of Saudi Arabia. Other than its oil, it produces very little and must import nearly everything.

THE GREATEST CITY OF IDOLATRY: Babylon "the great" is called "the mother of harlots and . . . abominations" (Rev. 17:5). She is the greatest source of false religion and idolatry ever known. Because Islam is the world's second-largest religion, with 1.61 billion Muslims, the city of Mecca is absolutely the unqualified greatest city of idolatry that has ever existed. No other city in human history can compare.

A RELIGIOUS CAPITAL AND MISSIONARY CENTER: The last-days Babylon is specifically a missionary-sending force, spreading her false religion all over the world and holding sway over "kings, . . . peoples and multitudes and nations and tongues" (Rev. 17:2, 15). Over the past forty years, the Kingdom of Saudi Arabia has spent well over $100 billion to spread Islam all over the world. No religious, political, or national evangelistic or propaganda campaign in human history has ever come close to equaling this.

A SEDUCER OF KINGS AND PEOPLES. That the harlot "reigns over the kings of the earth" (Rev. 17:18) and that they in turn "commit acts of immorality with her" (Rev. 18:3) makes it clear that the influence of this city is indeed global. Saudi Arabia exerts its influence over much of the world either through Islam or through outright bribery and oil blackmail. For the past few generations, no corporation, nation, or bank in the world has given a fraction of the money that the Saudi royal family has given to the past several American presidents.

A CITY OF EXCESS LUXURY. The last-days harlot is a city of extreme luxury and material excess (Rev. 17:4; 18:7). Saudi Arabia, unlike any other nation on earth, is specifically known for its absolutely excessive materialism and luxury. From gold-plated toilets to fleets of custom-made Rolls-Royces, the Saudi royal family's over-the-top excess is unparalleled and world renowned.

AN ECONOMIC SEDUCER. The harlot Babylon's material excess serves to greatly amplify her seduction and influence far beyond what she can accomplish through her religion alone. Both "merchants" and "shipmasters" have "become rich through the abundance of her luxury" (18:3, 9). All of this material wealth is directly responsible for the kings of the earth joining in with her spiritual corruption and bloodshed (17:2; 18:3). Needless to say, Saudi Arabia has not only corrupted the "kings of the earth," but she has also seduced innumerable banks, corporations, "great men of the earth" and, in fact, "all the nations" (18:23).

A CITY OF SLAVERY. The last-days Babylon is an importer of "slaves and human lives" (Rev. 18:13). Literally one-third of the entire population of Saudi Arabia are foreign workers, many of whom are treated worse than slaves. Secular human rights groups report endless stories of poor treatment, abuse, imprisonment, and rape that affect the roughly nine million foreign workers living in Saudi Arabia.

A CITY THAT MURDERS BOTH JEWS AND CHRISTIANS. The Scriptures state that the Harlot is "drunk with the blood of the saints, and with the blood of the witnesses of Jesus. . . . In her was found the blood of prophets . . . and of all who have been slain on the earth" (Rev. 17:6; 18:24). Saudi Arabia is not only the single greatest financier of the Palestinian Intifada, and the greatest lobbying power at the UN against the State of Israel, but it is also the primary ideological and financial fountainhead of nearly every radical Islamist jihadi organization in the world. ISIS, al-Qaeda, Boko Haram, and other jihadist groups that murder Christians, are all the fruit of Saudi Arabia's global Wahhabi influence.

SHE REPRESENTS ROYALTY. The harlot is "clothed in purple and scarlet, and adorned with gold and precious stones and pearls" (Rev. 17:4). These colors and adornments speak of the woman as royalty. Saudi Arabia is not a nation in the traditional sense; rather, it is a kingdom. The House of Saud is indeed a royal monarchy.

SHE IS HIDDEN IN PLAIN SIGHT. The harlot brags, "I sit as queen" (Rev. 18:7). This is a direct allusion to Isaiah 47, which reflects the attitude of the last-days Babylon, who in her wickedness also says, "No one sees me" (Isa. 47:10). The picture is of a city governed by both arrogance and secrecy. Despite all of her abundant sins, she somehow manages to fly under the radar of most. This describes Saudi Arabia nearly perfectly. Even as the Saudi royals have bought nearly every major American politician, they now also control various media outlets. Thus the Saudis have corrupted the most powerful nation in the world, and then they have bought that nation's silence.

THE SPIRITUAL AND FINANCIAL CAPITAL OF THE ISLAMIC WORLD: The Scriptures reveal that Babylon is the capital of the seventh and eighth beast empires, which arguably is a reference to the Islamic empire, the only empire to have followed the Roman Empire. If the Islamic end-time theory is true, then identifying the final Babylon is as simple as identifying the spiritual and financial capital of the Islamic world. Mecca is the religious heart of the Islamic world, and Saudi Arabia is the financial heart of the Muslim world, providing over 90 percent of the global funding of Islam.

CONCLUSION

As I stated at the beginning of this book, my most sincere hope was that this work would contribute to the larger discussion concerning the great harlot. Having both carefully assessed the prophecy and considered the primary interpretations that have been offered, I believe I have sufficiently demonstrated that Mecca/Saudi Arabia seems to fulfill all of the scriptural requirements of the harlot Babylon. To be clear, this is not to say that another option, a new city entirely, could not emerge in the future. For now, however, the view that Mecca is the last-days Babylon is not only a very legitimate view, but it would also seem to be the best option. Of course, even if the Kingdom of Saudi Arabia is not the ultimate last-days Babylon, it is clearly one of the greatest fulfillments in human history, and the greatest "Babylon" of this present time. Needless to say, the eschatological, pastoral, and missiological implications are profound.

On a personal note, if you've read this whole book, then it is probably obvious that in writing it, I've taken on a very real beast and likely exposed myself to all sorts of potential repercussions, whether spiritual, financial, or otherwise. Of course, I wouldn't have written any of these things if I didn't think it was critical for the church to understand. I am firmly convinced that we are living in a moment where remaining silent is simply not an option. There are some issues that no one is speaking about, yet they truly need to be shouted from the rooftops. I believe this is one such issue. That said, I do ask for your prayers for both myself and my family. I genuinely appreciate them.

Until the Day of Christ Jesus, may the Lord bless you and keep you!

AFTERWORD

WE WOULD BE ABSOLUTELY REMISS if we did not conclude this book with some very practical and proper responses to all of the information that we've covered. I want to begin by specifically addressing those readers who have never committed their lives to Jesus Christ. While this book is principally an interpretation of a prophecy from the Christian Scriptures, I know that many who read it may not necessarily be Christian. Perhaps someone handed you this book or you were simply interested by the information about Saudi Arabia and the many profoundly important political implications. Whatever the reason may be, I trust that God Himself had a purpose in getting this book into your hands.

If this is you, then quite simply, the first proper response is to get both your life and your soul in right standing with your Creator. This is simple wisdom. The fact of the matter is that "we must all appear before the judgment seat of Christ, so that each of us may receive what is due us for the things done while in the body, whether good or bad" (2 Cor 5:10 NIV). The day is coming when "God will bring every deed into judgment, including every hidden thing, whether it is good or evil" (Eccl. 12:14 NIV). As Jesus said, "There is nothing concealed that will not be disclosed, or hidden that will not be made known. What you have said in the dark will be heard in the daylight, and what you have whispered in the ear in the inner rooms will be proclaimed from the roofs" (Luke 12:2–3 NIV). God Himself will hack Google, as it were, and everyone's lives will be laid bare before an all-powerful and Holy God.

On its face, this is both terrifying and terrible news. The truth, after all, is that neither you nor I are clean. As the apostle Paul rightly said, "All have sinned and fall short of the glory of God" (Rom. 3:23 NIV), or as Isaiah the prophet expressed it, "We all, like sheep, have gone astray, each of us has turned to our own way" (Isa. 53:6 NIV). Worse yet, the Scriptures declare that "the wages of sin is death" (Rom. 6:23 NIV). Then, whosoever's "name [is] not found written in the book of life [will be] thrown into the lake of fire," where they "will be tormented with burning sulfur in the presence of the holy angels and of the Lamb. And the smoke of their torment will rise for ever and ever. There will be no rest day or night" (Rev. 20:15; 14:10–11 NIV). Jesus Himself described the lake of fire as a place of "eternal punishment" (Matt. 25:46 NIV), where "there will be weeping and gnashing of teeth," both anguish and eternal bitter regret (Matt. 13:42 NIV).

GOD SO LOVED THE WORLD . . .

There is good news, however—very good news! It is quite literally the best news that has ever been told—*if we will hear it.* This good news is summarized well in the famous Bible verse: "God so loved the world that he gave his one and only Son, that whoever believes in him shall not perish but have eternal life" (John 3:16 NIV). Our Creator loved us so deeply, so passionately, that He sent His very Son, His very essence, His very Heart—He sent Himself into the world to take on human flesh, to actually become one of us, ultimately to be mutilated in our place, and to make atonement for our sins. The Bible says that "he was pierced for our transgressions, he was crushed for our iniquities; the punishment that brought us peace was on him, and by his wounds we are healed . . . and the Lord has laid on him the iniquity of us all" (Isa. 53:5–6 NIV).

Peter the apostle appealed to his countrymen:

Repent and be baptized, every one of you, in the name of Jesus Christ for the forgiveness of your sins. And you will receive the gift of the Holy Spirit. The promise is for you and your children and for all who are far off—for all whom the Lord our God will call. (Acts 2:38–39 NIV)

If any of us desire to be saved from our sins and to be spared from being cast forever into the lake of fire, then there is only one way of escape. The Bible tells us that we must acknowledge, turn away from, and renounce our sins. This is the meaning of "repentance." As part of our public confession, we are to be baptized in water, signifying our choice to put to death our old sinful selves, and as we rise from the water, we are raised to new life. As Jesus said, "Whoever believes and is baptized will be saved, but whoever does not believe will be condemned" (Mark 16:16 NIV). We must transfer our faith and confidence from "our righteous acts [which] are like filthy rags" (Isa. 64:6 NIV) to Jesus Christ, placing all of our faith in His shed blood and the atoning work He accomplished for us on the cross. It is this way, and this way only, that we may be washed clean and forgiven. Whoever does this will receive the Holy Spirit. This is the very Spirit of God, who will testify "that we are

God's children" (Rom. 8:16). He will strengthen you to live a holy life, pleasing to God, and He will confirm that on the day of judgment, you will be raised unto eternal life, "guaranteeing what is to come" (2 Cor. 1:22 NIV). You will be spared from the punishment of "everlasting shame and contempt" (Dan. 12:2).

If you have never done this before, but would like to make this most important decision, please contact me through my website, joelstrumpet.com, and I will be happy to pray with you and help you to get started in your new life as a disciple of Jesus Christ. I assure you that though this may be a difficult decision, it will absolutely be the best decision you have ever made. If the Holy Spirit is touching your heart, do not ignore His voice. Do not miss this moment. As the author of the Letter to the Hebrews reminds us all:

> See to it that you do not refuse him who speaks. If they did not escape when they refused him who warned them on earth, how much less will we, if we turn away from him who warns us from heaven? (Heb. 12:25 NIV).

Along with the apostle Peter, I appeal to you from the bottom of my heart, "Save yourselves from this corrupt generation" (Acts 2:40).

THE CHRISTIAN RESPONSE

Now, I would like to speak to those who are already disciples of Jesus. I'm sure that a large percentage of those who read this book—maybe even you—did so simply because they were fascinated, or perhaps just interested, in understanding biblical prophecy. The fact is that the study of biblical prophecy is not merely about revealing secret knowledge and unlocking mysteries. Like any other aspect of biblical theology, this topic has very real application and should very legitimately affect the way that we live.

Unfortunately, the most natural, carnal response to what we've learned about the role of Islam in the last days is to allow fear and dread of what is to come into our hearts. If the theory presented in this book is true, then the fact of the matter is that until Jesus returns, Islam is not going away. Terrorism is not going to dissipate. Quite to the contrary, Islam will continue to expand and force itself onto the world. It will get worse. Whether we like it or not, there is nowhere to hide from what is coming upon the earth. The relevance of the Muslim world and the Middle East specifically will continue to force itself onto all of us. Whether we are speaking of the war in Syria, the global refugee crisis, the transformation of Europe, or who knows what might come next, the contours of the landscape of the end times as described by the biblical prophets are certainly beginning to come into very clear focus.

REJECT FEAR AND HATRED

Some of the most significant warnings in all of Scripture are found in Jesus' Olivet Discourse. The first warning concerns the issue of fear. Speaking of the last days, Jesus said, "There will be signs in sun and moon and stars, and on the earth dismay among nations, in perplexity at the roaring of the sea and the waves, *men fainting from fear and the expectation of the things which are coming upon the world*; for the powers of the heavens will be shaken" (Luke 21:25–26; emphasis added). The second warning concerns another heart issue—the most important heart issue of all, in fact. Again, speaking of the last days, Jesus warned, "Because lawlessness is increased, *most people's love will grow cold*" (Matt. 24:12; emphasis added). I am thoroughly convinced that one of the primary reasons the love of so many will grow cold is specifically because of the fear that will grip the world. Quite simply, fear is crippling. When fear gets ahold of the human heart, it snuffs out the ability to truly love as Jesus did.

In this age of increasing lawlessness, wickedness, and bloodshed, my heartfelt appeal to anyone who will listen is to resist the temptation to allow fear or hatred into your heart. Whether we like it or not, we can either live lives of safety or we can live like Jesus. We cannot do both. In the days ahead, the bloodshed is going to explode across the nations. The more it does, the more many voices will arise, claiming to speak on behalf of wisdom, claiming to have all of the answers, to know all the solutions. The push for more conservative legislation and greater military action will increasingly be the cry of many throughout the West. To be very clear, I am a constitutional conservative. I believe in responsible stewardship. Striving to elect leaders of integrity, pushing for righteous laws, and making wise decisions militarily are matters that are all very important to me. No doubt, I could speak extensively about freeing ourselves from dependence on Middle Eastern oil, and breaking away from the corrupting influence of Saudi Arabia. We could speak at length about wise immigration policies and intelligent border security. Certainly all of these things are incredibly important. The truth, however, is that neither military, nor legal, nor political solutions will ever actually solve the ultimate problems that we are facing. The Bible is clear that apart from the return of Jesus, our present situation is rather hopeless. It doesn't mean we do not do what needs to be done. We do not, however, place our hope in these things. We fix our hope in Jesus and the age to come. The return of Jesus is our only hope. Until He returns, we must move forward as wise as serpents, faithfully stewarding all that He has entrusted to us, but to be blunt, we need to die to the notion that we can save this world. To be clear, in no way am I advocating abandonment or abdication. I am simply saying that our anchor of hope should not be in temporal efforts or solutions. Without giving up on political activism, as Christians Jesus has given us a far greater mandate. Our emphasis is to be on something far more important, and having far more permanence.

PUT THE GOSPEL FIRST

As obedient disciples of Jesus, our primary emphasis must be to "go into all the world and preach the gospel to all creation" (Mark 16:15). We are to give a faithful witness concerning the Day of the Lord, the judgment of all mankind, the atonement Jesus has provided, and the glorious kingdom to come. This is the good news! This is "the power of God for salvation" (Rom. 1:16). It is only this message that can save anyone from sin. It is only this message that delivers anyone from the eternal lake of fire. This then, more than any other issue, needs to be our driving emphasis, our burning passion. Ten thousand years from now, who won the next election or won the next war will be irrelevant. Those who were won to Christ in these days, though, will be eminently relevant. Now, while most might agree that the gospel is to be premier, the truth is that actually making it a priority is never going to happen unless we are willing to embrace the cross.

EMBRACE THE CROSS

There is only one way forward: the way of the cross. The way of the cross, however, is not a popular message, particularly in American culture, including American Christian culture. Simply stated, the way of the cross is the way of laying down one's life. This is part of the reason Paul spoke of "the offense of the cross" (Gal. 5:11 NIV). No one enjoys suffering. No one desires to die or to make sacrifices. Yet this is precisely what Jesus has called us to: "For whoever wishes to save his life will lose it, but whoever loses his life for My sake and the gospel's will save it" (Mark 8:35). How much more offensive is it, then, that Jesus calls us to actually lay down our lives for our enemies? As He said, "Love your enemies and pray for those who persecute you. . . . Do good to those who hate you" (Matt. 5:44; Luke 6:27). The reason is simple. The Scriptures teach that "while we were enemies we were reconciled to God through the death of His Son" (Rom. 5:10). "God demonstrates His own love toward us, in that while we were yet sinners, Christ died for us" (Rom. 5:8), and we are called to imitate Him. As Peter wrote, "[we] have been called for this purpose, since Christ also suffered for you, leaving you an example for you to follow in His steps" (1 Peter 2:21).

To be very clear, I fully believe that Islam is that which was spoken of by the Lord through the prophets and that what we are seeing unfold throughout the world right now is the fulfillment of prophecy. I believe that in the days ahead, radical Islam will continue to expand and explode throughout the nations. I also want to state emphatically, however, that if this information leads you to withdraw into fear, hatred, or self-protectionism, then you have not responded as the Lord wants you to. If you are a Christian, then imitating and following Jesus is the only response. As Paul solemnly warned the believers in Rome:

> The hour has already come for you to wake up from your slumber, because our salvation is nearer now than when we first believed. The night is nearly over; the day is almost here. (Rom. 13:11–12)

The more that Satan seeks to raise up an army of his own from among the sons of Ishmael, the more the followers of Jesus should make it their priority to snatch as many from the fire as possible. Now is not the moment to make self-preservation our highest priority. Now is the hour when giving ourselves to see Muslims come to faith must become one the highest priorities of the body of Christ!

CONCLUSION

If the things that we've discussed in this book are true, then yes, the days ahead are only going to become much more difficult. As the great storms of the last days sweep through the nations, we must take comfort in the conclusion of the prophecy. For as much as the things spoken throughout the book of Revelation are real, so also is the Lord's great victory that will follow. It is for this reason that at the fall of Babylon, the angels break out in such exuberant rejoicing. With the angels, let us also rejoice in the soon-coming day of God's great victory:

> "Hallelujah! Salvation and glory and power belong to our God; Because His judgments are true and righteous; for He has judged the great harlot who was corrupting the earth with her immo-

rality, and He has avenged the blood of His bond servants on her." And a second time they said, "Hallelujah! Her smoke rises up forever and ever. And the twenty-four elders and the four living creatures fell down and worshiped God who sits on the throne saying, "Amen. Hallelujah!" And a voice came from the throne, saying, "Give praise to our God, all you His bond-servants, you who fear Him, the small and the great." Then I heard something like the voice of a great multitude and like the sound of many waters and like the sound of mighty peals of thunder, saying, "Hallelujah! For the Lord our God, the Almighty, reigns. Let us rejoice and be glad and give the glory to Him, for the marriage of the Lamb has come and His bride has made herself ready." It was given to her to clothe herself in fine linen, bright and clean; for the fine linen is the righteous acts of the saints. Then he said to me, "Write, 'Blessed are those who are invited to the marriage supper of the Lamb.'" And he said to me, "These are the true words of God." (Rev. 19:1–9)

To which we all shout ten thousand amens.

NOTES

CHAPTER 1: THE HISTORY OF THE MYSTERY

1. Victorinus of Pettau, *Commentary on the Apocalypse of the Blessed John*, in *The Ante-Nicene Fathers*, vol. 7, *Fathers of the Third and Fourth Centuries: Lactantius, Venantius, Asterius, Victorinus, Dionysius, Apostolic Teaching and Constitutions, Homily, and Liturgies*, eds. and; trans.(Buffalo, NY: Christian Literature Company, 1886), 357–58.
2. Marvin Richardson Vincent, *Word Studies in the New Testament*, vol. 2 (New York: Charles Scribner's Sons, 1887), 545.
3. Andrew of Caesarea, in *The Ancient Christian Commentary on Scripture, New Testament*, vol 12, ed. William C. Weinrich (Downers Grove, IL: IVP, 2005), 226.
4. Nicholas of Lyra, *Nicholas of Lyra's Apocalypse Commentary*, trans. Philip D. W. Kay (Kalamazoo, MI: Medieval Institute Publications, 1997), 189.
5. Ibid., 194.
6. William Tyndale, *The Obedience of a Christian Man*, in Richard Kenneth Emmerson, *Antichrist in the Middle Ages: A Study of Medieval Apocalypticism, Art, and Literature* (Seattle, University of Washington Press, 1981), 205.
7. Alexander Hislop, *The Two Babylons: The Papal Worship Proved to Be the Worship of Nimrod and His Wife*, repr. (London: S. W. Partridge, 1919), 218.
8. C. I. Scofield, ed., *The Scofield Reference Bible: The Holy Bible Containing the Old and New Testaments* (New York; London; Toronto; Melbourne; Bombay: Oxford University Press, 1917), 1347.
9. Douglas W. Kreiger, Dene McGriff, and S. Douglas Woodward, *The Final Babylon: America and the Coming of Antichrist* (Oklahoma City: Faith Happens, 2013), 59–60.
10. Cf. David Chilton, *The Days of Vengeance: An Exposition of the Book of Revelation* (n.p.: Dominion, 2006), 445–66.
11. P. W. L. Walker, ed., *Jerusalem: Past and Present in the Purposes of God*, 2nd ed. (Grand Rapids: Baker, 1994), 58.
12. Chris White, *Mystery Babylon: When Jerusalem Embraces the Antichrist: An Exposition of Revelation 17 & 18* (Ducktown, TN, CWM Publishing, 2013), back cover.
13. John F. Walvoord, "Revelation," in *The Bible Knowledge Commentary: An Exposition of the Scriptures*, eds. J. F. Walvoord and R. B. Zuck, vol. 2 (Wheaton, IL: Victor Books, 1985), 971.
14. "False Ministries (2): Occult Hand Signs—Part 2" *Olivet Journal*, accessed January 30, 2016, http://hebraicprophecyforum.olivetjournal.com/viewtopic.php?f=22&t=371, no longer accessible.
15. Ibid.

16. Joel Richardson, "Standing Firm in the Face of Slander," World Net Daily, August 7, 2012, http://www.wnd.com/2012/08/standing-firm-in-the-face-of-slander/. (The original comment has since been removed.)
17. "Joel Richardson: Double Secret Crypto-Jew?" *Incog Man* (blog), November 7, 2011, http://incogman.net/2011/11/joel-richardson-double-secret-crypto-jew/.
18. Ibid.
19. "False Ministries (2): Occult Hand Signs - Part 2" Olivet Journal, accessed January 30, 2016 http://hebraicprophecyforum.olivetjournal.com/viewtopic.php?f=22&t=371.

CHAPTER 2: THE GREAT CITY

1. A metaphor is simply a figure of speech in which a word or phrase literally signifying one type of thing is said to be another, different thing, to suggest that they are similar in some way. One might say for instance, "Life is a roller coaster." Of course life is not literally a ride at a theme park. The term *roller coaster* is simply used to indicate that life has many emotional and circumstantial ups, downs, and sometimes stomach-churning twists and turns.
2. Robert L. Thomas, *Revelation 8–22: An Exegetical Commentary* (Chicago: Moody, 1995), 290, says, "It is a city, but it is also a vast religious system that stands for everything God does not tolerate."
3. The word "wilderness" is used in the ASV, ESV, KJV, NASB, NET, NIV, NKJV, RSV, and many other translations.
4. Robert L. Thomas, *New American Standard Hebrew-Aramaic and Greek* Dictionaries, upd. ed (Anaheim: Foundation Publications, 1998).
5. Beale comments: "The evil nuance of 'desert' is also suggested by the contrast with the Lamb's bride in 21:9–10, where the 'great and high mountain' is associated with heaven, especially because it is from there that John is able to see the divine city descending from heaven itself." G. K. Beale, *The Book of Revelation: A Commentary on the Greek Text, New International Greek Testament Commentary* (Grand Rapids; Carlisle, UK: Eerdmans; Paternoster Press, 1999), 852.
6. Beale, *The Book of Revelation*, 859.
7. See the classic work on the subject by E. W. Bullinger, *Figures of Speech Used in the Bible, Explained and Illustrated* (London: Messrs. Eyre and Spottiswoode, 1898), 613–52, which has thirty-nine pages of examples of synecdoche in the Bible.

CHAPTER 4: THE NIMROD MYTH

1. C. D. Yonge, trans., *The Works of Philo: Complete and Unabridged* (Peabody, MA: Hendrickson, 1995), 231.
2. Ibid., 157.
3. Ibid.
4. Ibid., 840.
5. Nimrod before and after the Bible, http://www.michaelsheiser.com/PaleoBabble/NimrodHTR.pdf.
6. Charles Duke Yonge with Philo of Alexandria, *The Works of Philo: Complete and Unabridged* (Peabody, MA: Hendrickson, 1995), 840.
7. Ibid.
8. Flavius Josephus, *The Works of Josephus: Complete and Unabridged*, trans. William Whiston (Peabody, MA: Hendrickson, 1987).
9. Ibid.
10. Ibid.
11. As quoted by Josephus, in ibid.
12. Pseudo-Philo called Nimrod's grandfather Ham "Cham"; his father, Cush, "Chus"; and Nimrod "Nebroth."
13. M. R. James, ed., *The Biblical Antiquities of Philo* (New York: KTAV, 1971), 84.
14. Ibid., 90–91.

15.   Ibid.

16.   Ibid., 90–95.

17.   Louis Ginseberg, *The Legends of the Jews*, vol. 1, Classic Reissues (Philadelphia: Jewish Publication Society, 2003), 161.

18.   Ibid.

19.   Ibid., 162–63nn77–87.

20.   Augustine of Hippo, "The City of God," in *St. Augustine's City of God and Christian Doctrine*, ed. Philip Schaff, trans. Marcus Dods, vol. 2, *A Select Library of the Nicene and Post-Nicene Fathers of the Christian Church*, 1st ser. (Buffalo, NY: Christian Literature Co., 1887), 313.

21.   *The Apocalypse of Pseudo-Methodius: An Alexandrian World Chronicle*, Dumbarton Oaks Medieval Library 14, trans. and ed. Benjamin Garstad (Boston, Harvard University Press, 2012), 85.

22.   Also sometimes referred to as *The Apocalypse of Simon*, Clement, *The Testament of Our Lord*, or *The Testament of Our Savior*. The text is extant in Garshuni, Arabic, and Ethiopic and appears to have been written by Arabic Christians in Egypt around 800 CE.

23.   *Kitāb al-Magāll or the Book of Rolls. One of the Books of Clement*, accessed September 9, 2016. http://www.sacred-texts.com/chr/aa/aa2.htm.

24.   *Ancient Book of Jasher: A New Annotated Edition*, ed. Ken Johnson (USA, Biblefacts Ministries/CreateSpace, 2008), 21.

25.   Ibid., 22.

26.   Ibid., 56–57.

27.   Enrique Baez, "Nimrod, Son of Cush," ed. John D. Barry et al., *The Lexham Bible Dictionary* (Bellingham, WA: Lexham Press, 2012, 2013, 2014, 2015).

28.   The 1599 Geneva Bible, margin notes on Genesis 10:8–9. See http://biblehub.com/commentaries/genesis/10-9.htm.

29.   Martin Hengel, *Judaism and Hellenism* (Philadelphia: Fortress, 1981), 2.60n244.

30.   Ginzberg, *Legends of the Jews*, 162n77.

31.   John Chrysostom, Homilies on Genesis 29.29 as quoted in Andrew Louth, ed., *Ancient Christian Commentary on Scripture*, bk. 1, *Genesis 1–11* (Downer's Grove, IL: IVP, 2001), 165.

32.   Ephrem the Syrian, Commentary on Genesis 8.1.2.6 as quoted in Louth, *Ancient Christian Commentary on Scripture* 1.164.

CHAPTER 5: ALEXANDER HISLOP'S TWO BABYLONS

1.   Alexander Hislop, *The Two Babylons: or The Papal Worship Proved to Be the Worship of Nimrod and His Wife* (London, S. W. Partridge, 1858), 35.

2.   Hislop also argued that Nimrod's descent from Cush meant that he was black. The biblical account, however, says no such thing, nor does it logically follow that all of Cush's children were black. Much evidence exists that Asians, for example, are also descendants of Ham, the father of Cush.

3.   Hislop, *The Two Babylons*, 124.

4.   Ralph Woodrow, *The Babylon Connection?* (Palm Springs, CA: Ralph Woodrow Evangelistic Association, 1997), introduction.

5.   Woodrow's books can be purchased through the Ralph Woodrow Evangelistic Association, http://www.ralphwoodrow.org/.

6.   Hislop, *The Two Babylons*, 44.

7.   Ibid.

8.   Ibid., 47.

9.   Ibid., 177.

10.   Ibid., 178.

11.   Ibid., 180.

12.   Ibid.

13.   "Did Jesus Die on a Cross?" Jehovah's Witness Bible Teachings, accessed September 21, 2016, https://www.jw.org/en/bible-teachings/questions/did-jesus-die-on-cross/.

14. Woodrow, *The Babylon Connection?*, 60.
15. Joshua J. Mark, "Semiramis," *Ancient History Encyclopedia*, August 18, 2014, http://www.ancient.eu/Semiramis/.
16. Ibid.
17. Warren Wiersbe, *The Wiersbe Bible Commentary: New Testament*, new ed. David C. Cook (Colorado Springs: Wiersbe Bible Commentaries, 2007), 1073.
18. John Walvoord, *Every Prophecy of the Bible* (Colorado Springs: Chariot Victor, 1999), 605.
19. Paul McGuire and Troy Anderson, *The Babylon Code: Solving the Bible's Greatest End Time Mystery* (New York: Faith Words, 2015), 172.
20. Ibid., 76.
21. Ibid., 45.
22. Ibid.
23. Walvoord, *Every Prophecy of the Bible*, 605.
24. Lectures on Genesis 11.6 as quoted in John L. Thompson, ed., *Reformation Commentary on Scripture Book I, Genesis 1-11* (Downer's Grove, Illinois, IVP 2012), 329.

CHAPTER 6: THE MOTHER OF ALL HARLOTS

1. G. K. Beale, *The Book of Revelation: A Commentary on the Greek Text, New International Greek Testament Commentary* (Grand Rapids; Carlisle, UK: Eerdmans; Paternoster Press, 1999), 857–58.
2. Matthew Henry, *Matthew Henry's Commentary on the Whole Bible: Complete and Unabridged in One Volume* (Peabody, MA: Hendrickson, 1994), 2481.
3. *The American Heritage Dictionary of Idioms*, 2nd ed. (Boston: Houghton Mifflin Harcourt, 2013), 299.
4. R. C. H. Lenski, *The Interpretation of St. John's Revelation* (Columbus, OH: Lutheran Book Concern, 1935), 490.
5. Cf. Ex. 34:15–16; Lev. 20:5–6; Deut. 31:16; 1 Chron. 5:25; Judg. 2:17; 8:27, 33; Ezek. 6:9; 16:17–21, 35–36; 20:30. See also Beale, *The Book of Revelation*, 859.
6. Beale, *The Book of Revelation*, 859.
7. Lenski, *The Interpretation of St. John's Revelation*, 494.
8. The term "daughter of Babylon" is simply a synonym for "Babylon." Zephaniah 3:4, for example, uses multiple similar expressions to refer to Israel or Jerusalem: "Shout for joy, O daughter of Zion! Shout in triumph, O Israel! Rejoice and exult with all your heart, O daughter of Jerusalem!" (cf. 2 Kings 19:21; Isa. 37:22; Lam. 2:13, 15; Mic. 4:8; Zech. 9:9).

CHAPTER 7: THE WOMAN AND THE BEAST

1. The preterist interpretation, which seeks to identify the seven heads simply as seven historical Roman emperors, is fraught with both linguistic and historical problems. As G. K. Beale has stated, "The attempt to identify the seven kings with particular respective world empires may be more successful, since it is more in keeping with the 'seven heads' in Dan. 7:3–7, which represent four specific empires. The first five kings, who 'have fallen,' are identified with Egypt, Assyria, Babylon, Persia, and Greece; Rome is the one who 'is,' followed by a yet unknown kingdom to come." G. K. Beale, *The Book of Revelation: A Commentary on the Greek Text, New International Greek Testament Commentary* (Grand Rapids; Carlisle, UK: Eerdmans; Paternoster Press, 1999), 874.
2. Cf., Ernst Wilhelm Hengstenberg, *The Revelation of St. John: Expounded for Those Who Search the Scripture*, vol. 2, Classic Reprint Series (n.p.: Forgotten Books, 2016), 245–46; J. A. Seiss, *The Apocalypse*, 3rd repr. (Grand Rapids: Zondervan, 1957), 391–93; George Eldon Ladd, *A Commentary on the Revelation of John* (Grand Rapids: Eerdmans, 1971), 227–29; John F. Walvoord, *Revelation*, rev. ed. (Chicago: Moody, 2011), 251–54; see also Friedrich Hermann Christian Düsterdieck and Henry Eyster Jacobs, *Critical and Exegetical Handbook to the Revelation of John* (BiblioBazaar, 2009), 433–34, for a survey of older German commentators who also hold this view.

3. For a more thorough explanation of Daniel 2 and 7, see my book *Mideast Beast: The Scriptural Case for an Islamic Antichrist* (WND, 2012).
4. Although the Parthians and the Sassanids controlled the region, these were Persian kingdoms that should be seen as an extension of the Persians that first conquered Babylon. The Islamic empire was the one that finally concurred with the Persians.
5. R. C. H. Lenski, *The Interpretation of St. John's Revelation* (Columbus, OH: Lutheran Book Concern, 1935), 494.

CHAPTER 8: THE ISLAMIC EMPIRE

1. If you are interested in a more exhaustive presentation, I would encourage you to read my book *Mideast Beast: The Scriptural Case for an Islamic Antichrist* (WND, 2012).
2. James E. Smith, *What the Bible Teaches about the Promised Messiah* (Nashville: Thomas Nelson, 1993), 38; Walter C. Kaiser Jr., *The Messiah in the Old Testament* (Grand Rapids: Zondervan, 1995), 38.
3. Robert Jamieson, Andrew Robert Fausset, and David Brown, commentary on Numbers 24, in *A Commentary, Critical and Explanatory, on the Old and New Testaments*, vol. 1 (Hartford: S. S. Scranton, 1871), 113.
4. John Walvoord, *Daniel: The Key to Prophetic Revelation* (Chicago: Moody, 1989), 68–69.
5. It is my view that Daniel 9:26 is simply speaking of the things that will occur under the future reign of the Antichrist and has nothing to do with the events of 70 AD whatsoever. Nevertheless, because of the overwhelming popularity of the preterist perspective here, I have only endeavored to show that even if the passage is speaking of 70 AD, it still points to the Middle East and not Rome.
6. Tacitus, *The History*, New Ed., bk. 5.1, ed. Moses Hadas; transs. Alfred Church and William Brodribb (New York: Modern Library, 2003).
7. Flavius Josephus, *The Complete Works of Josephus, The Wars of the Jews or The History of the Destruction of Jerusalem*, bk. 3, chap. 1, par. 3.
8. Ibid., chap. 4, par. 2.

CHAPTER 9: THE CITY OF SATAN

1. Strabo, *The Geography of Strabo*, bk. 16, chap. 1, 739.
2. Cassius Dio, *Roman History: Epitome of Book LXVIII*, par. 30, line 1.
3. Ignatius of Antioch, "The Third Epistle of Ignatius to the Ephesians," in *The Apostolic Fathers with Justin Martyr and Irenaeus*, ed. Alexander Roberts, James Donaldson, and A. Cleveland Coxe, vol. 1, *The Ante-Nicene Fathers* (Buffalo: Christian Literature Co., 1885), 103.
4. Tertullian, "The Prescription against Heretics," in *Latin Christianity: Its Founder, Tertullian*, ed. Alexander Roberts, James Donaldson, and A. Cleveland Coxe, trans. Peter Holmes, vol. 3, *The Ante-Nicene Fathers* (Buffalo: Christian Literature Co., 1885), 260.
5. Irenaeus of Lyons, "Irenæus against Heresies," in *The Apostolic Fathers with Justin Martyr and Irenaeus*, vol. 1, 461.
6. *Unger's Bible Dictionary* 3rd ed. (Chicago: Moody, 1960), 850.
7. Eusebius of Caesaria, "The Church History of Eusebius," in *Eusebius: Church History, Life of Constantine the Great, and Oration in Praise of Constantine*, eds. Philip Schaff and Henry Wace, trans. Arthur Cushman McGiffert, vol. 1, *A Select Library of the Nicene and Post-Nicene Fathers of the Christian Church*, 2nd ser. (New York: Christian Literature Co., 1890), 116.
9. These certainly include Sibylline Oracles, bk. 5; the Apocalypse of Baruch 11:1, and possibly 2 Esdras (also commonly referred to as 4 Ezra) 3:31; 15:43–60; 16:1.
10. James H. Charlesworth, *The Old Testament Pseudepigrapha*, vol. 1 (New York; London: Yale University Press, 1983), 397. For further discussion on the Sibylline use of the Babylon motif for Rome, see G. K. Beale, *The Book of Revelation: A Commentary on the Greek Text, New International Greek Testament Commentary* (Grand Rapids; Carlisle, UK: Eerdmans; Paternoster Press, 1999), 903.
11. Beale, *The Book of Revelation*, 593.

12. William C. Weinrich, ed., *Tyconius's Commentary on the Apocalypse of John*, from *Ancient Christian Commentary on Scripture, New Testament*, vol. 12, *The Book of Revelation* (Downer's Grove, IL: IVP Academic, 2006), 225.

13. Kendell H. Easley, *Revelation*, vol. 12, *Holman New Testament Commentary* (Nashville: Broadman & Holman, 1998), 314.

14. Ibid., 303.

CHAPTER 10: THE QUEEN OF LUXURY

1. R. C. H. Lenski, *The Interpretation of St. John's Revelation* (Columbus: Lutheran Book Concern, 1935), 493.

2. G. K. Beale, *The Book of Revelation: A Commentary on the Greek Text, New International Greek Testament Commentary* (Grand Rapids; Carlisle, UK: Eerdmans; Paternoster Press, 1999), 854.

CHAPTER 12: ROME

1. Marvin Richardson Vincent, *Word Studies in the New Testament*, vol. 2 (New York: Charles Scribner's Sons, 1887), 545.

2. Andrew of Caesarea, in *The Ancient Christian Commentary on Scripture, New Testament*, vol 12, ed. William C. Weinrich (Downers Grove, IL: IVP, 2005), 226.

3. The general view that the book of Revelation has been fulfilled in history, known as the preterist interpretation, is largely dispelled simply by establishing a later date for the prophecy as having been written after the fall of Jerusalem. See Pastor Mark Hitchcock's December 2005 PhD dissertation (Dallas Theological Seminary) on the later dating of Revelation, titled *A Defense of the Domitianic Date of the Book of Revelation*, at http://www.joelstrumpet.com/wp-content/uploads/2013/11/hitchcock-dissertation.pdf.

4. Grant R. Osbourne, *Revelation, The Baker Exegetical Commentary on the New Testament* (Grand Rapids: Baker Academic, 2002), 228.

5. G. K. Beale, *The Book of Revelation: A Commentary on the Greek Text, New International Greek Testament Commentary* (Grand Rapids; Carlisle, UK: Eerdmans; Paternoster Press, 1999), 874.

6. Sarah Eekhoff Zylstra, "Pope Francis Quiet on Catholic Persecution of Protestants in Mexico," *Christianity Today*, February 18, 2016, http://www.christianitytoday.com/gleanings/2016/february/pope-francis-catholic-persecution-protestant-mexico-chiapas.html.

7. Dave Hunt, *A Woman Rides the Beast: The Roman Catholic Church and the Last Days* (Eugene, OR: Harvest House, 1994), 74.

8. International Theological Commission, "Memory and Reconciliation: The Church and the Faults of the Past," December 1999, http://www.vatican.va/roman_curia/congregations/cfaith/cti_documents/rc_con_cfaith_doc_20000307_memory-reconc-itc_en.html.

9. Steve Kloen, "Pope Repents, Seeks Forgiveness for Social Sins Through the Ages," *Toronto Star*, March 13, 2000; Ontario Consultants on Religious Tolerance, "A Roman Catholic Apology for the Past Sins Of Its Members: Overview, the Document, Verbal Apology," ReligiousTolerance.org.

10. "Pope Apologises for Church Sins," BBC News, March 12, 2000, http://news.bbc.co.uk/2/hi/europe/674246.stm.

11. Associated Press, "Pope to Visit Sweden, Apologizes for Catholic Wrongs," *Daily Mail*, January 25, 2016, http://www.dailymail.co.uk/wires/ap/article-3415549/Pope-visit-Sweden-commemorate-500-years-Reformation.html#ixzz49E0w8oUh.

CHAPTER 13: JERUSALEM

1. Joel McDurmon, *Jesus v. Jerusalem: A Commentary on Luke 9:51–20:26, Jesus' Lawsuit Against Israel* (n.p.: American Vision, 2016), as quoted in McDurmon, "Who is Babylon the Great, The Mother of Prostitutes?" American Vision, August 8, 2016, https://americanvision.org/6461/babylon-the-great-the-mother-of-prostitutes/.

2.   N. T. Wright, *Jesus and the Victory of God* (Minneapolis: Fortress, 1996), 354, 356.
3.   Eusebius of Caesarea, "The Church History of Eusebius," in *Eusebius: Church History, Life of Constantine the Great, and Oration in Praise of Constantine*, eds. Philip Schaff and Henry Wace, trans. Arthur Cushman McGiffert, vol. 1, *A Select Library of the Nicene and Post-Nicene Fathers of the Christian Church*, 2nd ser. (New York: Christian Literature Co., 1890), 138.
4.   G. K. Beale, *The Book of Revelation: A Commentary on the Greek Text, New International Greek Testament Commentary* (Grand Rapids; Carlisle, UK: Eerdmans; Paternoster Press, 1999), 889.
5.   Venerable Bede, *The Explanation of the Apocalypse*, trans. Edward Marshall (Oxford: James Parker, 1878), 121–22.
6.   J. A. Seiss *The Apocalypse*, 3rd repr. (Grand Rapids., Zondervan, 1957), 386.
7.   Beale, *The Book of Revelation*, 889–90.
8.   See also 2 Chron. 21:11 and Ezek. 16:28, among others.
9.   Beale, *The Book of Revelation*, 859.

CHAPTER 14: THE ILLUMINATI / NEW WORLD ORDER
1.   Paul McGuire and Troy Anderson, *The Babylon Code: Solving the Bible's Greatest End Time Mystery* (New York: Faith Words, 2015), 172–73.
2.   Ibid., 124.

CHAPTER 15: NEW YORK CITY / USA
1.   Douglas W. Kreiger, Dene McGriff, and S. Douglas Woodward, *The Final Babylon: America and the Coming of Antichrist* (Oklahoma City, Faith Happens, 2013), 59-60.
2.   Ibid., 60.
3.   Steve Cioccolanti, "Is America Mystery Babylon?" YouTube video, 19:11, from a sermon series titled "21 Future Events Predicted in the Book of Revelation," posted by Discover Ministries TV, January 16, 2014, https://www.youtube.com/watch?v=nOL_Ozm4P90.
4.   Kreiger, McGriff, and Woodward, *The Final Babylon*, 45.
5.   Woodward made this argument in a radio discussion/debate he and I had on Southwest Radio Network. See "The Antichrist: Islamic or Not? with: Larry Spargimino and Joel Richardson, S. Douglas Woodward," YouTube video, 49:42, posted by Dave Flang, June 1, 2016, https://www.youtube.com/watch?v=-B8yfgRZW2c.
6.   *Lexham Bible Dictionary*, s.v. "Daughter of Zion" (Bellingham, WA: Lexham Press, 2012, 2013, 2014, 2015).
7.   Walter A. Elwell and Barry J. Beitzel, *Baker Encyclopedia of the Bible* (Grand Rapids: Baker, 1988), 2204.

CHAPTER 16: LITERAL BABYLON
1.   Mark Hitchcock, *The Second Coming of Babylon: What Bible Prophecy Says about Iraq in the Last Days* (Sisters, OR: Multnomah, 2003), 91.
2.   Joel C. Rosenberg, *Epicenter: Why the Current Rumblings in the Middle East Will Change Your Future* (Coral Stream, IL: Tyndale, 2006), 171.
3.   Ibid., 173.
4.   Alec Motyer, *The Prophecy of Isaiah: An Introduction & Commentary* (Downers Grove, IL: InterVarsity Press, 1996), 140.
5.   Michael Brown, *The Expositor's Bible Commentary: Jeremiah–Ezekiel* (Grand Rapids: Zondervan, 2010), 531.
6.   Herodotus, according to Brown, *The Expositor's Bible Commentary, Jeremiah–Ezekiel*, 554.
7.   *Easton's Bible Dictionary*, s.v. "Tyre" (New York: Harper & Brothers, 1893).
8.   *Ancient History Encyclopedia*, s.v. "Tyre," accessed September 14, 2016, http://www.ancient.eu/Tyre/; "Countries: Tyre," MiddleEast.com, accessed September 14, 2016, http://www.middleeast.com/tyre.htm.

9. G. K. Beale, *The Book of Revelation: A Commentary on the Greek Text, New International Greek Testament Commentary* (Grand Rapids; Carlisle, UK: Eerdmans; Paternoster Press, 1999), 849–50.

10. Ibid., 929.

11. Ibid., 884–85.

12. Chris White, *Mystery Babylon: When Jerusalem Embraces the Antichrist, An Exposition of Revelation 17 & 18* (Chris White Publishing, TN, 2013).

13. *Holman Illustrated Bible Dictionary*, s.v. "Shinar, Plain Of" (Nashville: Holman, 2003), 1489.

14. Stu Roberts, "The Bride: Basra's Ambitious Vertical City to Become World's Tallest Building," New Atlas, November 25, 2015, http://newatlas.com/bride-vertical-city-basra/40588/.

15. Steve Rose, "The world's Tallest Building Planned—in Ex-Warzone Basra," *Guardian*, November 20, 2015, https://www.theguardian.com/artanddesign/2015/nov/20/the-worlds-tallest-building-planned-in-ex-warzone-basra-iraq.

CHAPTER 17: MECCA / SAUDI ARABIA

1. Laurent Murawiec, *Princes of Darkness: The Saudi Assault on the West* (Lanham, MD: Rowman and Littlefield, 2003), 145.

2. "Leading Saudi Cleric Says IS and Saudi Arabia 'Follow the Same Thought'" Assyrian International News Agency, January 28, 2016, http://www.aina.org//news/20160128183033.htm.

3. Midrash Tanchuma, Qedoshim.

4. *E. J. Brill's First Encyclopaedia of Islam, 1913–1936*, ed. M. Th. Houtsma et al., vol. 4, (Leiden, NL: Brill, 1927), 590.

5. Haaretz, September 6, 1995; *Jerusalem Post*, September 7, 1995.

6. Barry Shaw, "Original Thinking: Palestinian Flags over Jerusalem" *Jerusalem Post*, January 3, 2013, http://www.jpost.com/Opinion/Columnists/Original-Thinking-Palestinian-flags-over-Jerusalem.

CHAPTER 18: THE GREAT PAGAN CITY

1. S.M.R. Shabbar, "The Ka'aba, the House of Allah," from the book *Story of the Holy Ka'aba and Its People*, Al-Islam.org, accessed June 10, 2016, https://www.al-islam.org/story-of-the-holy-kaaba-and-its-people-shabbar/kaaba-house-allah.

2. Ibid.

3. James Hurd, *Temples of Tamilnad: Travels in South India* (Bloomington, IN: Xlibris, 2010).

4. Jayram V, "Hindu God Lord Shiva (Siva)—the Destroyer," Hinduwebsite.com, accessed September 15, 2016, http://www.hinduwebsite.com/hinduism/siva.asp.

5. Bharath K., "Why Do We Do Pradakshina or Parikrama? (Going around Deities and Temples)," IndiaDivine.org, May 14, 2014, http://www.indiadivine.org/why-do-we-do-pradakshina-or-parikrama-going-around-deities-and-temples/.

6. Bahsarat Peer, "Modern Mecca: The Transformation of a Holy City," *New Yorker*, April 16, 2012, http://www.newyorker.com/magazine/2012/04/16/modern-mecca.

7. Tafseer al-Qurtubi 2/271, Fatul Bayan 1/293, in Sh. Abdullah Hasan, "The Meaning of the Word Ramadan," muslimmatters.org, July 22, 2012, http://muslimmatters.org/2012/07/22/the-meaning-of-the-word-rama%E1%B8%8Dan/.

8. Al-Tirmidhi, 877; al-Nasaa'i, 2935.

9. Al-Tirmidhi, 877; Ahmad, 2792.

10. Al-Tirmidhi, 959.

11. Al-Tirmidhi, 961; Ibn Maajah, 2944.

12. John of Damascus, *Against Heresies, Writings, The Fathers of the Church*, vol. 37, trans. Frederick Chase Jr. (Washington, D.C.: Catholic University of America Press, 1958), 156.

13. Ibid., 157.

14. *E. J. Brill's First Encyclopaedia of Islam, 1913–1936*, ed. M. Th. Houtsma et al., vol. 4, (Leiden, NL: Brill, 1927), 590, 590.

15. "Ka'Ba," Inter Religious Federation for World Peace, accessed June 10, 2016, http://www.irfwp.org/content/archives/000219.shtml.

16. Shoshana Kordova, "Word of the Day Bulbul: Just Don't Confuse the Bird With the Man," Jul 13, 2014 Haaretz, http://www.haaretz.com/jewish/features/1.604755.
17. Muhammad Wajid Akhter, "Ten Things You Didn't Know about the Kaaba," muslimmatters. org, November 15, 2012, http://muslimmatters.org/2012/11/15/ten-things-you-didnt-know-about-the-kaaba/.

CHAPTER 19: THE KINGS OF LUXURY
1. Gerald Posner, *Secrets of the Kingdom, The Inside Story of the Saudi-U.S. Connection* (New York: Random House, 2005), 23.
2. Laurent Murawiec, *Princes of Darkness: The Saudi Assault on the West* (Lanham, MD: Rowman and Littlefield, 2003), 2.
3. Robert Baer, *Sleeping with the Devil: How Washington Sold Our Soul for Saudi Crude* (New York, Three Rivers Press, 2003), 76.
4. Keiligh Baker, "EXCLUSIVE: Best friends with Dr Dre and an entourage of six 'minders' wherever he goes: How Saudi billionaire playboy, 23, with a fleet of golden cars spends his summer in London," *DailyMail.com*, upd. May 24, 2016, http://www.dailymail.co.uk/news/article-3567339/MailOnline-meets-billionaire-Saudi-playboy-owns-gold-supercars.html#ixzz4ABtmoHlw.
5. Posner, *Secrets of the Kingdom*, 74.
6. Ibid.
7. Ibid.
8. Baer, *Sleeping with the Devil*, 25.
9. Sara Clemence, "The World's Most Expensive Homes" *Forbes*, August 2, 2005, http://www.forbes.com/2005/07/29/expensivehomes-world-realestate-cx_sc_0729home_ls.html.
10. *Forbes*, "Billionaires Own Homes Worth Their Riches," NBC.com, March 18, 2006, http://www.nbcnews.com/id/11827230/ns/business-forbes_com/t/billionaires-own-homes-worth-their-riches/#.V9r8Y4YrKUk.
11. Megan Willett, "The 11 Most Expensive US Homes Ever Sold," *Business Insider*, May 5, 2014, http://www.businessinsider.com/the-11-most-expensive-us-homes-ever-sold-2014-5?op=1/#-a-historic-bel-air-estate-was-scooped-up-for-94-million-2.

CHAPTER 20: SEDUCER OF NATIONS
1. After pressure from the United States, the Saudi government discontinued the free Quran program.
2. Dawood al-Shirian, "What Is Saudi Arabia Going to Do?" *Al-Hayat*, May 19, 2003.
3. Laurent Murawiec, *Princes of Darkness: The Saudi Assault on the West* (Lanham, MD: Rowman and Littlefield, 2003), 200.
4. Center for Religious Freedom, *Saudi Publications of Hate Ideology Invade American Mosques* (Washington, D.C.: Freedom House, 2005), https://freedomhouse.org/sites/default/files/inline_images/Saudi%20Publications%20on%20Hate%20Ideology%20Invade%20American%20Mosques.pdf.
5. Katherine Clad, "Group Cites Saudi 'Hate' Tracts," *Washington Times*, January 29, 2005, http://www.washtimes.com/world/20050128-100245-8571r.htm.
6. Ibid.
7. Ibid.
8. As quoted in Robert Spencer, "The Swine Are Christians and the Apes Are Jews," *FrontPageMag.com*, May 23, 2006, http://archive.frontpagemag.com/readArticle.aspx?ARTID=4320.
9. Clad, "Group Cites Saudi 'Hate' Tracts."
10. Gilles Kepel, *Jihad: The Trail of Political Islam* (London: I. B. Tauris, 2006), 72.
11. "Prince Alwaleed Bin Talal Centers," Georgetown University School of Foreign Service website, accessed September 15, 2016, https://acmcu.georgetown.edu/centers.
12. Gitika Ahuja, "Saudi Prince Donates $40 Million to Harvard, Georgetown Universities," ABC News, December 13, 2005, http://abcnews.go.com/International/story?id=1402008.

13. Kenneth Timmerman, *Preachers of Hate: Islam and the War on America* (New York: Three Rivers Press, 2004), 119.

14. Saudi Tolerance Watch, "750 Lashes for Teacher Who Discussed Bible and Spoke Positively of Jews," *Justify This* (blog), November 15, 2005, http://justifythis.blogspot.com/2005/11/saudi-tolerance-watch-750-lashes-for.html.

15. Rachel Ehrenfeld, "Saudi Dollars and Jihad," *FrontPageMag.com*, October 24, 2005, http://archive.frontpagemag.com/readArticle.aspx?ARTID=6835.

16. Yousaf Butt, "How Saudi Wahhabism Is the Fountainhead of Islamist Terrorism," *Huffington Post*, January 20, 2015, http://www.huffingtonpost.com/dr-yousaf-butt-/saudi-wahhabism-islam-terrorism_b_6501916.html.

17. Guest blogger, "IMB Questions (Thomas L Law)," *SBC Voices*, September 2, 2015, http://sbcvoices.com/imb-questions-thomas-l-law/.

CHAPTER 21: CORRUPTER OF KINGS

1. Gerald Posner, *Secrets of the Kingdom, The Inside Story of the Saudi-U.S. Connection* (New York: Random House, 2005), xi.

2. Prince Bandar bin Sultan, quoted in Craig Unger, *House of Bush, House of Saud: The Secret Relationship Between the World's Two Most Powerful Dynasties* (New York: Scribner: 2004), 87.

3. Robert Baer, *Sleeping with the Devil: How Washington Sold our Soul for Saudi Crude* (Santa Barbara: Three Rivers Press, 2003), 60.

4. Laurent Murawiec, *Princes of Darkness: The Saudi Assault on the West* (Lanham, MD: Rowman and Littlefield, 2003), 120.

5. Baer, *Sleeping with the Devil*, 44.

6. Ibid., 54.

7. Posner, *Secrets of the Kingdom,* xi.

8. Murawiec, *Princes of Darkness*, 200.

9. See Kris Broughton, "Sharia Prince Owns Stake in FOX News Parent," Big Think, accessed September, 16, 2016, http://bigthink.com/Resurgence/sharia-prince-owns-stake-in-fox-news-parent.

10. Baer, *Sleeping with the Devil*, xviii.

11. Ibid., 212.

12. See the Carter Center Annual Report 1998–1999, https://www.cartercenter.org/documents/520.pdf, 30; the Annual Report for 2006–2007 (https://www.cartercenter.org/documents/annual_report_07.pdf), 60; and "Carter Center Featured Partner: The Alwaleed Bin Talal Foundation," September 2011, https://www.cartercenter.org/donate/corporate-government-foundation-partners/archives/alwaleed-bin-talal-foundation.html.

13. CAMERA, *Bearing False Witness: Jimmy Carter's Palestine: Peace Not Apartheid*, ed. Andrea Levin (Boston: CAMERA, 2007), 89.

14. Alan Dershowitz, *The Case Against Israel's Enemies: Exposing Jimmy Carter and Others Who Stand in the Way of Peace* (Hoboken, NJ: John Wiley, 2008), 33.

15. Murawiec, *Princes of Darkness*, 51.

16. CAMERA, *Bearing False Witness*, 69.

17. Ibid., 40.

18. Ibid., 89.

19. Unger, *House of Bush, House of Saud*, 200.

20. Paul Craig Roberts, "9/11 Disinformation: Saudi Arabia Attacked America," *Foreign Policy Journal*, May 28, 2016, http://www.foreignpolicyjournal.com/2016/05/28/911-disinformation-saudi-arabia-attacked-america/.

21. Philip Shenonm "Saudi Officials Were 'Supporting' 9/11 Hijackers, Commission Member Says," *Guardian*, May 12, 2016, https://www.theguardian.com/us-news/2016/may/12/911-commission-saudi-arabia-hijackers.

22. *Richard Pollock,* "Persian Gulf Sheikhs Gave Bill & Hillary $100 Million," *Daily Caller*, May 11, 2016, http://dailycaller.com/2016/05/11/exclusive-persian-gulf-sheikhs-gave-bill-hillary-100-million/.

23. Tom Kertscher, "Hillary Clinton Took Money from the Kings of Four Countries, GOP Chief Reince Priebus says," Politifact, April 20, 2015, http://www.politifact.com/wisconsin/statements/2015/apr/20/reince-priebus/hillary-clinton-took-money-kings-four-countries-go/.

24. Bryan Schatz, "Hillary Clinton Oversaw US Arms Deals to Clinton Foundation Donors," *Mother Jones*, May 28, 2015, http://www.motherjones.com/politics/2015/05/hillary-clinton-foundation-state-arms-deals.

CHAPTER 22: DRUNK ON THE BLOOD OF THE SAINTS

1. Albert Hourani, *A History of the Arab Peoples* (n.p.: Faber and Faber, 1991), 23.

2. These figures come from a composite analysis of the following works: Bat Ye'or, *The Decline of Eastern Christianity under Islam: From Jihad to Dhimmitude* (Cranberry, NJ: Fairleigh Dickinson University Press, 1996); Andrew Bostom, *The Legacy of Jihad: Islamic Holy War and the Fate of Non-Muslims* (Amherst, NY: Prometheus, 2005); and Imam al-Waqidi, *The Islamic Conquest of Syria* (Ta-Ha, 2005).

3. Ibid.

4. Maimonides, quoted in Andrew Bostom, *The Legacy of Islamic Antisemitism* (Amherst, NY: Prometheus, 2008), front matter.

5. "Key Context Missing in Globe Article about Saudi Donor to Harvard and Georgetown," CAMERA, December 21, 2005, http://www.camera.org/index.asp?x_article=1043&x_context=2.

6. William Mayer and Beila Rabinowitz, "CAIR, Georgetown University, John Esposito and Keith Ellison Participate in Bin Talal Wahhabist Puppet Show," PipelineNews.org, accessed September 16, 2016, http://www.pipelinenews.org/2008/apr/08/cair-georgetown-university-john-esposito-keith-ellison.html.

7. MEMRI Special Report—Saudi Arabia / Jihad & Terrorism Studies, July 3, 2003, no. 17, Steven Stalinsky, "The Saudis: $4 Billion to the Palestinians (1998–2003)," *Jewish Post*, http://www.jewishpost.com/archives/news/the-saudis-4-billion-to-the-palestinians.html.

8. Gerald Posner, *Secrets of the Kingdom: The Inside Story of the Saudi-U.S. Connection* (New York: Random House, 2005), 44.

9. Edward Clifford, "Financing Terrorism: Saudi Arabia and Its Foreign Affairs," *Brown Political Review*, December 6, 2014, http://www.brownpoliticalreview.org/2014/12/financing-terrorism-saudi-arabia-and-its-foreign-affairs/.

10. Posner, *Secrets of the Kingdom*, 4.

11. See Jack Shafer, "The PowerPoint That Rocked the Pentagon," *Slate*, August 7, 2002, http://www.slate.com/articles/news_and_politics/press_box/2002/08/the_powerpoint_that_rocked_the_pentagon.html. Jaime Holguin, "Pentagon Blasts Saudi Arabia Report," CBS News, August 6, 2002, http://www.cbsnews.com/news/pentagon-blasts-saudi-arabia-report/.

12. Robert Baer, *Sleeping with the Devil: How Washington Sold Our Soul for Saudi Crude* (Santa Barbara: Three Rivers Press, 2003), xxix.

13. "Saudi Arabia Executes Nigerian Man, Marking 95th Execution This Year," Al Bawaba News, May 30, 2016, http://www.albawaba.com/news/saudi-arabia-executes-nigerian-man-marking-95th-execution-year-846196.

CHAPTER 23: THE PROSTITUTE OF THE DESERT

1. Sylvia Smith, "Saudi Arabia's New Desert Megacity," BBC News, March 20, 2015, http://www.bbc.com/news/world-middle-east-31867727.

2. "#KAEC—King Abdullah Economic City 2015," YouTube video, 8:29, posted by KAEC Saudi, January 19, 2015, https://www.youtube.com/watch?v=cjyn5BP38_4.

3. Laurent Murawiec, *Princes of Darkness: The Saudi Assault on the West* (Lanham, MD: Rowman and Littlefield, 2003), 3.

4. Robert Baer, *Sleeping With the Devil: How Washington Sold Our Soul for Saudi Crude* (New York, Three Rivers Press, 2003), 161.

5. Saudi Arabia: Foreign Workers Abused: Torture, Unfair Trials and Forced Confinement Pervasive," Human Rights Watch, July 15, 2004, http://hrw.org/english/docs/2004/07/15/saudia9061.htm.
6. Human Right Watch Saudi Arabia: Foreign Workers Abused Torture, Unfair Trials and Forced Confinement Pervasive July 5, 2004
7. Murawiec, Princes of Darkness, 3.
8. Daniel Pipes, "Islamist Calls for Slavery's Legalization," Daniel Pipes Middle East Forum (blog), October 15, 2014, http://www.danielpipes.org/blog/2003/11/saudi-religious-leader-calls-for-slaverys.
9. Ibid.
10. "Issue 12: Arabian Peninsula and the International Sex Slave Trade," Sauduction.com, accessed September 16, 2016, http://www.sauduction.com/issues/12.

CHAPTER 24: THE HATED HARLOT OF THE MIDDLE EAST
1. Robert Baer, *Sleeping with the Devil: How Washington Sold Our Soul for Saudi Crude* (New York: Three Rivers Press, 2003), 161.
2. Ibid.
3. Gerald Posner, *Secrets of the Kingdom, The Inside Story of the Saudi-U.S. Connection* (New York: Random House, 2005), 41.
4. Ibid., 40.
5. Ibid., 33.
6. Ibid.
7. Baer, *Sleeping with the Devil*, 24.
8. Ibid., 28.
9. "Sheikh Nimr al-Nimr: Saudi Arabia Executes Top Shia Cleric," BBC News, January 2, 2016, http://www.bbc.com/news/world-middle-east-35213244.
10. "Iran: Saudis Face 'Divine Revenge' for Executing al-Nimr," BBC News, January 3, 2016, http://www.bbc.com/news/world-middle-east-35216694.
11. Joel Richardson, *The Islamic Antichrist* (WND, 2009).
12. Baer, *Sleeping with the Devil*, 11.
13. Ibid.

INDEX OF ILLUSTRATIONS

INDEX

Islam, 4, 74, 88, 90, 92, 95, 100, 112, 157, 167,
    197–205, 209–10, 214, 225–31, 235, 239,
    243–50, 256, 261–64, 267–70, 274–75,
    277–78. *See also* Islamic empire
    the Christian response to the last-days role
        of, 274–75
    the Illuminati not related to, 157, 167
    meaning of the word, 95
    slavery a part of, 256
    the womb and heart of, 197–98
    the womb and heart of radical Wahhabi,
        198–99
    the world's second-largest religion, 267
Islamic Affairs Department of Saudi Arabia,
    225
Islamic Antichrist (Richardson), 264
Islamic Antichrist theory, 97
Islamic Caliphate, 74, 76, 79, 92, 93, 95–96,
    100, 103, 110, 167, 172, 186, 264. *See*
    Islamic empire
Islamic creed (Shahada), 216
Islamic empire (Islamic Caliphate). *See chapter
    8, "The Islamic Empire"* (81–101). *See also*
    74–77, 80, 131, 270, 284ch7n4
    the seventh head (kingdom), 74–76
    the eighth kingdom: the revived, 75, 77–78
Islamic State of Iraq and Syria. *See* ISIS
Israel, 8, 23, 24, 25, 29, 26, 66, 73, 74, 82–83,
    85–86, 87, 88, 91, 96, 113, 116, 124, 133,
    139–41, 145, 147, 150, 151, 165, 166, 167,
    168, 174, 175, 180, 182, 183, 185, 197,
    201–3, 208, 218, 219, 230, 235, 236, 237,
    238, 245, 269, 283n8
    centrality of (in the story of the Bible), 82,
        100, 201–2
    the Saudi war against the Jews and, 245–47
Israelites, 15–16, 65–66
Italy, 85, 98, 108

J

Jabhat al-Nusra (terrorist organization), 247
Jackson, Michael, 224
Jacob (patriarch), 85, 140, 151, 201, 211
Jeddah, 196, 252–53, 254, 260, 263, 267
Jehoiachin (king), 23
Jehovah's Witnesses, 55
Jeremiah (prophet), 23, 24, 140, 149, 175–76,
    177, 178, 179
Jerome (church father), 4, 107, 129
Jerusalem. *See in general chapter 13, "Jerusalem"*
    (138–52). *See also* 7–8, 16, 23–26, 54, 55,
    73, 82–83, 89, 94, 95, 97–100, 108–10,
    130, 168, 169, 178, 184–85, 200–3, 211,
    215, 216, 217, 244, 285ch12n3

the center of the earth, 201
two distinct views concerning, 138
the fall of Babylon versus the fall of, 141–42
as the "great city" of Revelation 17–18,
    143–44
Jerusalem Targum, 85
Jesus, return of, 81, 87–90, 119, 188, 275
Jesus versus Jerusalem (McDurmon), 139
Jews, 26, 27, 28, 29, 94, 96, 99, 103, 108, 116,
    123, 135, 142, 165, 166, 169, 180, 200,
    201, 227, 228, 230, 237, 269
    Islam's war against the, 244–45
    the Saudi war against Israel and the,
        245–46
jihad, 166, 199, 207, 219, 228, 246, 247, 248,
    269
Joel (prophet), 82–83, 140
John (apostle, the Revelator), xii, 4, 13, 15,
    16–17, 63, 65, 70, 77–78, 106, 109, 111,
    121, 148, 150, 167, 179, 243, 281ch2n5
John of Damascus, 214–15
John Paul II (pope), 135
Jonah (prophet), 143
Jordan, 85, 87, 89, 90, 95, 96, 175, 244
Josephus, Flavius, 33, 34, 41, 99
Judah, 23–24, 25, 26, 73, 83, 87, 89, 151, 185
Judaism, 37, 143, 216, 226, 227
Judea, 25, 99
Julius Caesar, 132t
Jupiter (Roman god), 94

K

Kaaba, 186, 198, 204, 205–6, 209–10, 212–17,
    218–19
Keating, Karl, 47
Kelly, John, 237
Kenya, 148
Kepel, Gilles, 228
Khalid ibn al-Walid, 244
Khilafa, 74. *See* Islamic Caliphate; Islamic
    empire
King Abdullah Economic City (KAEC), 196,
    252–53, 254, 267
Kingdom of Saudi Arabia. *See* Saudi Arabia
Kitab al-Magall (*Book of Rolls*), 38–39
Koresh, David, 264
Kreiger, Douglas W., 6–7, 161, 168

L

Lactantius, 3, 4, 107, 129
Ladd, George Eldon, 73
"Lady Liberty," 164
Lang, G. H., 8–9, 170

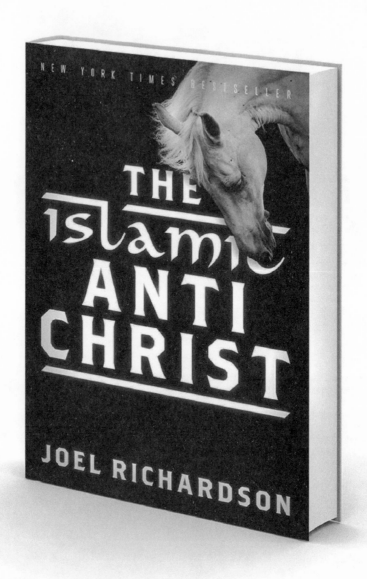

In THE ISLAMIC ANTICHRIST, Joel Richardson exposes Western readers to the traditions of Islam and predicts the end times may not be here. Richardson's revelations will stun readers who are unaware of the similarities between the Antichrist and the Islam's expectations about a returning Jesus. This is the book to read for insights on the world's fastest-growing religion and the future of the world.

WND BOOKS • A *WND* COMPANY • WASHINGTON DC • WNDBOOKS.C

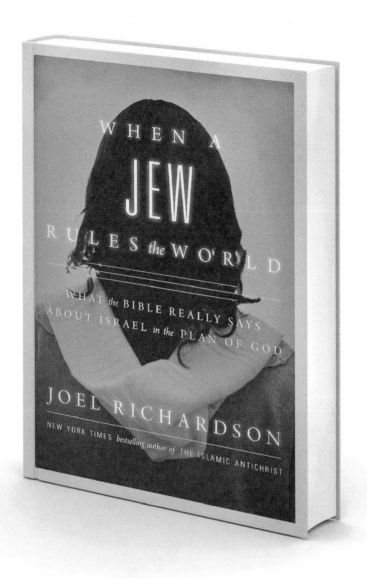

In the past thirty years, the trend among American evangelical's view of Israel has shifted dramatically. There is a sudden rise of anti-Israel and anti-Semitic sentiment among Christians today. WHEN A JEW RULES THE WORLD sets the record straight regarding the New Covenant, the millennium, and what every Christian must know about Israel.

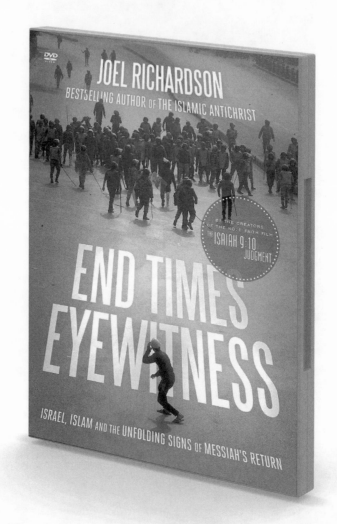

"There is a sense in the world that things are unhinged."
—JONATHAN CAHN

Is the return of Jesus closer than you think? What are the most powerful prophetic signs being fulfilled on the earth today? How is the new Middle East after the Arab Spring aligning with the testimony of the biblical prophets? What are the little-known prophetic signs that few are paying attention to? END TIMES EYEWITNESS takes you on a firsthand journey to the front lines of the ongoing Middle Eastern revolutions, to discover the shocking answer to all of these questions.

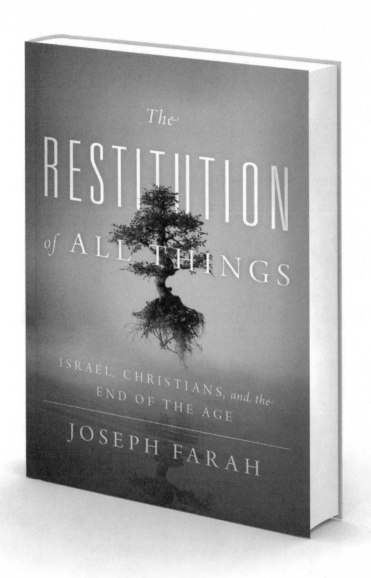

THE RESTITUTION OF ALL THINGS exposes the spiritual traditions of men that often overshadow the commandments of God. It lays bare the pernicious lie that has become known today as "replacement theology." It is a wake-up call to the world regarding the ever-present truth of the Bible, and of the reality of Jesus-Yeshua, the Messiah, the King, the High Priest, the Redeemer, and Son of God.

WND Books • A **WND** COMPANY • WASHINGTON DC • WNDBOOKS.COM

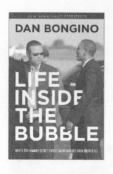
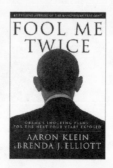

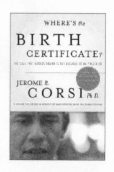
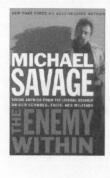
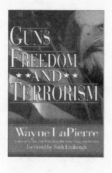
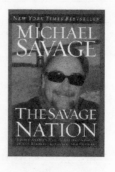